# THE SEVERAL LIVES OF CHESTER HIMES

*the several lives* *1* *of*

*chester* **h** *imes*

*Edward Margolies & Michel Fabre*

University Press of Mississippi  *Jackson*

Copyright © 1997 by the University Press of Mississippi
All rights reserved
Manufactured in the United States of America
00   99   98   97      4   3   2   1
The paper in this book meets the guidelines for permanence and
durability of the Committee on Production Guidelines for Book
Longevity of the Council on Library Resources.

Library of Congress Cataloging-in-Publication Data

Margolies, Edward.
    The several lives of Chester Himes / by Edward Margolies and Michel
Fabre.
        p.   cm.
    Includes bibliographical references and index.
    ISBN 0-87805-908-3 (alk. paper)
    1. Himes, Chester B., 1909–    —Biography.   2. Afro-American
novelists—20th century—Biography.   3. Afro-American prisoners—
Biography.   4. Afro-Americans—Europe—Biography.   I. Fabre,
Michel.   II. Title.
PS3515.I713Z685   1997
813'.54—dc21
    [B]                                                        96-39330
                                                                    CIP

British Library Cataloging-in-Publication data available

Photographs not otherwise credited are courtesy of Michel Fabre.

*For Jacob, Peter, William, Julien, Jessica, and Plume*

# Contents

# PREFACE

MEMORY IS A FRAGILE INSTRUMENT, and Chester Himes's was no exception. The two volumes of autobiography he wrote when he was well past sixty are fraught with errors of fact, incorrect sequences of events, and even incorrect dates of central experiences. Further, Himes was not averse to putting a romanticized or ideological "spin" on some of his accounts. This is not to say these books are not useful, but often they represent a state of mind as much as a life lived.

This is a pity because Himes's years not only tell us what literary lessons he drew from the flagrant contrasts in his life but also tell of the little-known worlds and societies he passed through in his quest to attain celebrity—a celebrity, be it acknowledged at once, far greater in France than in America. (The enthusiastic reception in France of African American artists and intellectuals is, of course, a story in itself, and Himes, as we shall see, had some acerbic observations in this regard.) Himes's American successes did not come early or easily, doubtless in part because of racial barriers, but also because he contained within himself so many of the contradictory impulses, desires, and aspirations of his American upbringing. Himes is mainly known in the United States today as an author of Harlem thrillers, but his other works also deserve serious attention. Although no one would wish to claim Himes as an American Everyman, or even as a black American Everyman, surely he mirrors in himself the social, cultural, and racial conflicts of the America he wrote about. Indeed his most powerful writings express these unresolved tensions.

Born in 1909, the youngest and fairest-skinned of three brothers, Chester Himes passed his first eleven years in the genteel surroundings of the southern black middle class. His "professor" father taught mechanical skills in land-grant colleges in Missouri, Mississippi, and Arkansas, and his mother, a gifted musician, occasionally taught young people as well. During his childhood years—years which coincidentally saw more and more anti-Negro violence—Himes seldom moved beyond protective southern black communities. It would be a mistake, however, to deduce that the young Chester was isolated from the larger America. Despite distance, his family situation reflected outside clashes.

Chester's mother was light-complexioned and took immense pride in her white ancestors, whose genealogy she traced back through slavery to the American Revolution. Herself the daughter of prosperous South Carolina Presbyterians who rose from slavery to become successful in business, she tried to impress on her children a kind of Victorian gentility and self-help ethic, which she equated with religiosity. So fearful was she of her children associating with other Negro children whom she regarded as social and cultural inferiors that for the most part she tutored her sons at home almost until their teenage years. Throughout her marriage she was frequently at odds with her much darker-skinned husband, who knew next to nothing about his ex-slave parents but had nonetheless acquired an education despite a childhood of poverty. Unlike his wife, Professor Himes took some pride in his Africanness and was probably among the first southern pedagogues to teach Negro history. Nevertheless, as his son related, he was also capable of appearing obsequious to authorities, white and black, on whom his economic survival depended. Thus, in their different ways, both of Himes's parents had assumed the divided loyalties and cultural ethos of the larger America, and conveyed these to their children who subconsciously internalized them.

Given Himes's emotional contradictions, readers of his works would want to discover how they manifested themselves in his life and career. In one sense the task does not seem daunting since, by his own admission, very nearly all of Himes's writings (with the exception of his Harlem thrillers) are autobiographical. Here we as his biographers tread cautiously, however, suggesting now and then the real-life plausibility of some of his fictional accounts. Nearly from the start, Himes expressed a love-hate perception of America and a deep ambivalence about race, his own as well as that of the whites who surrounded him. Inner conflicts reveal themselves most flagrantly in his relationships with white women, whom he often loved, pitied, and identified with as Negro-like victims—and yet seemingly perversely manipulated and abused.

It follows that Himes's views of blacks, both men and women, were also deeply mixed. At times he regarded African Americans as hopelessly mired in self-delusion, degradation, and brutishness—and he would have nothing to do with them; at other times he saw them as fellow sufferers, heroic rebels, and potential revolutionaries. Politically he came to believe that extreme black violence on a seriously organized level could succeed in achieving justice.

One of the great paradoxes of Himes's life was that he ultimately won the kind of popular artistic recognition he had always yearned for—not in America but in Europe, and not for his classically traditional novels, but for the Harlem detective thrillers he had begun writing in Paris simply to earn a living. Perhaps it was because he did not at first take these works seriously as "literature" that he granted so much free range to his dark humor, his surreal imagination. Only in his later years did he come to realize that these works may have constituted his best and most lasting contributions.

If there exists a persistent thread in Himes's life, it is his constant restlessness. The several worlds he passed through in his American years—a childhood in the deep South, adolescence and manhood in northern cities, and nearly a decade in prison—served only to exacerbate his frenetic search for peace of mind. He found no repose in Europe, even after gaining his long desired recognition. Finally, it was only the act of writing that provided him with the catharsis he sought—and when his strength failed him, when he was no longer able to write, he lost the will to live. Yet for his readers he left behind a record of his struggle—a struggle which in its fashion perhaps mirrors the divided American soul.

# ACKNOWLEDGMENTS

WE BEGAN THIS BIOGRAPHY IN 1985 in collaboration with LeRoy S. Hodges, Jr., a friend and colleague. Hodges's sudden and untimely death in 1986 undoubtedly slowed our work, but we hope his spirit and enthusiasm have infused this book. We remember him here in fond appreciation.

The research for this book was based in part on our personal acquaintance and correspondence with Himes over the last twenty years of his life and on conversations with persons mentioned below, and is largely derived from material in Himes's archives and correspondence. The bulk of the archives are now divided between the Beinecke Library at Yale University, where since 1946 the James Weldon Johnson Collection has held the Himes–Van Vechten correspondence, related letters, and practically all extant manuscript versions of Himes's published works until 1972, and the Amistad Research Center at Tulane University, where the rest of the drafts, manuscripts, correspondence, and copies of correspondence are deposited along with the Joseph S. Himes papers.

Sundry other correspondence may be found at the University of Rochester Library (the John A. Williams archive), the Spingarn-Moorland Collection of Howard University (mainly letters to Walter Freeman), the Ohio State University Library, the Schomburg Center for Research in Black Culture of the New York Public Library (Henry Lee Moon–Himes correspondence), and the recipients' private collections (e.g., Yves Malartic, Ishmael Reed, Michel Fabre).

All these sources have been used extensively, although we have tried not to make the critical apparatus too burdensome. Thus, footnotes and references are kept to a minimum. We have provided a chronological list of

Himes's published works, based on *Chester Himes: An Annotated Primary and Secondary Bibliography,* compiled by Michel Fabre, Robert E. Skinner, and Lester Sullivan (Greenwood Press, 1992).

Before any other individual, we wish to thank Mrs. Lesley Himes for her invaluable assistance and friendly hospitality. She spent a week at the Margolies home and earlier allowed Michel and Geneviève Fabre to sort and photocopy many items in her husband's papers at Moraira in February 1985 before they were acquired by the Amistad Research Center at Tulane University, and she has made herself available for questions ever since. Chester Himes's two brothers have also been greatly cooperative. The late Joseph Sandy Himes, assisted by his hospitable wife Estelle, granted Fabre a long interview in Greensboro, North Carolina, in 1986 and opened the family papers to him; Edward Himes in New York City granted an interview to Fabre and Hodges. Jean Johnson Himes spoke at length to Edward Margolies on the telephone in 1988. Among Himes's friends, John A. Williams generously shared his memories in extensive interviews and correspondence over fifteen years, as did Yves and Yvonne Lamour-Malartic, Daniel Levin, Ishmael Reed, and Roslyn and William Targ.

We have also benefited from conversations and interviews (some conducted before starting this project) with James Baldwin, Horace Cayton, Schofield and Rosette Coryell, Marcel and Germaine Duhamel, Ralph Ellison, Ronald Fair, Hoyt Fuller, Emilio Garcia, Herbert Gentry, Richard Gibson, Ollie Harrington, Celia Hornung, Helen Johnson, Ambroise Kom, Claude Julien, Constance Webb Pearlstien, Stephen Rosen, Ruth Seid, William Gardner Smith, Darwina Troller, Ellen Wright, and Frank Yerby.

Thanks are due to the helpful staff of the following institutions and publishers: the Amistad Research Center at Tulane University for early access to the Joseph S. Himes archive; the Beinecke Rare Book and Manuscript Library at Yale University; the Federal Bureau of Investigation in Washington, D.C.; the library of Alcorn University, Mississippi; the Ohio State University Library in Columbus and the Western Reserve Historical Society in Cleveland; the Schomburg Center for Research in Black Culture in New York City; Editions Gallimard, Editions Buchet-Chastel-Corréa, Editions des Autres, and Editions Lieu Commun in Paris.

During his research, Fabre benefited from a summer fellowship from the Beinecke Library, Yale University, in 1988 and received a travel and documentation grant in 1991 from the Centre National des Lettres in Paris. Margolies was given a release from teaching time at the College of Staten Island, City University of New York, to work on this project.

*Acknowledgments*

Assistance in securing sources and documents was provided by Esme Bhan, Come N'dongo, Geneviève Fabre, Ellistine and Kermit Holly and their family, Donald Gallup, Keneth Kinnamon, Geraldine Matthews, Christine McKay, Stephen Milliken, Gloria Rose, Ruth Seid, and Robert E. Skinner.

Rachida Chbihi and Patrick Salès, of the CETANLA at the Université de la Sorbonne Nouvelle in Paris, tracked down and verified information regarding places and book reviews. At the final stage, we benefited from the valuable advice and help of Seetha Srinivasan, our editor at University Press of Mississippi, and the close scrutiny and editorial assistance of Lys Ann Shore and Claire Margolies.

Finally, we thank Robert E. Skinner of Xavier University of Louisiana, a Himes scholar in his own right, who read our manuscript, asked pertinent questions, and provided us with inestimable help.

M. F. and E. M.

THE SEVERAL LIVES OF CHESTER HIMES

# 1

# GENEALOGY

LOOKING BACK ON HIS LIFE at the age of sixty, Chester Himes sought some meaning, some pattern. It seemed almost from the start that he and people close to him were always on the move, sometimes on the run. Rarely staying long enough to put down roots, to find value in their environment, purpose in their culture. What *was* his culture? American? African American? He bitterly rejected both at times, though in the deepest sense, he recognized that he was the unhappy hybrid of both. He could not be other than what he was. America had made him. Despite his expatriate status, his writings embodied American cultural contradictions.

Himes had once hoped that writing would be a means of resolving his confusion, yet, paradoxically, his greatest strengths came out of his unresolved conflicts. Thus, in his later years, when he sat down to write his autobiography, he could only say that he had been deeply hurt and that his life was absurd— indeed, if one is a Negro, he ventured, one is absurd.[1]

But such views were a far cry from what his mother had tried to teach him. Estelle Bomar Himes was a genteel woman, a churchgoer, a believer in culture, and perhaps above all, ardently ambitious for her husband and children. For these reasons she held it important that her children possess a sense of the past, a genealogy. This was not an easy task when one's ancestors had been born in slavery, but the difficulty did not deter Estelle; in fact, it spurred her on. In a curious way it was a matter of pride. Look, she seemed to say, see how far we've come, how far we may yet go by virtue of our superior blood, our bourgeois ideals. Ironically, Chester, her favorite son who was perhaps the most successful, achieved his success by utterly rejecting his mother's ethos—although one might argue that his disavowals echoed the ferocity of his mother's spirit. In the end, Chester was truly his mother's son.

Estelle loved nothing better than to tell her children about their ancestors. On occasion these accounts differed, and it is difficult now to determine their degree of accuracy. Suffice it to say that one of her grandmothers was the daughter of either an Indian squaw or an African princess, and an Irish overseer. Her light-skinned mother, Malinda, was a maidservant to a South Carolina doctor named Cleveland, who could trace his lineage to the British aristocracy, as well as to a general who fought the redcoats during the Revolution.

Despite laws that forbade literacy to slaves, Malinda was taught to read by Miss Sunie, presumably her master's daughter. While still a slave, Malinda gave birth to three children, two of whom may have been sired by Doctor Cleveland and a third by an Indian slave. After the Civil War, Malinda married Chester Bomar, himself the son of a beautiful octoroon, "Grandma Mary," and her master, John Earl Bomar. Since there already existed considerable intermarriage between the white Clevelands and the white Bomars, Malinda's marriage to Chester now also brought the "colored" branches of the family together.[2]

Chester and Malinda and Malinda's three children lived on an acre of land donated by Chester's former master near Spartanburg, South Carolina. Malinda took in washing and worked as a wet nurse while Chester learned to become a brick mason. After three years they decided to sell their land and move to Dalton, Georgia, with money the Freedmen's Bureau provided for their transportation. There Chester found jobs as a mason for nearly eight years. Malinda meanwhile gave birth to three more children, the youngest being Estelle, who was born in February 1874.

Estelle was two years old when her father moved his large family to Atlanta in hopes of finding steadier work. They established a home on Marietta Street, where Malinda gave birth to her second son, Chester, Jr. Her husband then fell ill, and became so incapacitated that it was left to Malinda to support the family. Once more she took in washing, and on some days she worked in other people's homes as a cleaning woman. Despite their travails, however, the Bomars managed to send their oldest daughter, Maggie, to Maryville College where she met her future husband, a Presbyterian minister. Upon his recovery, Chester returned his family to their first home, Spartanburg, and began a business as a builder, helped now by an older son, Tom, who proved to be a strong and astute mason. In time, their enterprise prospered, and when Chester, Jr., grew old enough, he joined them as a partner. Among their achievements were the first large brick cotton mills built in the region. Her parents' sacrifices and dogged perseverance were not lost on Estelle, who one day would endeavor to convey these virtues to her own children.

By the early 1890s the Bomars had become solid members of the upper bourgeoisie. Chester was elected deacon of his Negro Presbyterian Church, acting both as superintendent of the Sunday school and financial advisor. One story Estelle enjoyed telling about him concerned the time their minister asked him to lead the congregation in prayer. Chester drew himself up and said, "You lead us yourself, Reverend; that is what we are paying you for." Clearly, Chester was a commanding figure.

Meanwhile, Malinda did her best to inculcate into her children all the middle-class values she revered. Estelle, regarded as the most musically gifted in the family, was given piano lessons. Later, as a young woman, she was sent to study at the Scotia Seminary in Concord, North Carolina, which at the time was considered an elite institution for black women in the South. Here, the largely white missionary Presbyterian faculty aimed to imbue their students with a high sense of purpose as well as a "cultural" education. Estelle acquired her diploma in 1895. The document stated that she had earned it "by virtue of her literary attainments and good moral behavior." Estelle stayed on at the seminary for two years as a teacher, although she took a year off to pursue her musical education at a Philadelphia music conservatory. As befitted her social status and religious upbringing, she felt it her duty to uplift the less fortunate members of her race. She fulfilled this goal by teaching music and academic subjects in public schools in North and South Carolina, at the North Carolina School for the Deaf, Dumb and Blind, and at the Tuskegee Institute in Alabama.

If Estelle entertained a high opinion of herself, she was not altogether unjustified. How many nineteenth-century American women—white or black—were as well educated and attractive as she? Not surprisingly, she valued her white ancestors as well as her light complexion, and although she was small and dressed daintily, there was something undeniably forceful in her manner. She could easily "pass" with her auburn hair, fair skin, gray eyes, and aquiline nose, but she seldom thought of doing so. She was who she was. As regards her social views, she was not opposed to barriers, but felt that barriers ought to be erected on the basis of culture and refinement rather than race. On its face, therefore, her marriage to Joseph Sandy Himes in 1901 was most curious.

To begin with, Joseph Sandy could scarcely trace his ancestry. He came from a poor black family in North Carolina, and neither he nor his brothers and sisters knew their father's first name. He did know that in slave times his father, as a very young boy, had been bought by someone named Heinz or Himes to apprentice as a blacksmith, and that his father did not even know who his parents were. When the Civil War ended, he was in his mid-twenties and the father of four. He decided to remain on the plantation of his former master, where one day he had a row with an overseer whom he may have killed. He fled, and his wife and children never saw him again. Some time later, a traveling evangelist held a wedding ceremony for him and an ex-slave from Georgia named Mary. Mary bore him five children before dying of consumption. Joseph Sandy, her third child, was fourteen at the time. Leah, an older sister, took charge of him and two younger siblings, but all the impoverished Himes children had to find work in order to survive.

Among their family, Joseph Sandy and Leah were the only ones to acquire college educations; both became teachers. Joseph Sandy attended Claflin College, a Methodist institution in Orangeburg, South Carolina, where he played football and helped support himself by taking menial jobs. Later, according to his sons, he may have studied at the Boston Mechanical Institute and taken a summer course at Cornell University. In any case, by the time he met Estelle he was trained in the teaching of mechanical skills and obviously capable of teaching at the Negro technical and agricultural colleges.

Whatever else attracted Estelle to Joseph Sandy, she must have admired his ambition. After all, had not her own parents, whom she adored, also risen above poverty by dint of hard work and relentless drive? Moreover, she fancied she saw in Joseph not simply a teacher, but a future Negro college dean or president. She knew that there was a touch of condescension in her attitude, but the truth was that she was descended from a "good," affluent family, and he was not. By marrying him, she felt that she could further his career, and if asked, he would probably have agreed. From a physical standpoint, they were a marked contrast to one another. He was dark-skinned and broad-shouldered, with rather large arms, and a barrel-chested torso above slightly bowed legs. His bright, glittering blue eyes were deep-set above a large hooked nose. If not exactly handsome, he was at least arresting.

In the fall of 1901 the young couple joined the faculty of Georgia State College in Savannah. Joseph Sandy taught his specialized skills—blacksmithing and wheelwrighting—as well as an occasional history course. Estelle taught English composition and music. The following year their first son, Edward, was born. Estelle now tried to use her influence among the light-skinned black southern elite, centered at the time in Charleston, to obtain an administrative position for her husband. She apparently failed, because later they moved to Greensboro, North Carolina, where they both taught at the Agricultural and Technical College. By 1906 Joseph Sandy had obtained a faculty post teaching blacksmithing and wheelwrighting at the more prestigious Lincoln Institute in Jefferson City, Missouri. The move was advantageous, but it meant that Estelle had to give up her valued network of social relationships.

At Jefferson City in 1908, Estelle gave birth to her second son, Joseph, Jr. Her third son, Chester, was born the following year on July 29.[3] Estelle would have liked a daughter.

For Chester and his brothers, their parents' contrasting histories bore heavily on their consciousness throughout their early years. Long afterward, they discovered that Estelle and Joseph had managed to protect them from some of the worst ravages of southern racism. Because as children they never learned to defer to whites, they would refuse to do so as adults. Surely this was one ironic consequence of their upbringing in the deep South.

# 2

# THE SOUTH

WHILE ESTELLE WAS STILL learning the ways of white gentility at the Scotia Academy, southern state legislatures were passing laws segregating and disenfranchising their Negro citizens. The result was a slow but steady drift of mainly poor southern blacks to the north and west. The migration became a flood by the 1910s, as more and more African Americans left the South in hope of finding a more secure life.

By the time Chester was born in 1909, an agricultural depression, race riots in northern and southern cities, and nearly a thousand lynchings had further aggravated the precariousness of black lives. The Himeses were by no means impoverished, and because Jefferson City was something of a border community, they hoped they could find there a stability that had hitherto eluded them.

Six months before Chester's birth, the Niagara Movement was born in New York City—an organization that later became the National Association for the Advancement of Colored Peoples (NAACP). An important leader of that movement, the Harvard-educated sociologist W. E. B. Du Bois, challenged the accommodationist views of the nationally recognized Negro leader, Booker T. Washington. In effect, Du Bois called for immediate access to the ballot box and legislation that would end racial violence. It is a measure of the times that Du Bois and his movement were then widely perceived as radical, though their views fell far short of the radical militancy Himes would advocate during his adult years.

Despite disappointments, Estelle Himes was not about to give up her dreams of bourgeois fulfillment, even though the means by which blacks might attain such success were now greatly diminished. The black middle class, such as it was, would now have to depend more on the Negro community for its sustenance and prestige. Rarely now was it possible for African Americans to overcome poverty as the Bomars had done, by constructing buildings and cotton mills for white businessmen. To add to their difficulties, rapidly developing technologies and expanding industrialization were rendering obsolete the kind of independent artisan Joseph Sandy Himes was teaching. Yet to all appearances, Lincoln Institute, Himes's new post, stood apart from the turmoils of the world it was educating its five hundred students to enter. A land-grant college for Negroes, it was situated on a thirty-six-acre campus overlooking the city.

The Himeses looked forward to their new situation. Joseph Sandy would teach blacksmithing and wheelwrighting. Estelle would care for the couple's three children, and would also be able to attend Lincoln's frequent concerts and recitals. She hoped that the small liberal arts faculty, the undergraduate debating and literary societies, and the fine college library would provide her with intellectual stimulation. She may have regretted that she was not offered a position on the music faculty, but she had her young family to occupy her.

The Himeses soon got to know their neighbors, some of whom, like President Allen and his family, may inadvertently have encouraged Estelle's ambitions for her husband. Perhaps someday Joseph Sandy, too, would become a college president. Joseph Sandy himself shared his wife's aspirations. When occasion warranted, the ambitious professor could ingratiate himself, even to the point of being obsequious. The couple's hopes ran high.

The children, during these years, were happily oblivious to their parents' dreams and obsessions. By and large, life for them was pleasant. They lived in an ample, comfortable house facing the campus and played together a great deal. They did not associate much with their neighbors' children, whom Estelle regarded as culturally inferior. She complained that they spoke poor English, while she was determined to keep her children's language "clear." She was especially protective of Chester.

Estelle's efforts to maintain standards of refinement are evidenced by a photograph that long remained in her son Joseph's possession. The Himes brothers and Estelle are sitting on a lawn in front of a brick house with white gingerbread woodwork and trellis, among a group of children, including those of President Allen. Toddlers Joseph and Chester are dressed alike in white dresses decorated with flowers and lace, and neatly tied shoes. Estelle clearly dotes on Chester, her favorite, with his cherubic smile, round face, fair complexion, and almost blond curls. The image is not unlike a turn-of-the-century photograph of a similarly dressed young Ernest Hemingway, who in later years became a manly idol of Himes's. Perhaps, in part, the two authors were reacting to their genteel mothers' strictures.

A most unhappy moment for Estelle came when Chester was three or four. She discovered to her horror that he and Joseph had painted each other's hair green with old house paint that had been lying about the premises. Estelle cut Chester's tresses, but his hair never grew back as she would have liked.

The pastoral serenity of the Himeses' life came to an abrupt halt in 1913 when Joseph Sandy resigned his professorial post. The reasons for the resignation are somewhat obscure. His aggressive behavior and airs of superiority may well have alienated colleagues. Possibly Estelle, who had been prodding her husband to seek a higher administrative post, caused him to overstep himself. Years later, in an early draft of Chester's autobiographical novel *The Third Generation,* the protagonist's father resigns in a rage upon learning that a younger man, specializing in automobile mechanics, is to be made dean over his head.

Professor Himes moved his family of five to Cleveland, where they lived with his now married sister, Leah. But a few months later he obtained a new teaching position and moved his family south again to Alcorn College in Mississippi, a state-supported secondary school for Negroes, which had known better times, first as an antebellum plantation house and later as a Presbyterian secondary school for white males. It now stood remote from major transportation routes. To get there, the Himeses took a train to Lorman, some fifteen miles distant. From Lorman they journeyed by buggy along gravelly roads, looking out at isolated farms and cotton fields tilled by black sharecroppers. On their arrival they found a general store, where foodstuffs and a few other essentials could be bought. Most of their shopping would have to be done at Port Gibson, a declining city on the Mississippi bluffs some seventeen miles to the northwest.

Still, in some respects Alcorn was an improvement over Lincoln. Its antebellum buildings were elegant, its tree-lined campus spacious, its laboratories and classrooms well equipped, and its extensive farm acreage more than adequate for training agricultural students. Moreover, the college provided the Himeses with a large house whose wide veranda fronted a generous expanse of lawn.

Joseph Sandy was an excellent craftsman and built much of their furniture. In addition, he promised to teach Sunday school in nondenominational classes, which the Himes children, among others, would attend. As for Estelle, she now had a servant who cooked and cleaned, allowing her more time for cultural activities.[1]

As the years passed, the social life of the Himes family revolved around picnics, barbecues, and croquet games with other faculty families; from time to time the older men would go on hunts. Though the Himes boys were too young to join the hunts, a compensating joy was the general store where they could gawk at the fascinating displays of country goods and listen to their elders chat and joke and gossip. As with so many other authors of southern origin, black and white, Chester Himes may well have acquired some of his storytelling proclivities here. Doubtless he had his share of childhood accidents and illnesses, but to Chester the Alcorn years seemed almost idyllic, and he later portrayed them as such in unpublished versions of his autobiographical novels.

But Estelle soon grew restless. Although she gave piano and violin lessons to her children and others, she felt that Mississippi was a cultural wasteland. Her husband bought her a Victrola on which she played classical and semiclassical recordings, but this was small recompense.

She feared for her sons' sensibilities, and because there were no public elementary schools for Negroes, she taught them herself. The brothers did not attend regular classes with other children until they were nine or ten years old. Their first schoolroom was the Himes living room or the Himes library. Their reading material was the mail-order English and American classics—Dickens, Thackeray, Longfellow, Poe, and the like—that Professor Himes had shipped to him.

Estelle would often read her sons adventure tales from Greek and Roman classics, and on occasion their father would join them, poring over articles in volumes of the *Encyclopaedia Britannica* as he prepared for his classes. Other kinds of reading material were scarce in the Himes household. Estelle subscribed to the *Ladies Home Journal* and the *Woman's Home Companion,* and Professor Himes read daily the *New Orleans Times Picayune.* Militant Negro newspapers were conspicuously absent from the household.

As they had done in Jefferson City, the boys played chiefly with each other since Estelle still feared the "vulgarity" of other black children. Indeed, she did what she could to bring out the "white" in her sons. Chester in his autobiography recalled her pressing her hand against his nose in an effort to suppress his Africanness. Her favorite word, he wrote elsewhere, was "ugly," which she used in both a moral and physical sense. Chester, the fairest yet moodiest of the three brothers, was confused and angry at being both black and white.

If Estelle was excessively protective, neither she nor her husband shrank from disciplining the children, although their transgressions were relatively infrequent. When their mother whipped them, Joseph would cry, but not Chester. He would take additional beatings rather than surrender to tears. On one occasion, Joseph recalled, their mother chased the brothers across the fields with a rattan switch for attending a baseball game she had forbidden them to watch. Estelle regarded baseball as "common."

Joseph Sandy, too, had his standards. One evening Chester uttered a rapt "damn" while reading a Poe story. The taboo word evoked a visceral response in his father, who pursued the child about the house with a razor strap for having uttered the obscenity. Still, Joseph Sandy was less the martinet than the teacher. Periodically he would take his sons to the shed out back or to the college machine shop, where he taught them the principles of carpentry, as well as the use of tools and machinery. These lessons stood Chester in good stead during the 1940s when he worked in the California shipyards. From the boys' point of view, though, their father's crowning achievement was his purchase in 1917 of an old Studebaker automobile. He used to service it from time to time while the boys looked on, fascinated. When their father was not about, Chester and Joseph loved to sit behind the wheel and pretend they were driving.

The boys rarely, if ever, left Alcorn before America's entry into World War I, and in their small back-country community they experienced few of the war's racial and political reverberations. Once during the war years, Joseph recalled, their father took them to the entirely Negro-populated Mound Bayou, Mississippi, a town whose ambiance delighted the brothers. They had been invited to stay at the home of a Mr. Moseley, the principal of a local school, whose son was one of Joseph Sandy's students. The town looked to be booming. A bank had long been established, and there were several schools and churches, as well as a Carnegie library. Located in rich delta country, Mound Bayou shone as a beacon of black economic achievement. Several very wealthy Negro families—cotton farmers, merchants, and businessmen—lived there, but what most astonished the Himes boys were the up-to-date electrical appliances and farm implements they saw and the brand-new automobiles. They also attended a Sunday service in a small white-painted church and heard their first fire-and-brimstone sermon, quite different from the staid Presbyterian homilies they knew at Alcorn. Here they began to experience some of the contradictions and varieties of southern Negro life.

Late in the summer of 1917, Estelle prevailed upon her husband to let her take Chester and Joseph to Cheraw, South Carolina, where she had been offered a teaching position in a small missionary school. Her decision to leave was an act of desperation. She felt culturally deprived at Alcorn, and she feared for her children's education.

Whether or not her separation from her husband was also caused by animosity between them is hard to say. Chester, in what he once called his "dishonest" autobiographical novel, *The Third Generation,* described his hero's light-complexioned mother as becoming increasingly resentful of her husband's blackness, a blackness, she felt, that held them back. Chester's brothers admit to emotional strains between their parents, but reject the view that the tension was racial.[2] Yet given Estelle's preference for things white, Chester's fiction may well have caught an unstated premise of her discontent.

Estelle's return to teaching was not a very happy one. She found Cheraw too isolated, and the constant rain depressed her. After a few weeks, she and her children trundled off to Augusta, Georgia, where two of her nieces, Margaret and Mabel, then in their early twenties, taught at the Haines Normal and Industrial School. The school was a missionary Presbyterian institution that embraced both elementary and high schools. Many of the six hundred students were "Geechies," pure-blooded descendants of African slaves from the Georgia Sea Islands, whose strong dialect astonished the Himes boys. Chester and Joseph were placed in the eighth grade despite their lack of formal schooling. Their mother had educated them well. They performed beyond their years.

The months the brothers passed at Haines were again different from anything they had known. For one thing, they enjoyed more freedom. They could associate now with other students on the campus without arousing their mother's anxiety and earn their fellow students' respect by absorbing their share of whippings for unscholarly behavior. Young Chester fell in love with his two lovely, light-complexioned teacher cousins. There were also barbecues and baseball and football games and even a Maypole dance. As new students, the Himes brothers had to prove their mettle. Chester and Joseph—"Cat" and "Goat," as they were called—fought their challengers as a team, the latter tackling them and the former pummeling them on their heads and chests.

Estelle, too, appeared more forthcoming. She had obtained a temporary position on the music faculty, which lifted her spirits. She told them more stories about their ancestors, revealing once again her strange mix of racial pride and revulsion, noblesse oblige, and racial defiance.

Chester's more immediate impressions were of a school mule that bit him on the nose while he was trying to steal an ear of corn, the "funny" ungrammatical diction of the Geechie children, and perhaps more portentously a terrible conflagration during which he observed the inhabitants of a Negro slum neighborhood scatter in efforts to save their belongings and themselves. Something about that fire (he had witnessed another such event years before in Alcorn), and a far worse one he later experienced in prison in 1930, would serve as a metaphor for the absurdist, all-consuming violence he depicted in many of his later writings. For the present, however, his stay at Haines meant that he was finally attending school with other black children, and that among his new acquaintances were the Geechies who brought him face to face with his African roots.

Estelle brought the boys back with her to Alcorn in the early summer of 1918. That September, both Chester and Joseph enrolled as students at Alcorn College. Edward, in the interim, had left home to attend Atlanta University. The family would see him infrequently from then on. Seven years older than Chester, he was never as close to his parents as his brothers were, and he was less close to his younger brothers than they were to each other. In the course of years, he made his own way in the world without them and eventually found a post for himself in the waiters' union in New York.

Edward's departure made little impression on his brothers. Their main business was to adjust themselves to their changed school environment. First, they had to endure the taunts of their darker classmates who made fun of their pale complexions and their physiognomy. Joseph remembered their being called "tadpoles" and "flatheads," among other epithets. Once again the brothers fought back as a duo, proving themselves capable of giving as much as they got. Crises always brought them closer. However, ten-year-old Chester was the more vulnerable and the more trusting of the two. Joseph recalled a classmate telling him that an absent student had gone out chasing whores. Chester, believing that the forbidden word meant "hoers," since so many of his fellow students were the children of farmers, enthusiastically relayed the information to his teacher, who slapped him for being sassy. Poor Chester stood puzzled by life's injustices.

At the end of the school year, Professor Himes again resigned suddenly. The bewildered children accompanied their parents to St. Louis, where their father had purchased a house some time before as a rental investment. The causes of Professor Himes's second resignation are not known. He does not seem to have affronted anyone; indeed, he was a popular teacher. Nor was Estelle the ferocious maverick she was portrayed as being in *The Third Generation* as Professor Taylor's wife, or as the gun-toting rebel in Himes's *The Quality of Hurt*. Indeed, according to Chester's brothers, Estelle was the last person in the world one would expect to carry a gun. Joseph thought there was reason to believe that Professor Himes might have irritated some envious white farmers by driving his Studebaker along country roads; a few had complained that he was disturbing their livestock. Edward, however, agreed with Chester's version in *The Third Generation:* that Estelle unsuccessfully tried to pass herself off as a white woman on public transportation and that Joseph Sandy was dismissed for his wife's misconduct.

In any case, Professor Himes's unemployment did not last long. The following September, he was appointed to the Branch Normal School, another state-supported Negro institution, in Pine Bluff, Arkansas. But his circumstances were, by now, considerably reduced. The school's plant and facilities were inferior to the ones he had known, and much of Pine Bluff was impoverished. Nonetheless, the family traipsed south again, finally settling in a house some distance from the campus. As before, Joseph Sandy taught mechanical arts and Sunday school, but one of his new responsibilities was the teaching of black history, which probably made him one of the first southern teachers to do so.

Professor Himes's efforts were not lost on his sons, who attended his classes. Joseph glowed with new pride, while Chester buried himself deeper in his books, unable to resolve his internalized conflicts. In one draft of his autobiographical novel, he spoke of the figures in Greek classics, especially the sulky Achilles, as being more real to him than persons in his immediate environment. His brothers remember him as being forever immersed in Poe. Perhaps Chester's later fictional heroes bear a faint psychological resemblance to the injured Achilles, not to mention the self-tormenting protagonists of Poe.[3]

Despite its drawbacks, Pine Bluff improved Estelle's morale. She involved herself in church activities and found a job as a public school teacher. Joseph believes that her haughty demeanor offended her husband's college president, J. B. Watson, who on one occasion threatened Joseph Sandy with dismissal.

Tensions in the family rose again, but the boys remained as close as ever. They would play tennis together a great deal and cross town from time to time to participate in school games. Estelle, of course, still did her best to protect them from sordid realities, but her efforts were now less successful. To get to school they had to pass through slums where prostitutes openly solicited customers. Their new schoolmates were not especially welcoming. Once more the boys were the objects of racial teasing, hooted at for their Caucasian features. Chester's reactions at these times were volatile. He could charm a roomful of people, but he was equally capable of exploding into fits of anger. Yet he excelled in his studies and especially benefited from the attentions of his English teacher, Miss Ernestine Copeland, a stickler for correct grammar and syntax, who also managed to convey to him a deep love of literature. To please her he decided he would become a writer.

The most traumatic event in the lives of both brothers occurred on their graduation day in June 1923. Joseph stood before an assembled audience of parents and children exhibiting his chemistry skills. His aim, he said, was to demonstrate how gunpowder was made. Ordinarily, Chester would have helped him in the preparation, but on this day he was sulking over something his mother had said to him. The gunpowder blew up in Joseph's face, blinding him. A few days later, Estelle rushed him off to the Barnes Hospital in St. Louis, which specialized in the treatment of eye injuries. Chester blamed himself for the accident. Although he was not at fault, he could not forgive himself. Had he transgressed against God, or was it because he had disobeyed his mother? He was not sure, and he never forgot.

Images of blindness, social and physical, recur several times in Himes's fiction. One of the celebrated detectives in his crime series is blinded by a young thug who throws acid at him. Significantly, Himes's penultimate published American work is titled *Blind Man with a Pistol.*

The explosion that took Joseph's eyes foreshadowed the end of the Himeses' southern years. Chester remained with his father that summer in Arkansas, but Professor Himes once again resigned his post. In September father and son returned to St. Louis, where the unhappy family reinstalled themselves in their house on Taylor Avenue.

# 3

# ADOLESCENCE

THE DISINTEGRATION OF THE HIMES family was now well under way. Chester and his parents lived in far smaller quarters than before, the rest of the house being let out to tenants. Estelle would take Joseph daily to the Barnes hospital for treatment and then return him to the Missouri State School for the Blind, where he shared a room with two other black children and ate with them at a table set apart from that of the white children. On weekends he was allowed to go home.

Chester once remarked that the school for the blind was the only nonsegregated institution in St. Louis at that time. In point of fact he was mistaken: the Barnes was nominally for whites, although some exceptions were made.

On their arrival north, Joseph Sandy had spoken grandiosely of going into business for himself, but hard times and tense race relations made him settle for odd jobs carpentering and wiring buildings for electricity. He also had difficulties with his fellow blacks, one of whom, Frank Williams, a community leader and principal of the all-Negro high school, rejected him for a teaching position. The two men took an immediate dislike to each other, and their antagonism may have been exacerbated by Chester's behavior at school. In his autobiography Chester wrote that he was "insufferably belligerent" and that he was understandably disliked by all the teachers and students he had come into contact with. His state of mind may be deduced by what he described as the "suicidal intensity" with which he engaged in high school sports.[1] His fellow students, he stated, used to gang up on him, injuring him when possible. One result was a dislocated shoulder blade that never healed properly.

Most of the time Chester felt himself friendless, and he used to wander the streets of the city alone. In a blue mood, he would walk to the railroad station and watch the trains pull in and out. He remembered intensely cold winter days when he would stand by himself on the Eads Bridge as horse-drawn beer drays crossed the frozen Mississippi. His solitude disoriented him. In *The Third Generation* Charles, his fictional counterpart, describes the loss of a coherent past. "There was no pattern, no continuity, no rational deletions," and hence no perception of an understandable present. "Meaning [was] all distorted as if coming suddenly and unexpectedly into a street of funny mirrors."[2]

At fourteen, too, Chester was becoming sexually aware. His sense of his own physical attractiveness was curiously muddled by the proximity of the Overton Beauty Company on Taylor Avenue, whose outdoor advertisements touted skin lighteners and hair straighteners for black people. His mother still tried to imbue the children, especially Chester, with the notion that "white" features were desirable, although by now Chester's skin and hair had darkened.

Chester missed his brother's companionship and continued to brood about his own guilt. Joseph, however, was making progress. If he did not learn very much at the state school for the blind, he did at least learn to read Braille and to play the clarinet. At the same time the doctors at Barnes had managed to scrape enough scar tissue from one of his eyes so that he could discern light from dark and faintly make out large objects. It was now possible for Joseph to take steps on his own, and Chester remembered lovely winter weekends when the brothers took long bobsled rides down the hills of the city.

Yet on the whole, the Himeses' nearly two and a half years in St. Louis were unhappy. Joseph Sandy's continuing failure to provide a reliable income aggravated Estelle's irascibility. He was even compelled to work part-time as a waiter in a speakeasy. In April 1924 he sold the house on Taylor Avenue to buy a small family flat on Sarah Avenue. Still, money remained scarce, and at one point Estelle swallowed her pride and sent son Joseph out into the streets to sell copies of a poem she had written:

> *The Blind Boy's Appeal*
> 1. Say, friend, do you ever stop to think
> "Suppose I should lose my sight,
> And should have to dwell, for the rest of my life
> In a land of perpetual night.
> 2. Never to see God's sunlight again.
> Nor the beauties which nature unfolds,

Nor the great inventions which men have worked out,
That challenge my eyes to behold."
3. Do you think if this cross you were called on to bear,
You could still face the world with a smile?
We face it that way; then give us a lift
To something in life that's worth-while.

In June 1925 Joseph Sandy sold the St. Louis flat and moved the family
to Cleveland, where his brother and two married sisters lived. He hoped
for steadier employment, but the principal inducement was a public school
system that also served the blind. The classes Joseph attended in St. Louis
made too few demands on him. All family decisions now centered on
Joseph—a situation that he felt tended to infantilize him. Chester, for his
part, resented the attention his older brother was getting. He, after all, had
once been his mother's favorite.

The Himeses first stayed with Joseph Sandy's married sister, Fanny
Wiggins, and her husband, Wade. They lived on East Seventy-ninth Street
in a racially mixed, working-class neighborhood near the Cleveland In-
dians' ballpark. Estelle disapproved of this arrangement, as did her sons,
because she regarded the Wigginses as a cut below them socially (Wade
was a fireman for Standard Oil). Their country manners and Fanny's dark
skin especially rankled. Both Chester and Joseph disliked the Wigginses'
sixteen-year-old son, Gerald, whom they thought fat, pampered, and not
very bright. They may also have resented Gerald's business acumen in gar-
nering tips for parking cars in the Wiggins front yard during the baseball
season.

Meanwhile, Joseph Sandy's efforts to find permanent employment were
no more successful than they had been in St. Louis. He and Wade concocted
elaborate schemes for going into business together, but, as before, much
of their planning was bluster. Finally, Estelle, exasperated, fled the house
with Joseph and found quarters elsewhere in the city. Chester and his father
remained with the Wigginses, but sometime later Joseph Sandy bought a
house on Everton Avenue in the Glenville section of Cleveland, a Jewish
middle-class neighborhood and the location of Joseph and Chester's high
school. The move could not have come at a better time, since Chester had
recently smashed up his Aunt Fanny's car in an accident, the first of many.

How could the hard-pressed Himeses have afforded such an investment?
Joseph thought his father probably made the down payment with the pro-
ceeds of the sales of his St. Louis property, hoping to rent out most of his
new Glenville rooms to tenants. Whatever the arrangements, the family came

together once more, though even in their new surroundings Estelle was not placated.

The Himeses were not isolated in Glenville; among their neighbors were Leah and Rodney Moon, Joseph Sandy's older sister and her husband, a federal meat inspector and part-time real estate agent. Estelle, however, felt the Moons condescended to them because of her husband's straitened circumstances. One result was that she turned her wrath on Joseph Sandy, who in earlier, easier times had given money to his sisters to help them move north. More recently, he had helped Rodney pay for his son's college expenses. Furthermore, the devout Joseph Sandy was also donating whatever extra money he had to his church. Given their precarious finances, Estelle's outrage was understandable. Joseph Sandy was foolish and profligate, she complained. Still, the two families maintained relations. Twenty years later Henry Lee Moon, Rodney's son, helped Chester establish himself as a writer in New York; Henry's wife, Molly, served as the model for Mamie Mason, the oversexed hostess in Chester's scandalous 1961 novel, *Pinktoes*.

Chester and Joseph were both enrolled in Cleveland's predominantly white East High School, even while they were living far outside the district at their Aunt Fanny's. The high school provided special services for the blind, and somehow Professor Himes managed to persuade the appropriate authorities to accept both his sons, despite the distance they would have to travel. Joseph later speculated that Chester was able to gain admission because he had to accompany Joseph on the long trolley ride. Another reason that an exception was made in his case was that Chester needed only three more months of schooling to graduate. When the family moved to their new home in Glenville, the school was practically across the street. Well into his sixties, Himes remembered his sixteen-year-old self masturbating behind the parlor curtains as the white high school girls passed in front of his house.[3]

In *The Third Generation* the protagonist, Charles (Chester), is overly sensitive and fancies rejections when it is quite likely he is only being teased. The few Negro students he encounters do not seem friendly, preferring the company of white students, and Charles determines that he will never again allow himself to be hurt. In effect, he will not allow himself to trust others. Still, granting Chester's Byronic self-portrayal, his brother recalled quite another Chester: a handsome young man, popular with whites and Negroes ("the girls ate him up"), one who danced the Charleston at school dances despite his mother's disapproval. In all likelihood both Chesters existed, given the wide polarities and mixed nature of adolescence. Indeed, the gregarious fellow and the supersensitive brooding individual existed as well in Chester's adult persona.

At about this time Chester's academic performance began to suffer, much to his mother's chagrin; his more permissive father did not comment. For the first time Chester found himself competing with other children as well educated as he was himself. Nonetheless, his entire secondary school record indicates that he had taken a full range of college preparatory courses. His university entrance transcript reveals that he had fulfilled requirements in English literature, rhetoric and composition, classics, American history, Greek and Roman history, political science, and mathematics. Chester said that he failed elementary Latin, but that his grade was somehow erroneously transcribed in his favor, making him eligible for admission to Ohio State University. He graduated from high school in January 1926, fully a year and a half before Joseph, who had to make up for lost time.

Chester's January graduation gave him a head start in looking for jobs. Sometime in February his uncle Andrew Himes, a waiter, helped him find work as a busboy in the Wade Park Manor Hotel, a fashionable establishment in the eastern part of the city. Chester hoped to save money to defray his college expenses. The job, however, proved a disaster. In *The Third Generation* we read of Charles Taylor's mix of feelings during his first days at work. To an extent, he reflects his mother's snobbery. The work is below him. As a busboy for waiters and waitresses, he'd be the "servant of servants." On the other hand, he is intimidated and made uneasy by many of the working-class help who sense that he is not one of them. Soon, however, his spirits pick up, and the pretty white waitresses clearly like him and flirt with him. In his autobiography Himes wrote that these experiences filled him with sexual desire. At opportune moments he raced to Cleveland's worst black slums to avail himself of prostitutes.

One of Chester's jobs was to remove the dirty room-service dishes from the guest rooms. On one occasion he strode into what he thought was an open elevator door. It was an empty shaft, down which he plummeted some thirty or forty feet. He suffered multiple injuries: one arm was nearly broken off at the wrist, three vertebrae were fractured, his jaw was broken, several teeth were lost, and there were other, lesser injuries. The physical pain was unbearable. He was heavily dosed with morphine in one hospital, and was then taken to another for treatment. He spent four months in the hospital, most of that time lying immobile in a body cast. After his release he wore a back brace that he would use for the rest of his life.

The psychological implications of his trauma were equally dramatic. Well past middle age, Himes still remembered the names of the doctors who treated him. To be sure, his fall looked to be accidental, but it did occur immediately after he had made overtures to a white waitress who he at once sensed was about to turn him down. Was it a rejection not unlike his mother's before Joseph's accident? The reality of refusal was now deflected by the greater pain of his own physical suffering, a kind of inadvertent castration in his own defense. One consequence was that Chester now recaptured the attention of his mother, who had been lavishing so much of her energies on his older brother.

The accident had consequences for Chester's parents as well. Joseph Sandy persuaded him to accept the seventy-five-dollar monthly compensation the Ohio Labor Industrial Board offered him. Estelle felt the settlement was not nearly enough and said that he should sue the hotel. Eventually the hotel did add a small stipend, but the differences between Chester's parents on the issue aggravated their mutual hostility.

In retrospect Chester believed his mother was right, that he should have sued the hotel for more money. But was Chester responsible for his parents' constant bickering? In *The Third Generation* he seems to suggest as much. Here lay new possibilities for guilt, rage, and self-punishment for his own role (desires?) in the family romance. But Chester now dreamed of leading a much different life in Columbus at the state university, hoping—in vain, as it turned out—that the whole messy business of family now lay behind him.

# 4

# OHIO STATE

CHESTER ENTERED OHIO STATE UNIVERSITY in September 1926. His first months on the Columbus campus were far from auspicious, but his education in American race relations really began here. The bewilderment and contradictions of his consciousness he could now blame on the absurdities and contradictions of the Negro's role in a race-conscious world. The guilt and rage he felt about himself could, with some justification, be directed away from himself. There was more than a germ of truth to his rationalizations, but somewhere inside he also knew that he was too complicated an individual to be defined merely as a product of society.

Up until now, Chester had been protected from outright prejudice. He had known or seen few whites in the South, and had lived for the most part in enclosed black communities in St. Louis. In Cleveland his situation was reversed, but the few blacks in the largely white school he attended aroused little racial hostility.

Columbus was another matter. There were shops, restaurants, movies, and recreational facilities that did not admit blacks, or admitted them only reluctantly. The university, for its part, denied the 800 Negro students both dormitory space and use of the student union. This was the policy even though, as Himes noted in his autobiography, one of Ohio State's football heroes was black.[1] Chester boarded in a house in the Negro quarter of town, some distance from the campus. There were two off-campus Negro fraternities, one of which Chester pledged for, but even these, he said later, admitted students on the basis of skin shadings, with men of lighter complexion being viewed as more desirable.[2]

The injustices of Jim Crow did not fully register on Himes's consciousness until long past his prison years, but it was as if his mother's self-contradictions were objectified by his environment. Paradoxically, it was precisely because he had experienced so little racism as a child that he became so enraged as an adult. For better or for worse, his upbringing had not conditioned him to exclusion.

At Ohio State Chester played at being both black and white without being fully aware of what he was doing. He bought a raccoon coat and a Model T Ford, smoked a pipe, drank bootleg whiskey, and dated pretty Negro coeds. In effect, he did what typical white college boys did, or what he believed they did. Among his friends was Stanton DePriest, the son of a member of Congress, Rep. Oscar DePriest. Chester took his meals with this friend and said later, "I felt important to be considered Stanton's friend and I used to lend him my car." If it is true, as he later claimed, that he didn't care whether white people liked him or not, and that he himself did not like, or have any use for, white people, he was nonetheless behaving in a fashion that mirrored the larger white world. There is no indication, at this time or afterward, that Himes ever identified himself with black culture, except with that of the black underworld. Neither black writers (except perhaps Richard Wright) nor black music (although he knew a few black musicians in his lifetime) figured strongly as writing models or subject matter for Himes's fiction. A sometime champion of black militancy and black separatism, he seems often to have preferred the company of whites as friends and lovers. The ambivalence he felt throughout his life was not unlike his mother's.

At first Chester found Columbus exhilarating. Black students had a social life of their own, and Chester joined the more popular of the two Negro fraternities, Alpha Phi Alpha. Normally initiates were paddled and thrown into the middle of a lake in Franklin Park, an upper-class Negro community, but members made an exception of Chester because of his injury. Along with his fraternity friends, Chester loved to attend football games. He recalled the buzz of excitement when Ohio State played Michigan. He reminisced fondly of football heroes: Benny Friedman and Benny Osterbann of Michigan; Wesley Ferrel of Ohio State; Red Grange, the "galloping ghost" of Illinois; and Red Cagle of Army. One of Chester's black friends, Tommy Thompson, played spectacularly for Ohio's freshman team and unlike other Negroes was allowed to move into the Stadium Tower dormitory.

Now Chester became more familiar with black popular culture. Most public entertainment remained segregated—at best, blacks could sit only in the balcony or in reserved sections of theaters—though Columbus had two black movie theaters. The more opulent of these was the Empress on Long Street. Himes vividly recalled a homosexual pianist who played wonderfully, while a singer named Hawkins could "knock the women out" crooning "Moonlight on the Ganges." The other theater, the Pythian, had a ballroom upstairs for large affairs and public dances, though Chester more often went downstairs to see black musicals and road shows—among them, *Lucky Sambo, 4-11-4, Brownskin Models,* and *Running Wild.* Such shows, he said, made stars of Ethel Waters and Josephine Baker. He also enjoyed minstrel performances and passed hours ogling the chorus lines of lithe, sensuous dancers. A few times, he went backstage to try his luck, but without success.

In *The Quality of Hurt* Himes wrote that he entered Ohio State with hopes of studying medicine, enrolling as an arts and science major. He was proud of possessing the fourth highest IQ of entering freshmen that year, but his intellectual capacities exceeded his performance. "[Had] rows with cracker instructors," he wrote John A. Williams in 1962, and while his back injury exempted him from military science and physical education courses, the highest grade he attained during his first term was a C in English. Elsewhere he noted that other students were better prepared than he. In chemistry, for example, he was unfamiliar with the equipment and quarreled with the lab instructor. His favorite lectures were those of a Professor Day, who would freeze cherries in liquid oxygen and throw them at students who napped during his course. In physics Chester lacked the mathematical background and needed more trigonometry and advanced algebra. In German, his knowledge of grammar was weak. Understandably, classes made him tense. On December 26, 1926, he was placed on academic probation.

Much of his time in Columbus, Himes wrote, was passed in the Negro slums visiting brothels, where he may have contracted a venereal disease. Near the start of his second term in early February 1927, he took several student couples to a combination speakeasy-whorehouse to drink bootleg beer and dance to phonograph records. A jealous prostitute broke up the party, cursing the girls and smashing their records. The students fled, and one reported Chester to the dean of students. Shortly afterward he was called into the dean's office and told to withdraw. His transcript spares him the ignominy of describing the reasons, recording merely poor health and failing grades.

Chester's return to Cleveland did not make his life easier. His parents argued over how he should be disciplined. The fury intensified. Joseph Sandy, now reduced to janitorial work, abdicated responsibility. Himes wrote that in his heart his father felt that Joseph's blindness was the result of

Chester's earlier infractions. However involuted the reasoning, Joseph Sandy adamantly resisted demands that he "do something" about his younger son's behavior. Estelle, for her part, was convinced of Chester's debauchery, but without her husband's cooperation, she could do little. Chester, meanwhile, fell ill. His "back froze up," and he required a doctor's care. After several weeks he drifted back to Cleveland's worst neighborhoods, resuming his dubious associations. So frequently did he visit brothels, gambling halls, and whiskey houses that he was eventually employed in several of these in one capacity or another.

At one point Chester did find work outside the ghetto as a bellhop in one of Cleveland's fancier hotels. Here, his main tasks were to furnish prostitutes to hotel guests who asked for them, and to sell bootleg whiskey on the side at outrageous prices. The rather complicated logistics of these arrangements were controlled by the black underworld, to which the young college dropout had become apprenticed. Chester drew most of his income from illegal enterprises inside the black community, associating with persons known by such monikers as Bunch Boy, Hotstuff, Red Johnnie, Cateye, Chink Charlie, Big Katzi, Dummy, Abie the Jew, and Four-Four. Himes later transferred some of their activities as well as their names to his hard-boiled Harlem crime novels of the 1950s and 1960s.

Despite his shady activities, Chester apparently still had time for his family. Joseph remembered Chester picking him up in a big car in September 1927 to drive him to Oberlin College, some thirty-six miles away. Joseph had graduated from East High with the highest honors in his class, which won him a full college scholarship. Chester thereafter spoke of Joseph with reverence, though his brother's example did little to stem his own drift toward the black underworld.

In late 1927 and well into the following year, Chester ran "important" blackjack games for Bunch Boy, whom he called his father figure. He also noted the arrival of Italian gangsters around this time, who eventually took over "policy" gambling operations from Negroes, Bunch Boy included. Chester himself gambled a great deal, especially at Hotstuff Johnson's dice parlor across the street from Bunch Boy's blackjack house. When he won, he would typically go on a clothes-buying binge. Clues to Himes's divided personality—adolescent, college student, gangster, dandy—may be gathered from his description of his purchases:

> I kept my hair pasted down with a white pomade . . . which I had learned to use during my last term in high school . . . my taste in clothes . . . was partly influenced by the collegiate style and partly by the clothes Bunch Boy wore.

I bought very expensive suits, shirts, ties, shoes and coats—stylish but not outlandish . . . I liked tweeds, Cheviots and worsteds . . . My most daring venture was a pair of square-toed yellow pigskin bluchers by Florsheim . . . I got to know the expensive men's stores where blacks rarely ventured.[3]

As Bunch Boy's sidekick, Chester led a life that revolved chiefly around gambling and pimping. At one point during the late summer, however, Bunch Boy departed, leaving Chester more vulnerable to other criminal attractions. He began smoking opium and stealing cars to impress an adoring young sneak thief named Benny Barnett. Benny, who knew a lot of girls, in turn invited Chester to his parties. It was at one of these that Chester met his future wife, Jean Lucinda Johnson, then seventeen, whom he later described as "the most beautiful brownskin girl I had ever seen." She "looked vaguely like Lena Horne in her youth but her complexion was a darker brown. Her skin was the warm reddish brown of a perfectly roasted turkey breast the moment it comes from the oven. She had a heart-shaped face, thick hot lips, and brown eyes. What there was about me that attracted her so I never knew, but she fell desperately in love with my immortal soul."[4] In an unpublished version of his prison novel, Himes called her Joan—Joan "who had loved me more than anyone ever has or ever will and who still does . . . Joan who had come the closest ever to understanding me. She had said as we stood once watching a sunset leak into Lake Erie: 'Why do you try to be so tough and casual? You're not, really, you're different . . . You have a great, grand mind full of beautiful dreams.' "[5] In this version, Jean/Joan hints at Himes's frailty of character while encouraging his dreams. Perhaps it was this clear-eyed view of him, touched only slightly by romanticism, that so irresistibly moved him.

Jean and Chester became lovers, though Himes wrote that he often treated her badly, sometimes leaving her waiting on street corners for hours, and other times leaving her in rented rooms "in lieu of room rent." He imagined himself expressing a pimp's hardboiled indifference, but there were other occasions when he would become overly possessive. Chester and Jean were hired to run a whiskey house by a "land prop" (Himes's term for the proprietor of a shady enterprise) named Margaret. They could live there together, Margaret told Chester, and if he were hard pressed, he could always hire Jean out. "I moved her into the house," Himes wrote, "but I never made her a whore."[6]

Some of the rougher customers made persistent passes at Jean, and Chester, to protect his honor, bought his first gun, which he fired on several occasions. Fortunately for all concerned, he missed his targets, but Margaret, the proprietor, evicted her tenants.[7]

Although nearly a year had passed, Himes's expulsion from Ohio State still rankled. Late in September 1928, he stole a car and drove back with Benny to the Columbus campus. He wanted to see his old classmates, to show them that he had thrived, that he had not been humiliated. After a series of small adventures and misadventures, drinking, dancing, and driving, Himes stole another student's identity card and forged his name on "fifteen or twenty checks," which he used for purchases in shops along the business district. That he had not been immediately apprehended, he wrote, "should have made me suspicious of my success, for Columbus was a racist city."[8] In the last of the shops, a clerk withdrew to the rear to telephone the police, questioning the authenticity of his signature. "I could have run. I should have run. But unfortunately I never did run. Maybe that was my inspiration for my book *Run Man Run* I wrote thirty-two years later."[9] Paralysis, the inability to run, occurs again and again at critical moments in Himes's life, and often emerges as a theme in his fiction: the unconscious guilt of his protagonists who want to get caught. Chester was sentenced to five months' probation for forgery and for issuing a check to defraud.

Chester's court conviction heightened the tensions between his parents. Estelle wanted to take possession of his pension and have him sent to an institution for delinquent adolescents. Joseph Sandy again refused to go along. Estelle said she'd sue for divorce.[10] One night Joseph Sandy left home after a violent quarrel. The following day Chester moved out to live with Jean in Benny Barnett's apartment.

As roommates Benny and Chester egged one another on. They would start a small crime wave. The two friends and a third recruit, Thatch, planned to steal Colt automatics and ammunition from the Ohio National Guard Armory that were stored in the Cleveland YMCA. They would drive to Youngstown and Warren to sell their loot to black millworkers. The burglary went off smoothly, but on October 3, 1928, at a dance hall in Warren, Chester was involved in a near shoot-out with one of the workers. The following morning, the three friends were arrested. The police report indicates that several fur coats were found in their car, presumably stolen. Chester was returned to Cleveland, fined, and given a suspended sentence, due in large part to his mother's pleas for compassion to a sympathetic municipal court judge. Benny and Thatch were not so fortunate; they were sentenced to thirty days each.

Within a month Chester found himself in far more serious trouble. His parents were now divorced and he was sharing a double bed with his father in a rented room somewhere in the black slums. Joseph was living in other rented quarters across town with his mother when he was not in attendance at Oberlin. Himes wrote that he tried whenever he could to avoid staying with his father: "Anything to keep away from that room that stank of my father's fear and defeat."[11] He dreamed of getting away from it all—the squalor, his parents, his brother, America—"somewhere where black people weren't considered the shit of the earth." He had fantasies of going to Tijuana, gambling, living "a wild gay life," and sleeping with "hotbodied senoritas."[12] If only he had the money to make the fantasy a reality.

One day at Bunch Boy's old gambling club, Chester overheard a Negro chauffeur bragging about the possessions of his rich employer, one Samuel Miller, and, more intriguing, where Miller kept his money and jewelry. On the evening of November 25, 1928, a heavy snow fell. Chester hid out on the premises, awaiting the Millers' return home.[13] He knew it was the chauffeur's day off, so that he could escape unrecognized. When the Millers arrived, he confronted them with his revolver and took from them over three hundred dollars in cash and five thousand dollars in jewelry. He tried to escape in the Millers' Cadillac, but got stuck on a muddy road.[14] Abandoning the car, he caught a train to Chicago and attempted to pawn the watch and the rings with a known pawnbroker "fence." Like the clerk in Columbus, the fence retired to the back of his shop. Himes sensed that he was phoning the police, but once again he froze. He could not run. "I never could run. I have always been afraid that one stupid mental block is going to get me killed."[15]

Chester was arrested. The Chicago cops handcuffed his ankles, dangled him upside down from a door, and beat him. He confessed and was returned to Cleveland to face charges. Awaiting his day in court, Chester swore he would not "feel" anything. He thought that he succeeded. What followed was some kind of mix-up. His parents were not present for the sentencing. Only the Millers sat huddled together far back in the courtroom. Perhaps Chester's lawyer was incompetent. He had been advised to plead guilty. The judge, Walter McMahon, sentenced him to twenty to twenty-five years in the Ohio State Penitentiary.[16]

On later occasions Himes related how astonished, shocked, and infuriated he was at the severity of the sentence. He thought that his age (nineteen) and the fact that he had never before served a prison sentence might be mitigating factors. He was convinced that if he were white, the judge would have been more lenient. Perhaps, but the deed, committed with a gun and some psychological violence, was considered under law an aggravated crime. One must also remember that he had been previously arrested for three admitted crimes within a two-month period, and by his own account had committed others for which he had not been apprehended. It is well to note, too, that he gave the appearance of being dangerous. He wrote of himself, "I discovered that I had become very violent. I saw a glimmer of fear and caution in the eyes of most people I encountered: squares, hustlers, pimps, even whores. I had heard that people were saying, 'Little Katzi [his nickname] will kill you.'" At his hearing, he expressed no remorse. Judge McMahon, on sentencing him, said he had taken ten years off his victims' lives.[17]

If Himes was testing himself for his limit of self-hurt, he had very nearly reached it. He was remanded to the penitentiary in Columbus on December 27, 1928, little more than a week after his sentencing. He remained there until September 21, 1934, at which time he was transferred to the London Prison Farm. On April 1, 1936, he was paroled in custody of his mother.[18]

# 5

# THE PRISON YEARS

HIMES ENTERED THE OHIO STATE Penitentiary ten days after his trial, in late December 1928, as number 59623. He was taken through the Bertillon routine (a set of physical measurements), was led before the chaplain for religious affiliation and before a doctor for medical files (he was registered as partially disabled), and was handed a gray uniform with a hickory-striped shirt. The next day he was assigned to the "coal company," charged with bringing back from the planing mill shavings used to heat the building. The "coal company" was housed in the basement of a low building near the west stockade. When Himes entered the dormitory—rows of double-decked bunks—he was mildly surprised to see the convicts playing cards, chatting, making music, playing records, or "mushfaking" (making metal rings, cigarette holders, and other small objects).

In due course Himes discovered the setting that would become his limited universe: the tin shop and the woolen mill, the hospital, the barbershop over the correction cells (the "hole"), the bathhouse, the dining hall, and the west cell house whose main gate stood in the middle. Later he made a sketch of the west cell house with its five rows of barred windows. The yard, some 600 feet by 400 feet, was crisscrossed with brick sidewalks. He located the death house and the empty pool, two feet deep, where the Negro convict band stood on clear days to play as the inmates marched to dinner. There was also a sunken garden and a greenhouse, as well as a pool that held alligators in the summer.

One winter day, Himes refused to dig out more shavings under the snow, claiming he was totally disabled. The guards locked him out in the freezing cold and later took him to the hole, where they slapped him around.

Afterward he huddled all night long under skimpy blankets with two other convicts in a freezing, stinking cell. Himes vowed never again to resist openly, but this was only the first of several near-death experiences he managed to survive in prison.

The worst came on Easter Monday, 1930, when fire engulfed the entire building, killing more than 330 inmates. Himes counted himself lucky. He could well have been a victim. Only the week before he had been removed from a portion of the prison housing the "punishment company," where many of the "insubordinate" prisoners later perished. The fire had been set by a few convicts probably to deflect attention from an attempt to escape. Flames spread from the scaffolding of a block under construction, over a thirty-foot wall and into the upper tiers of a building where prisoners remained locked in their cells. Most were burned alive because keys could not be secured quickly enough. Prisoners in the yard below meanwhile rushed into the burning building to break down doors to try to save the trapped inmates. Himes lauded their efforts in his autobiography:

> Given freedom of the yard when the fire got out of control, convicts from other blocks braved death, asphyxiation, and injury to climb the steep steps of the burning cellblock through the dense black smoke, scorching heat, and leaping flames to rescue those convicts locked in the infernos of their cells.[1]

Himes portrayed the holocaust vividly in a story in *Esquire*, "To What Red Hell" (1934), and retold it in *Cast the First Stone* (1953). His fictional autobiographical protagonists are so stunned with fear that they appear as mere spectators. (Years after the event he told a friend that he had aided in rescue efforts.) Now with terrifying clarity he had to face the possibility of his own imminent death. From here on he would confront the meaning of his own life. His fiction would be a means of self-discovery.

Himes was more than a survivor, although in prison physical survival was never assured, given the sporadic unprovoked violence of other prisoners, sexual assaults, and the murderous sadism of guards. His prison years also offered him a kind of worldly education. He would no longer be surprised at people's bestiality and the depths of their irrationality. He learned something of the class relationships within the prison community. He read law, wrote letters to the governor petitioning for parole, and came to understand the system that held him incarcerated. He also came to understand how some of the institutions within the penitentiary functioned: the clinics, chapels, classrooms. He saw how they were distorted versions of the larger society outside the prison. At the same time, for short periods he oversaw gambling and card-playing operations among convicts, paying off guards to look the

other way. In sum, Himes learned in his prison years how the world works—
"absurdly" (a term he used later)—and especially the Negro's role in such a
world.

To maintain his equilibrium, Himes had to come to terms with his anger,
to redirect his furies to safer channels. He was not always successful. He flared
into paroxysms of rage, refused work details, disobeyed guards' commands,
and broke other unspecified rules, for which he had to endure beatings,
reduced food rations, and solitary confinement. Yet, curiously, imprisonment
also meant that the burden of personal guilt was lifted. He was in one world,
his parents and Joseph in another. He was no longer responsible. Perhaps in
prison he was expiating what he imagined he had done to them. During these
years Himes never saw his brothers. It is likely that Joseph Sandy visited him at
least once, although Himes made no mention of it in his autobiography.[2] His
only other visitors were the ever loyal Jean Johnson and his mother Estelle.[3]

The daily routine of prison life, its unremitting dreariness, the pun-
ishments to which he was subject, as well as his small triumphs and means
of survival, are seldom evoked in Himes's autobiography, but are recalled
in telling detail in his novel, *Cast the First Stone* (begun and revised several
times after he left prison). But because the novel advances the time of events
to the World War II years (probably on the advice of Himes's editors), the
account holds occasional anachronisms. Where the book rings true autobi-
ographically is in Himes's revelations of his white protagonist's psychology
over the grind of years: his terrors, his tedium, his shame, his narcissism,
his humiliations, his revulsion at the constant squalor he confronts, and of
course his rage and suicidal despair at ever getting out. There are, as well,
rare moments of tenderness and exhilaration with his companions. Prison
shaped Himes's manhood and urged him forward as a writer.

Himes also had to acclimate himself to the more or less overt homosexuality that permeated prison culture. Not only did he have to fend for
himself, he also, and more significantly, had to open himself emotionally
to others, give himself over once more to vulnerability, allow himself to be
"hurt." There is some suggestion that he succumbed to at least two convicts.
One of them, Prince Rico (Duke Dido in his novel), he loved deeply. He was
erotically attracted to the other man, a believing Catholic (named Lively in
one of his draft manuscripts). In "Present Tense," this inmate is called Bobby
Guy. He arrives in his company looking "like a doll, small and curly headed
with brown, limpid eyes and a lisp and a pure peach and cream complexion."
Bobby tells the protagonist, Jimmy, to kiss him and tries to room with him
but is taken to hospital the next day with appendicitis. When Bobby later tries

to sell himself for three dollars, Jimmy is disgusted.[4] It is not clear whether the actual relationship ever became carnal, though Himes seems to have given this inmate money and bought him clothes. He even took catechism classes to be able to attend Mass with him. (Himes may have converted to Catholicism at this time, although, judging from several of his stories, he struggled with his faith.)[5] Whatever the nature of the relationship, it seems to have ended unsatisfactorily. The character Jimmy also tells of being followed for awhile by a fellow who said he had fallen in love with him at the age of twelve when he had seen him on the train platform in Port Gibson. Jimmy finds him repulsive.

Himes met Prince Rico in 1933 at about the time Rico entered prison. Rico, a Georgia Negro, wrote and collected work and prison songs and planned to use this material for a folk opera he was composing. He made no pretense concerning his homosexuality, and he and Himes became lovers.[6] They read aloud to one another, wrote a play together, worked on an "opera" together ("Bars and Stripes Forever"),[7] encouraged each other's creative efforts, and exchanged ardent views about the movies they had seen and the authors they enjoyed (mostly O. Henry, Hemingway, Hammett, and Maugham). Once when Himes broke his arm playing baseball, Rico typed for him. Rico lovingly called Himes Puggy Wuggy. They met each other's mothers on visiting days, and Rico's mother later corresponded with Himes. What Estelle thought of this is unknown. Himes's love affair with Rico inevitably aroused the envy and suspicion of prisoners and guards who separated them.

Homosexuality, though frowned upon in theory, was unofficially sanctioned in the upside-down world of prison life. When Himes was transferred to the London Prison Farm the following year, he and Rico carried on a correspondence.[8] They met again in Los Angeles during the World War II years, but by that time each professed a preference for women. Nonetheless, Himes wrote Carl Van Vechten in 1952 that the most fulfilling relationship he had ever had was with the man whom he called Dido in *Cast the First Stone*.

One of the factors that drew Himes to Rico was their mutual need for fantasy. Movies especially entranced them. They lost themselves in Hollywood gossip, immersed themselves in movie magazine lore, and pretended to identify with the stars. But it was the films themselves—frequently shown in the prison—that most affected them, evoking images of life outside the walls and at the same time reminding them of where they were. The following fragment is drawn from one of Himes's discarded prison manuscripts. Jimmy Monroe is speaking:

Oh my God, how I used to live in those pictures . . . And what did we get when the picture came to the end? . . . Plenty of self pity anyway . . . They helped a lot. They made us softer, more human. They gave us a certain perspective in the grind of years. Oh, they did a lot for us, morally, spiritually, emotionally. But they hurt us too. Oh, my God, they hurt too. You had to come back to a cell . . . to the rooted, immovable, eternal prison of stone and steel, and to the gutless, stale, tawdry, callous convicts.[9]

In some four pages Himes listed the movies and stars he had seen: Clive Brook in *The Night of June 13th,* George Raft in *Taxi Dancer,* Cab Calloway in *Minnie the Moocher,* Nancy Carrol (a favorite) and Fredric March in *Laughter,* Richard Arlen (whom he calls "Dick" elsewhere) and Gary Cooper in *The Virginian,* Nancy Carrol and Buddy Rogers in *Follow Through,* Nancy Carrol and Cary Grant in *Hot Saturday,* Bing Crosby in *The Big Broadcast.* Himes also remembered stars like Helen Kane, Clara Bow, and Laurel and Hardy. In other passages he listed *Cimarron, Cavalcade,* and *Paramount on Parade,* and spectacles like *Ben Hur* and *Gold Diggers of 1933. Skippy* really made him cry.

Striking in this compendium is the absence of racial sensitivity, hostility, or resentment. The passion with which Himes invoked these names cannot be gainsaid. The films and the stars transcended race, became for him emblems of life. Even when color or race was mentioned, nothing was made of it. Jimmy Monroe longingly remembers Bing Crosby singing, "You have the soul of an angel, white as snow."[10] Rico, in a letter to Himes, wrote that he loved him with the poignancy of Al Jolson singing "Mammy."

Movies were not the only source of popular culture from which Himes drew sustenance during his prison years. In another section of his manuscript, Jimmy, the budding convict author, reads the "slicks"—*Cosmopolitan, The Saturday Evening Post, Liberty,* and *Colliers*—and tries to imitate their styles.[11] He sends his own stories to these magazines, but they are rejected. Jimmy observes ruefully that his own stories are replete with self-pity. Regardless, Jimmy is almost as addicted to the slicks as he is to the movies:

I read of these storybook characters' dilemmas and loves and hates and misfortunes, projecting myself into their storybook lives, and suffered with them, sympathized with them, pitied and fought alongside of them, experienced all the soft, mushy emotions which I could not experience in the brutal . . . days. I made lonely crusades into a fantastic dreamland that grew out of the written page . . . and I broke my heart every time a woman said goodbye to the man she loved.[12]

Afterward he would be ashamed of his sentimentality and become "invariably more vulgar, obscene, callous." The two parts of his ego "were very ashamed of each other."

Himes also read westerns and detective pulps. One of the latter was *Black Mask,* and one of the authors he alludes to in his manuscripts is the pre-Hammett writer of hardboiled private eye fiction, Race Williams. That Himes benefited by the terse, deadpan prose of writers of this genre is most evident in his first published novel, *If He Hollers Let Him Go* (1945). Traces of their involuted plots can be found in much of his later detective fiction. But beyond popular culture, Himes's taste was catholic. His mother and schoolteachers had imbued him with a love of literature, and in prison he read everything from dog stories to the classics—whatever he could get his hands on.

Once Himes had begun writing, he genuinely concerned himself with problems of craft. One of his prison novel manuscripts finds Jimmy and a companion reading Maugham's "The Narrow Corner" and arguing the merits of presenting character by means of someone's thoughts or by means of their actions. In actuality, the argument revolves around Maugham's methods as opposed to Hemingway's (though Hemingway is not mentioned by name). Jimmy is sympathetic to Maugham and likes his work, but he comes down solidly on the side of Hemingway.[13] This episode is clearly autobiographical. Later, in a letter to Van Vechten, Himes wrote:

> In the story of Jimmy and Rico, I have Jimmy develop an ambition to write and reveal the growth of emotional motivations for various short stories which he writes during that time. Which, of course, is more or less autobiographical. That is when I began writing.[14]

Himes probably began writing fiction in late 1931. His first pieces were published in 1932 and 1933 in Negro publications: *Abbott's Monthly and Illustrated News, Bronzeman, The Pittsburgh Courier,* and *Atlanta Daily World.*[15] A couple of them, such as "A Modern Marriage" and "Hero: A Football Story," told rather acidly of youthful chivalric delusions. Most were vignettes and sketches about convicts and prison life, although a few dealt with the criminal world outside. One, "Prison Mass," required three successive issues of *Abbott's Monthly* because of its near novella length.

More prestigious and lucrative was the publication in *Esquire Magazine* (April 1934) of "Crazy in the Stir," for which Himes was paid seventy-five dollars. Later that year *Esquire* published "To What Red Hell." For *Esquire,* Himes's principal figures are white and their author's race is not identified. Possibly Himes or Arnold Gingrich, the editor of *Esquire,* thought the magazine's readership would not be especially drawn to Negro characters different from the then popular Amos 'n' Andy stereotypes. Meyer Levin, Gingrich's assistant, told Himes that "To What Red Hell" received greater response than any other fiction published in *Esquire* that year.[16] This success did wonders for Himes's ego. He was now more than a prison number; he had a name, an identity. He was a writer. Wardens and guards had better be wary. Even his fellow convicts grudgingly respected him—although they seldom read his work.

Much of what Himes wrote during his prison years is apprentice fiction. Himes himself did not want to include any of his early prison pieces in his 1971 anthology, *Black on Black*. His reluctance is understandable. Often his prose very nearly caricatures the cliches of the popular magazine fiction he was trying so hard to emulate:

> He had searched for life in the gambling clubs, the vice dives, the gay night clubs—the fleshpots. He knew, now, that it was the lure of the synthetic gaiety produced by drink, the animal attraction in the hot eyes of prostitutes . . . He had realized that he had sought for gold among the tinsel, he had thought it to be gold for which he had sought . . . He should have known by that persistent yearning in his heart, that yearning for beautiful things, which would not be denied.[17]

Not surprisingly, Himes put much of his own experiences into his stories, but their tortured syntax and trite images suggest that he was not being quite honest with himself. He wrote what he thought his readers wanted to read, what he thought they expected, what he may even have believed he believed. Too much biographical exposition clutters his portrayal of characters, and the narratives themselves are often blatantly ironic and sentimental.

Yet granting all these faults, one also finds in his early fiction the seeds of the later Himes. For example, in "He Knew," one of two tough black cops kills a couple of burglars whom he later discovers are his sons. Oedipal implications apart, the story anticipates Himes's hardboiled policemen, Coffin Ed Johnson and Grave Digger Jones, twenty years hence. He was learning. He had an eye for chaos, for the grotesque and the absurd ("To What Red Hell"). He understood the anger, racism, and desperation of a white prisoner ("Crazy in the Stir"); the fear of execution ("His Last Day"); and the amorphous yearnings, rationalizations, and callow intellectualizing of three worshiping convicts in "Prison Mass." One sees him moving toward a more concise narrative in "A Modern Marriage," where a young man and woman pretend to each other they are romantic lovers. He was also capable of clearer, harder, less "literary" prose, influenced, as we have seen, by the tough-guy authors he liked to read in pulp magazines: "He frowned and flipped the cigaret against the wall at the back of the cell. He was conscious of a dull burning resentment at having been sold by a lousy frail. He didn't claim to be smart but he didn't usually act that dumb. Well a jane had been many a con's Waterloo."[18]

If his pieces were derivative, their predetermined structure did give form to his contradictions, allow for his tensions, provide some order for the meaninglessness he sensed around him. Moreover, because his work had to pass the prison censor (often the warden's daughter), there was much he could not say. Would he have been able to write about homosexual tenderness, the thievery and corruption of prisoners and guards, the racism, the sadism, the violence? A desperate letter Himes wrote to the prison censor in late 1933 reveals what he was up against: "I have a script which I have written especially for *Esquire Magazine* which I would like to consult you about before I send it out to you. It is a story which deals with the affection between two convicts. *It is not vulgar,* although it cannot be termed conventional either. There is the implication in one of the character's thoughts of sex perversion—but not the statement."[19] He went on to say that *Esquire*, a magazine for men, requested stories that were off the beaten track, adding, "I have had so many different upbraidings I would not like to have my stories discredited because some official does not personally care for my style of work."

The script was not sent out. But it was an achievement of sorts that several stories did pass beyond the prison walls. Indirectly they may have served other purposes. An investigation following the Easter Monday prison fire highlighted the terrible conditions in the penitentiary, and measures were taken to set up a special parole board. Himes was among those convicts who benefited from a review of their cases. He was obviously not the first convict author in the Ohio state pen (O. Henry had also begun his literary career there), yet the fact that Himes's work was published in a "respectable" magazine surely strengthened his argument for a shortened sentence.

# 6

# FREE AT LAST

HIMES'S RETURN TO CIVILIAN life was not altogether auspicious. Times had
changed, and when he emerged from prison on April 1, 1936, he found a
world very different from what he remembered. He had been arrested when
faraway Harlem Renaissance writers and artists were being celebrated, and
were celebrating themselves, for their presumed "primitive" qualities, their
spontaneity, and their distinctive pleasure culture. Had this mythology of the
easy life penetrated to the Midwest? By his own account, Himes had robbed
the Millers to take the money and have a good time. His years in prison were
devoted to survival, physical and emotional. Outside prison walls, there was
the Depression. The current political and popular culture apotheosized the
poor, the underdog, the ordinary citizen. Blacks and whites needed to link
arms and struggle for a just and equitable world. African Americans, for the
most part, remained skeptical, but many of their leaders, their intellectuals,
their literati, turned to the banners of the Left. After all, where else was there
to go? Notions of a black culture, a culture apart from the rest of America,
were now seen as a romantic fantasy.

None of this was easy for the newly freed Himes to assimilate. His
tendency was to rely on his own experiences to assess reality. Released into
his mother's custody, he tried to adapt to his environment as he remembered
the old days. Estelle had come north again with Joseph, who was now working
in Columbus. While Chester was still in prison, Joseph had gone from Oberlin
to Ohio State, where he earned a doctorate in sociology. At present he was
employed as an administrator for the Columbus Urban League. Mother
and son awaited Chester's arrival with trepidation. They loved him, but
feared a resurgence of the old rebelliousness, a falling back to his dissolute

ways. Their fears were not unfounded. Upon his arrival, Himes wrote, he was so sex-starved that he almost immediately repaired to the black slums to relieve himself with prostitutes. Memories recollected in tranquility are always suspect. Some thirty-five years later, Himes recalled that these women were so pleased with him they serviced him free of charge. It was not long before his mother noted the smell of sex about him, and disputes arose between them once again. Estelle would undoubtedly have been even more distressed had she known that Chester was also associating with ex-convicts, gamblers, and other marginal types.

The crowning blow came when Himes's disreputable new friends introduced him to marijuana. Chester, who had no idea of the weed's effects, cried out one morning that he was having a heart attack. The doctor who called at the house informed Estelle of the source of his symptoms, whereupon the outraged Estelle reported her son to his parole officer. Soon Chester departed for Cleveland to live with his father. Estelle returned to South Carolina.

Joseph Sandy now worked as a mechanics teacher for the Works Progress Administration and lived in a dreary two-room flat on Ninety-third Street off Cedar Avenue. Because he was "involved" with a woman, he had little time or money for his son. The changed environment may have reawakened Himes's literary ambitions. He resumed writing stories about the life he knew, that of criminals and prison, aiming them first at slick magazines. All but *Esquire* rejected them. *Esquire* published "The Visiting Hour" in September 1936, and "The Night's for Cryin' " in January 1937. Beneath their hard-boiled façade, these stories express a mix of melancholy and unrelenting fury.

Himes's accident compensation was discontinued in April 1936, which meant he now had to fend for himself. Ironically, his first job upon arriving in Cleveland in July was waiting on tables at the Wade Park Manor Hotel, the scene of his traumatic accident years before. His Uncle Andrew contacted the black headwaiter, Dick Smith, who took Chester under his wing. Himes's short story "Headwaiter" portrays Smith as trying to find a nice balance between his responsibilities, compassion for his Negro underlings, and his own rigorous work ethic, while dealing with abusive whites. Himes clearly liked Smith, but he looked also to other role models. Among these was the black politician and Congregational minister Grant Reynolds. Another was Sidney Williams, director of the Cleveland Urban League. Since Himes's work at the hotel was at best intermittent, he sought these men out in May 1937 in the hope that they would help him find steadier work. They offered only advice, but Himes did keep in touch with them long after to learn their views on race politics.

40

If Himes's return to Cleveland did not yield immediate literary success, he did make a couple of useful contacts, one of whom was Langston Hughes. Himes met Hughes sometime in August. Hughes, at the time, was living with his aunt, and writing and directing plays in the old Karamu settlement house on Central Avenue. Himes had rewritten a couple of his stories as plays ("To What Red Hell" and "Day after Day"), and tried to sell them to Hughes. Hughes did not take them, but the two men became friends, and in later years the always generous Hughes put Himes in touch with any number of influential people in Hollywood and New York.[1]

An unlikely source of literary encouragement was Himes's cousin Henry Lee Moon, a journalist, who during the late 1930s worked as a federal housing official in Washington, D.C. Over a period of eight years, the cousins socialized occasionally and exchanged letters, in which Henry would convey his reactions to Chester's stories and advise him where they might be published. Chester's letters to Henry during these years appear somewhat deferential, while at the same time assuming a kind of familial camaraderie. One gets the impression that Himes was not altogether comfortable addressing his "successful" cousin.[2]

By far the most important event for Himes during the summer of 1937 was his marriage in July to Jean Lucinda Johnson. Jean had remained devoted to him during his long incarceration, but she was not blind to the difficulties that lay ahead. She was familiar with Himes's erratic moods, his betrayals, and his sudden eruptions of anger. She knew as well about his other women and his relationship with Rico. In a discarded autobiographical manuscript, Himes's adolescent protagonist impregnates a seventeen-year-old girl, probably modeled on Jean, and suggests she marry someone else. The Himes character eventually goes to prison. How much of the manuscript corresponds to actual events is uncertain. In any case, Himes was twenty-eight years old at the time of his marriage; Jean was twenty-seven.

The nuptials were performed on August 13 before a justice of the peace. Estelle refused to attend because she felt the dark-skinned Jean was her son's inferior. After the ceremony Chester moved out of his father's flat and lived with Jean in a succession of rented rooms. Desperately poor, they leaped to accept dinner invitations from Chester's uncle Rodney Moon, who would also give them food to take to their rooms.

Clearly, what Himes really wanted was a steady job. Times were grim, and Himes was, after all, a black ex-convict. Ideally, he would have liked to earn a living as a writer, but he was realistic enough to recognize that this was not immediately feasible. Nonetheless, he thought of himself as a writer and never ceased writing and revising his stories, one of which he turned into a homoerotic play, "Idle Hours," dealing with two convicts. Meanwhile, he continued writing and rewriting his prison novel.

What especially rankled with Himes was his failure to provide for Jean.[3] He was still so upset by his parents' marital disputes that he believed his own shortcomings as a breadwinner compromised his manhood. The violent anger he used to turn on Jean, his drinking, and his subsequent womanizing reflected deep-rooted fears about himself. In time he came to identify poverty as a major source of these fears. His first semi-autobiographical novels of the mid-1940s portray racism as having deleterious economic, social, and deeply psychosexual effects.

Finally, in November 1937 Himes found WPA work in the suburbs, digging ditches and dredging sewers. The physical exertion affected his back, reminding him of his punishment details in prison. The pay was minimal, but beyond that, his pride demanded identification as a writer. He sent off numerous letters to state and local officials, who ultimately promoted him to research assistant at the Cleveland Public Library, where he wrote vocational bulletins. He had begun earning ninety-five dollars a month but aimed for higher things. By mid-1938, he achieved the official status of writer and busily engaged himself in churning out fragments of state and local history. Unhappily, he did not enjoy his new rank for long because, he said, a piece he wrote embroiled him in arguments with his new supervisors. Set in the nineteenth century, the work dealt with the acrimony that arose between Shaking Quakers and Mennonites, both of whom expected Jesus to visit their respective camps on the same day. Himes's supervisors evidently thought his treatment of the subject offensive, and demoted him to research assistant. Outraged, Himes wrote "long, intense, emotional and extremely angry letters to the state director, to the national director in Washington and finally to President F. D. Roosevelt personally. I think that was the beginning of my protest writing—at least those letters were long enough to make a book."[4] He may have been embittered, but he still believed the system capable of redressing injustice.

Himes's persistence paid off. Later in the year he was restored to the status of writer—here his cousin, Henry Lee Moon, may have helped—but he transferred to another project under the aegis of a "fat mannish woman who worked the hell out of me." He says he was assigned to write the first third of an Ohio history essay and then compelled to produce the entire piece, some seventy-five thousand words in length. His treatment, for some reason, was not printed, and its whereabouts remain a mystery. At the start of 1940, he also wrote and edited a Cleveland guide. The essay was never printed.

Himes's memories of exploitation notwithstanding, one of his colleagues remembered a more upbeat Himes. Ruth Seid, later known as the novelist Jo Sinclair, worked on a project with Himes in 1938. They took to each other immediately, she wrote, met every day on the job, and became good friends.[5] Seid was only twenty at the time. She recalled a good-natured young man who dreamed with her that one day they would both become famous writers. Seid had had two short stories published and told Himes about Richard Wright's first book of fiction, *Uncle Tom's Children.* Until then, Himes had not heard of Wright, who later played an important role in his life.

Seid and Himes worked for the most part alone on the second floor of the library at the John White Collection, "a quiet beautiful room with massive tables and special books for scholars." Between stints of work, they would talk about books, theater, movies, politics, and life in general. Himes was a charmer, Seid wrote, very handsome and articulate. She was especially taken by his account of the "heroic work" he had done during the prison fire.

In time, Seid began to meet the Himeses in the evenings. Jean she remembered as beautiful, intelligent, sweet, verbal, and "crazy" about Chester. They enjoyed much talk, a lot of walking, and eating cheap. On several occasions their supervisor, Miss Pearl Moody, a trained librarian on leave of absence, took the three of them out to dinner. Evidently Himes charmed her as well. Once Himes took Seid to an after-hours drinking spot in the ghetto. There was a police raid, but Himes got them out, coolly and efficiently, before any arrests could be made. Seid was impressed.

After about a year Seid was transferred to another project and subsequently saw little of Himes. On leaving, she remembered "some astute finagling on his part with money and in the end I gave it to him."[6] She would not be Himes's only friend who recollected him as a persistent borrower. Himes was not always as affable as Seid remembered. Warm and ingratiating one moment, he could flare into tantrums the next, not unlike Joseph's memories of his childhood. Penury, racial snubs, literary failures, and his ever-present anxieties about his wife and parents no doubt contributed to his volatile moods. Though not an alcoholic, he could on occasion drink heavily, which afforded him temporary relief but left sour depression afterward. At these moments Jean stood bravely by, aggravating his despair. Invariably he would turn his fury on her.

Another friend at this time, Dan Levin, offered different impressions of those years. Levin had advertised for writers for his new publication

*Crossroad,* and among the submissions sent him was Himes's angry fiction. He invited the Himeses to his apartment to get acquainted, and on their arrival Himes looked dreadfully ill at ease. He told Levin that he had been to jail for an adolescent theft, and seemed so angry that Levin wondered almost at once whether Himes could ever be capable of a frank and open relationship. In the course of months the two men did become good friends (Levin served as the prototype of Abe Rosenberg in *Lonely Crusade*), and Levin concluded that what he saw that first day was someone who was "basically hurt, high strung and brilliant."[7] He was also immediately impressed by Jean's "taut dignity" and poise. After the interview Levin stood with his wife at the window. Himes "strode off angrily," while Jean "walked calmly beside him as if steadying him to keep him from blazing away like an angry comet."

During the summer of 1939, Himes approached the editors of Cleveland's three daily newspapers for assignments. Louis B. Seltzer of the *Cleveland Press* put him off, but later that year reportedly told him, "I could not hire you if you were Jesus Christ re-incarnated." Himes said he was told much the same at the other papers. Negroes were not employed as writers, presumably because white reporters would object. Himes did, however, meet an editor whom he regarded as sympathetic. N. R. Howard of the *Cleveland Daily News* had read his stories in *Esquire* and liked talking with him about literature. They exchanged views on good writing, discussed the authors who interested them (Faulkner and Wright), and then got around to race relations. What Himes especially liked about Howard was that he absolved him of his guilt. He told Himes he had amply paid his debt to society, something Himes may not have been quite ready to acknowledge to himself.

By November 1940 Howard was secretly using Himes as a writer and paying him out of pocket. He was assigned to write vignettes about Cleveland's ethnic neighborhoods, which seems to have involved Himes standing on street corners to sop up the atmosphere. Himes's brief pieces reportedly appeared in a box on the editorial page under the heading "This Cleveland," signed "CH." In a letter to the black novelist John A. Williams years later, Himes said that he believed that these pieces were very popular, and that one or two may have been printed elsewhere.[8] After about ten weeks he quit, though Howard promised to keep him on at a steady fifteen dollars a week. Too much time was being consumed, and too little money was involved. More than anything, Himes wanted to get on with his own writing.

How much of Himes's unbridled anger and hurt was racially induced? According to Joseph Himes, it was never so fierce as it would become in later years. Himes himself wrote, "While on the Writers Project, I did not feel the racial hurt so much . . . My domestic life was happy and we were all, black and white, bound into the human family by our desperate struggle for bread."[9] But anxieties about himself are expressed in some of the stories he had begun writing for Levin's *Crossroad*. One story, a heavy-handed satire, tells of a worker who shoots a senator named McDull, who wants to terminate the WPA because he says too much money is being spent. Another piece tells of a married WPA worker, barely surviving, who deludes himself with drink that he is not so abject and humiliated as he generally feels himself to be. A third tale depicts the desperation of an impoverished unemployed industrial worker who prays for war in hopes of getting back to work. Revealingly, in the two latter stories, the protagonists' miseries are compounded by their feelings of failure as husbands.[10] In one sense, Himes's pieces conform to the protest-proletarian literary fashion of the times, but they differ from the trend in that their protagonists, rather than being noble or heroic, are angry and defeated. Indeed, these men seem without hope.

In March 1939 Himes petitioned the Ohio governor for restoration of his citizenship. Without full citizenship, he would not have been allowed to live outside Ohio, and he was hoping now to look for work out of state. Meanwhile, he continued reworking his prison novel, then titled "The Way It Was." To further remove himself from his white protagonist, he shifted his point of view from the first to the third person. Jean Himes, however, remarked that the novel was considerably more detailed and sophisticated in its first drafts than when it was finally published as *Cast the First Stone* in 1953.[11]

Himes was determined to make himself acceptable to publishers. He knew that his writing days on the WPA were coming to an end and that he would soon have to look elsewhere to support himself. The invigorated American labor movement, especially the newly formed Council of Industrial Organizations (CIO), seemed to offer him some hope. Around the start of 1940 he had begun writing and editing articles about CIO history for the *Yearbook of the Cleveland Industrial Council* and the *Cleveland Union Leader*.[12]

As Himes saw it, the emergence of the CIO provided African Americans with a means of asserting themselves. The new union recruited men and women on an industry-wide basis, as opposed to its older rival, the American Federation of Labor, whose members were drawn in accordance with their occupational skills. Since most blacks were confined to unskilled jobs, CIO affiliation would presumably allow them to bargain for the first time. Moreover, the CIO proclaimed its opposition to racism, while the AFL had a long history of racial exclusion. Himes's union pieces have not been found, but his optimism of this period stands in sharp contrast to his disillusionment only a few years later, when he deplored organized labor's failure to understand the psychology of the Negro.

Himes recognized that another means of getting on with his career would be to expand his contacts with the black artistic community. During the week of July 4, 1940, he and Jean journeyed to New York to pay their long delayed visit to Henry Lee Moon, who was by now closely involved with publications at the National Association for the Advancement of Colored People (NAACP). Moon had married the former Molly Lewis, herself a social celebrity in Negro circles, who in 1932 had gone with black writers and intellectuals to the Soviet Union to make a movie about the exploitation of blacks in America. The movie never materialized and Molly later went to live in Berlin. She departed Germany at about the time of Hitler's rise to power, and her 1938 marriage to Moon gave them both access to ever widening circles of political figures, authors, and artists. Himes appreciated the chance to meet some of New York's leading lights.

The Himeses stayed one night at the Theresa Hotel in Harlem, and perhaps a couple of days more with the Moons at their grand apartment on West 66th Street. Molly gave a party for Himes and invited several celebrities, among them Katherine Dunham and the journalist Ted Poston. But Himes was disappointed that Richard Wright could not come. Indeed, the only author who did show up that evening was his old friend, Langston Hughes. But if Himes's first attempt to reach out to the New York publishing world was not what he had hoped, he did get a glimpse of the exotic and sinister city that would become the setting for so many of his detective novels.

Himes returned to his WPA projects, and when his service period ran out, he went to work for a tea and coffee importer named Weill. He did not stay on the job very long, nor is it clear what his tasks were, but his wages were so low that he and Jean had to sell their furniture to pay debts.

Langston Hughes came to their rescue. Hughes spoke of Himes's plight to the Jeliffes who ran Karamu House, and the Jeliffes in turn contacted the best-selling novelist, Louis Bromfield, who hired the Himeses early in June 1941 to work on his farm called Malabar in Lucas, a small community southwest of Cleveland. That year the couple worked as butler and cook for Bromfield at a combined salary of 120 dollars a month. Bromfield knew of Himes's literary ambitions and his *Esquire* stories, but if Himes hoped Bromfield would give him time off to write, he was mistaken. The hours were long, Bromfield was demanding, and the Himeses had only Sundays and Thursdays to themselves. Himes may have resented being treated as a servant, though Bromfield did read his prison manuscript and evidently liked it well enough to say he would try to get it published or perhaps made into a movie. Himes was naturally delighted, and when in the fall Bromfield flew off to Hollywood to work on a screenplay, the Himeses followed him by bus.

Their arrival in Los Angeles was attended by small shocks. Race relations in southern California, never harmonious to begin with, were being further threatened by large influxes of southern whites fleeing the Depression. To compound matters, the imminent war brought thousands of soldiers and sailors to the state, many of whom had never lived outside Jim Crow regions of the country. Everywhere the Himeses looked, racial boundaries were drawn in housing, in public accommodations, and inevitably in employment. The atmosphere was tense and would worsen throughout the war years—roughly the length of the Himeses' stay.

Himes observed at once that Negroes were not the only ones to suffer discrimination and violence. Filipinos, Mexicans, and Japanese Americans were also vulnerable. The fragile sense of interracial fraternity he had known during his WPA years was all but dissipated. In stories, letters, and articles he tells of his fears and anger, and a terrible frustration at the inability to strike back. Added to this was a deep shame at not being able to provide Jean with the support he believed she deserved. During this period and throughout his life, Himes's ambivalent attitude toward women was complicated by the paradoxical Victorian view that a man's chief business was to protect and provide for his women. Ideally, he would have liked the women he loved dependent on him. This was seldom possible, since it was all he could do in his lifetime to take care of himself. But if this anguish never left him, he was at least capable of deflecting some of the pain onto his art. His first two novels of the 1940s, *If He Hollers Let Him Go* and *Lonely Crusade,* relate the raddled psychology of black war workers with stunning intensity.

Hollywood experiences reinforced Himes's convictions about American race relations. Sporadically for the next several years he went from studio to studio with his stories, but was turned down everywhere. At one point he was on the verge of being hired as a reader for screenplays but was afterward told that Jack Warner "didn't want any niggers on his lot." At another studio where he was being considered for a publicity position, he learned that the all-Negro cast of *Cabin in the Sky* was excluded from the whites-only commissary. His experiences at publishing houses were no better. Despite Bromfield's good will, his prison novel continued to be rejected.

Realizing that work in Hollywood was at best a chimera, Himes used the mechanical abilities he had learned from his father to help him find jobs in shipyards and war plants. Still, given his state of mind, he seldom kept these jobs for long, sensing racism and condescension, real or imagined, wherever he went. Langston Hughes had given him a list of people whom he might contact to help him find work. One of these was Wilford Wilson, a Communist who worked for the U.S. Employment Agency. Wilson sent him out mainly to war plants and businesses that did not employ Negroes. Himes began to feel (and quietly resent) that the Communist Party was using him to prove that Negroes were being discriminated against, especially when America's war needs were greatest. Even with this foreknowledge, such experiences were devastating.

> It wasn't being refused in plants so much . . . It was the look on people's faces when you asked them about a job. Most of them didn't say outright they wouldn't hire me. They first looked goddamned startled that I asked . . . It shook me . . . Los Angeles hurt me racially as much as any city I have ever known . . . It was the lying hypocrisy that hurt me.[13]

The party's efforts to recruit Himes, or at least to imbue him with the proper ideological spirit, were not confined to sending him out on fruitless job hunts. He was actively courted. He attended cell meetings, lectures, even parties. He was introduced to Spanish Civil War veterans, and to white radical writers, among them Dalton Trumbo and John Howard Lawson. By now Himes's cynicism regarding white motives was unabated. If capitalists were exploitative, Communists were manipulative. Once when he was out of work, he and another black man collected clothes from wealthy Hollywood leftists to be sold for salvage for Spanish Civil War refugees living in Mexico. Most of the "brothers" who did this, he wrote, appropriated the clothes for themselves. "I had more expensive clothes then than I've ever had since."[14] Yet though he made common cause with other blacks, he made few lasting friendships. On several occasions Prince Rico, his erstwhile prison companion, paid visits, but their affair was long over, and they parted, never to see each other again.

To trace Himes's work history and habitations during his California years is to trace a frantic, zigzag route that took him from the outskirts of Los Angeles to the outskirts of San Francisco. Although he lived for the most part at several addresses in Los Angeles, federal investigators—who had begun taking an interest in him in 1944 for potentially seditious activities— attempted to track his job history and uncovered what must have seemed to them an endless maze. A few citations in the files of the Federal Bureau of

Investigation (FBI) list him as a labeling machine helper for the California Sanitary Canning Company, a towel machine operator in Los Angeles, a shipfitter in Richmond, and a warehouseman at Kaiser-Hughes aircraft plant in Vernon. Himes himself spoke of working as a tire rebuilder in Los Angeles and as a trainee at the San Pedro shipyards.[15] In all, he claimed to have worked at twenty-three jobs in a span of four years, most of which the FBI never learned about. The jobs were mainly semi-skilled, and Himes probably quit most of them of his own volition. According to one FBI report, he told one of his bosses he was leaving because of race prejudice. Perhaps it would have been closer to the truth to say that he was torn between playing the bourgeois role of husband-provider and finding time to write his books.

Himes's writing was becoming more and more racially focused, although *Esquire* and *Coronet* still published a few of his crime and prison pieces. By 1942 he was so distressed at the plight of interned Japanese Americans that he published what purported to be part of a Nisei's diary in a black newspaper called the *War Worker*. In a *Crisis* article two years later he described the appalling treatment of Mexican Americans in Los Angeles who were attacked and beaten by soldiers and sailors during the Zoot Suit Riots of 1943. In one seemingly defiant article he wrote for *Crisis* (arousing FBI vigilance), Himes called for a revolution to fulfill the promises of the Constitution. His interpretation of the Constitution may have been debatable, but his long repressed militancy was beginning to show.[16]

Firsthand reports of racism in the armed forces only strengthened Himes's views. Sometime during his California years he once again encountered Grant Reynolds, the Congregational minister whom he had known in Cleveland. Reynolds, now an armed forces chaplain, told Himes of the slurs and injustices Negro servicemen were forever enduring. Hugo Johnson, Jean's brother, who served as a shore patrol officer in San Francisco, related similar tales. Himes dreamed of leaving America.

Jean's perception of life was different from her husband's. While Himes smoldered, she seemed to flourish, at least in his view. At first she found war work, at slightly higher wages than his, but her "friends," Himes wrote, found her a post as co-director of women's activities for the Los Angeles office of the United Service Organizations (USO). A newspaper item of the period also identifies her as community services head at the Pueblo del Rio Housing Project.[17]

Jean's success was a sore point with Himes, and her association with liberal whites and middle-class blacks, whom Himes savaged in his first novel, infuriated him. His status was now inferior to hers. "That was the beginning of the dissolution of our marriage. I found I was no longer a husband to my wife; I was her pimp. She didn't mind and that hurt all the more."[18] Himes hinted that Jean owed her successes to favors she had given others, women as well as men.

Himes himself was not above seeking out "establishment" institutions and organizations to advance his own career. He had become a member of the respectable Urban League, as well as the NAACP. He joined a group called Writers Mobilization and won a scholarship from the League of American Writers School. But his most signal achievement was obtaining a grant from the Rosenwald Foundation in 1944, for the purpose of completing a new novel. (In his autobiography Himes said that his cousin's wife, Molly Moon, used her influence to help him get this award.) For the first time, he felt free to write how he truly felt, not what he thought editors and readers might want. Ironically, the book was begun in a house abandoned by a Nisei.[19] Himes now began to distill his California experiences for their ultimate bitterness, and to produce what many readers still believe to be his most impassioned indictment: *If He Hollers Let Him Go.*

# 7

# ARRIVALS AND DEPARTURES

ONE MEASURE OF HIMES'S FURY may be gauged by his initial scheme for *Hollers.* He originally intended it as a mystery in which white people are being killed seemingly at random everywhere in Los Angeles. The novel ultimately became something quite different, but in a sense Himes's original intent may have lived on, as he transformed it more artfully into the murderous mix of fear and rage of his protagonist, Bob Jones, a black shipyard crew foreman. Jones's bitter anger is directed not only at "peckerwood" white coworkers who would deny him his place in the sun and the fatuous black bourgeoisie who rationalize their humiliating caste status, but also at easily manipulated Negro ghetto dwellers, upon whom he casts a condescending eye. In short, Jones is a loner, and his views are his author's.

Jones tells his story as a succession of confrontations with his seductive landlady, his "well-adjusted" girlfriend, her complacent bourgeois parents, and finally, snide and hostile white coworkers, both on and off the job. Among the last group is Madge, a southern migrant who refuses to take directions from Jones despite his "leaderman" status. In the course of events, it becomes clear that she desires Bob, yet is revolted by her own feelings. Jones, reflecting Himes's ambivalence toward white women, feels much the same way about her. A climax is reached when Madge unjustly accuses him of attempted rape, and he must choose between serving a prison sentence or enlisting in the marines. The irony is cut a bit thick, but Bob's teetering emotions are so compelling that the reader may forgive Himes for the rather predictable ending.

A reviewer at the time of publication described *Hollers* as being written in "gall and wormwood," but what saves it from self-pity is Himes's skilled use of a first-person narrative in terse, hard-boiled prose. The book echoes both

Hemingway and Hammett, whose fiction Himes admired. By now Himes was also well aware of Richard Wright's works, especially *Native Son*, to which *Hollers* has often been compared. Aside from its protest aspects, however, Himes's Bob Jones is very different from the inarticulate Bigger Thomas in that his subconscious lives very near the surface of his consciousness. Indeed, Bob awakens each day from dreams that he describes to us. The dreams foreshadow events and symbolically express the dreamer's fears of impotence, death, or rejection:

> I dreamed a fellow asked me if I wanted a dog and I said yeah, I'd like to have a dog and he went off and came back with a little black dog with stiff black gold-tipped hair and sad eyes . . . I was standing in front of a street car that was just about to start and the fellow led the dog by a piece of heavy stiff wire . . . I took the dog and got on the street car. I liked the little dog; but when I got home nobody else seemed to like it.[1]

In early 1944 Doubleday accepted the book for publication, subject to revision, and here again Henry Moon may have been helpful, since at the time he was one of Doubleday's readers. Himes visited New York in May, presumably to transact business with his publisher, and en route stopped off in Chicago, where he met Vandi Haygood, acting director of the Rosenwald Fund, the agency that had provided the grant that allowed Himes to write *Hollers*. Vandi was substituting for her husband William, then serving in the armed forces. She told Himes of her rocky marriage, and together they spent the weekend at her apartment. This was the start of a nine-year, on-and-off liaison, which lasted up to the time Himes left for Europe.

Back in Los Angeles, Himes continued writing. Several more of his stories, mainly in the protest mode, were printed in 1944 and 1945. *Esquire* bought two prison stories, and *Crisis* accepted "All God's Chillun Got Pride" and "The Song Says 'Keep on Smilin'.' " The newly founded *Negro Story* also published five stories, but paid the author nothing. The flurry of responses may well have encouraged Himes to think that he could survive as a professional author.

In September Himes returned alone to New York and stayed again with the Moons, who by now had moved to St. Nicholas Avenue in Harlem. Henry and Molly Moon were actively supporting Franklin Roosevelt's candidacy for a fourth term in the forthcoming presidential election. Henry worked for the CIO Political Action Committee, as well as the NAACP, and Molly, who had recently been made director of the New York chapter of the Urban League Guild, gave fundraising parties attended by all sorts of notables, black and white.

Here Himes met many of the important Negro luminaries whom he did not see on his first visit to New York with Jean in 1939, although one suspects they still did not accord him as much attention as he felt he deserved. Among the persons he mentioned were the labor leader Lester Granger, Urban League head Ralph Bunche, Walter White of the NAACP, the Winthrop Rockefellers, Reps. William Dawson and Adam Clayton Powell, and the celebrated sociologist E. Franklin Frazier.[2]

Despite their ostensible political purpose, Himes viewed Molly's parties primarily as springboards to interracial sexual liaisons. In this regard he mentioned later that he "took the bodies" of many women, some of them socially prominent, and while he may have indulged himself in "sex and drunkenness," he felt that he was being patronized by whites who assumed sexual favors were the same thing as social justice. One of the women he reportedly had an affair with had once worked for his cousin Henry in Washington. Himes berated Henry for overworking her, to which Henry took exception. Perhaps because of this, the relationship between the cousins grew testy, especially after Jean came to New York at the end of the year and learned of her husband's affairs.

Himes as always tried to reassure Jean of his love and may even have believed he would remain faithful. The strains on the marriage eased somewhat, and the couple remained together. Neither of them had much money, and for most of 1945 they lived precariously, often at the homes of friends. In September Estelle Himes died in Columbus, but there was not enough money for Jean to return with Chester for the funeral. Chester wept.

In his autobiography, Himes said of New York that it hurt him by accepting him, by taking him for granted. "I knew that as much as I had been hurt by then, I was sick. But New York accepted me as normal, and that made me sicker."[3] Still, there were moments of exhilaration. In a 1972 CBS address far different in tone, he portrayed himself as "the happiest man on earth" when he arrived in the city. He told of the thrilling views from his bedroom window while staying at the Moons' Sugar Hill apartment. He spoke of exciting visits to Molly Moon's Urban League friends who lived in fashionable apartment buildings and of walks along Harlem streets relishing the sights and sounds. He recited the names of business establishments, theaters, and places of entertainment:

> I could walk south down . . . past the Fat Man's Bar at 155th Street and Eddie's Chicken Shack, Lucky's Nightclub further on, and all the barber shops, restaurants, and beauty parlors which served the number barons and numbers writers and black bourgeois who lived in the 140s . . . I

would continue to 145th Street and turn past Elder "Lightfoot" Micheaux
Harlem Temple and turn south again into the neon jungle of Seventh
Avenue, the main street of Harlem (which I always thought of as the land of
dreams) past the Renaissance Ballroom, Small's Paradise Inn, Dickie-Wells
Restaurant-Bar.[4]

He also remembered churches, libraries, barbershops, undertakers, the Harlem YMCA, and the Apollo Theater, and waxed nostalgic about the old
Theresa Hotel at the intersection of Seventh Avenue and 125th Street in
whose "cool and intimate bar" he often had drinks with Langston Hughes
(and where he and Jean had once stayed). He dwelled on the famous
blacks who had stopped off at the Theresa: Florence Mills and Billie Holiday, the impresarios Miller & Lyles and Sissle & Blake, the comedians
Williams & Walker and Dusty Fletcher, the dancers Buck & Bubbles, and
the politicians William Dawson and Oscar DePriest. He even lingered on
warm memories of Ralph Ellison and the Moons and those "important"
blacks and whites whom he often derided to friends or caricatured in
his books.

Harlem was not then the wicked, voracious, violent region of Himes's
thrillers, but rather a vibrant and romantic place. "Everything I saw that year
was new and exciting, the many colored people, the variety of scenes, the
thousands of activities, the millions of expressions in the eyes and the faces
of the people."[5]

What undoubtedly bolstered Himes's ego, if not his professional career,
were his new literary acquaintances: Roy Ottley, Owen Dodson, Sterling
Brown, and two white scriptwriters, Dalton Trumbo and John Bright.

One of Himes's first New York friends was the novice author Ralph
Ellison, whom he visited often in his nearby St. Nicholas Avenue basement
apartment. Himes remembered Ellison experimenting with ideas and themes
that would later become *Invisible Man*. Ellison and his wife Fanny would
invite Himes, and later Jean, to dinner parties, and Himes reciprocated one
day by giving a party for them at the Moons' apartment while Molly was away.
Their friendship atrophied in later years, but while it lasted, they exchanged
ideas about politics, writing, and black culture.

Perhaps most important for Himes was his encounter with Richard
Wright, whom he met in July 1945 at a party that Hughes was giving for
W. E. B. Du Bois. A sporadic friendship grew up between them, a peculiar mix
of admiration, amusement, and envy. Ellison, who had known Wright since
1937, often talked about him, though he had never really been a close friend.
Himes's relationship with Wright was at once more intense. He and Ellison

acknowledged their indebtedness to Wright, not necessarily as a literary influence, but always as someone who had encouraged them, as unknowns, to write. Yet the differences among the three were striking. Wright, who had escaped the Deep South, Jim Crow poverty, and later the Communist Party, was a self-educated intellectual who sometimes sounded pedantic. Himes, and especially Ellison, both of whom had had more formal schooling and possessed a more middle-class sense of decorum, found Wright both dazzlingly impressive and relatively unsophisticated.

Wright, for Himes, also served as a source of financial help. On more than one occasion Himes borrowed money from him, and at least once Wright gave him more money than he had asked for. Before leaving for Europe, Wright's wife Ellen helped Jean look for a Greenwich Village apartment the Himeses could afford. The quest was unsuccessful.

As his November 1945 publication date approached, Himes remained hopeful, yet anxious. Informed that *Hollers* might be chosen as a Book of the Month Club selection, he was of course delighted, but he was also understandably dismayed to discover, almost at the last minute, that Doubleday was about to delete thirty pages of his manuscript. The offending portions portrayed a confrontation in "racy" language between Bob Jones and Madge in a hotel room—mild by today's standards. Himes, who had gone to California on a brief visit, rushed back to New York to defend his manuscript. His editor, Bucklin Moon, a white sometime novelist not related to Henry or Molly, had left for Florida, and Himes could not find the name of the editor responsible for the cuts. He nevertheless objected so strenuously that all was restored.

Things were beginning to look up again. Himes was promised Doubleday's George Washington Carver award for the best book on Negro life published in 1945, which assured an advance sale of ten thousand copies. At publication he was given a book party at the Moons' place, which made him uneasy because he was still on cool terms with his cousins.

Then came the letdown: The George Washington Carver prize was awarded to a white woman, Fannie Cook, the author of *Mrs. Palmer's Honey*, a novel about a domestic. Moreover, only 7,100 copies of Himes's book were printed, and when several of his friends told him they could not find *Hollers* in bookstores, he learned that Doubleday's publicity department had made scarcely any effort to get word out about it. To add insult to injury, he was offended by Doubleday's advertising copy for Fannie Cook's novel, which he believed made indirect and invidious references to his own book as being "a series of sledgehammer speeches punctuated by spit." He believed, not without some justification, that Doubleday had set out deliberately to subvert the book it had bought from him.

If Doubleday executives regarded Himes's novel as a manifesto of un-relenting anger, many newspaper critics dwelled on its sociological impli-cations, often overlooking its wit and sardonic humor. But for anyone who knew Himes, the wry twists of dialogue and plot recall something of his personality.

> When I got on the job I found Tebbel cursing out the Jews. I didn't want to listen, didn't want to argue . . . Tebbel said the Jews controlled all the money in the world; that the Jews had started the war to make money; and that all Jews were Communists.
>
> "That I gotta see," I said.
>
> But no one paid any attention to me. I supposed they were so happy to find somebody cursing out somebody besides the "niggers" they didn't want it interrupted.
>
> He said F.D.R. was a Jew, that his real name was Rosenveld; that all movie actors were Jews [citing movie actors' names and their presumed real names].
>
> "You left out Jesus Christ," I said. "What was his real name?" But nobody paid any attention to that either.[6]

At the end of the novel, when Bob Jones is about to be hustled into the marines, his "paranoia"—and, by extension, Himes's—is seen to be justified. Suggestive of his author, as well, is Bob's momentary paralysis in crises. Confronted by his white tormentors, male and female, in near life-and-death situations, he does nothing. Ultimately, his law-abiding passivity is what gets him into trouble.

On the whole, the reviews were favorable, though not ecstatic—leaving Himes disappointed. Still, he was comforted by the encouragement of Wright and Ellison and another acquaintance, the sociologist Horace Cayton, a friend of Vandi Haywood's whom Himes had first met in Chicago. He was pleased, he wrote Richard Wright, that they did not denigrate his achievement as so many other celebrated Negroes might well have done.

Even if the book was no great commercial success, it lent the peripatetic Himeses an aura of stability. By November they had found an apartment in Brooklyn,[7] and by year's end they were exchanging visits with the Wrights, the Ellisons, and new friends whom they had met at the Moons'.

Himes was once again in touch with his brother Joseph, whom he had last seen at his mother's funeral, and around Christmastime Joseph and his wife Estelle visited.[8] Joseph's vision was much improved since the dreadful days of their adolescence, and the brothers hit it off famously.

The new year of 1946 also saw some improvement in Himes's finances. He drew $2,000 in royalties for *Hollers* and another $2,000 as an advance toward a new book. Still, he remained so embittered by his Doubleday experience that he asked a new friend, Carl Van Vechten, to intercede with publisher Blanche Knopf on his behalf. Blanche and Alfred Knopf did ultimately buy out Himes's contract, and his new agent, Lurton Blassingame, negotiated still another $2,000 advance for his next novel. Dribs and drabs of money also came in from various publications, but Himes's main source of magazine income remained *Esquire,* which published another of his stories in January.

Chester's friendship with Van Vechten had begun sometime in late 1945, when Himes accompanied Wright to Van Vechten's studio to be photographed for his collection of famous Negro figures. Wright, according to Himes, behaved so pompously at the sitting that Himes doubled up with laughter.

Not long afterward Van Vechten photographed Himes. The two men took a liking to one another, and within a year Himes was affectionately addressing Van Vechten as Carlo. They corresponded even when both were living in New York, partly because of Himes's eternal money needs, and partly because he hoped that Van Vechten might wield some influence with publishers. Himes also sent Van Vechten manuscripts for his literary assessment, and Van Vechten could be critical as well as supportive. For his part, Van Vechten's only request was that, at appropriate times, Himes submit his manuscripts and related literary material to the James Weldon Johnson Collection at the Beinecke Library of Yale University. Himes promised he would do so and for the most part kept his promise.

In February 1946 Himes vented his anger publicly at what he regarded as the lukewarm reception of *Hollers.* In a short article for the *Saturday Review of Literature,* he assailed reviewers who suggested that it was not enough for black novelists to indict racial oppression, they also needed to offer solutions. Himes responded that the "Negro problem" was a white problem.[9] Since whites were the source of racism, let them solve it.

Himes's view was that it was not the province of the artist to play the role of anthropologist or sociologist, and yet, as we shall see, the protagonist of his next novel does indeed suggest answers, offending both blacks and whites on the political left. If Himes's "solutions" did not please everyone, at the very least they were probing Americans' divided feelings about race, as well as his own. To expect from Himes, or from any author, some blanket social wisdom would be to ask for a diminution of his art and to wish that Himes were other than what he was.

This time around Himes did not allow himself the indulgence of excessive self-pity in his reaction to what critics said about him. He knew that he had written a good book and that the next one was going to be better. He played with the idea of writing a novel from a black woman's point of view, but he put that notion aside. He began *Lonely Crusade* at about the time he received the first payment for *Hollers*. Like *Hollers*, the new work dealt with the experiences of a black wartime worker. But this time Himes hoped to treat more extensively and intensively themes he had only touched upon in his first book. Going beyond protest and interracial sex, he would break new ground in dealing, for example, with the relationships between black and white women, blacks and labor unions, blacks and Communists, blacks and Jews. He would focus not simply upon the neuroses of educated blacks, but also on the pathology of alienated proletarian blacks. He would tell harsh truths that would grate on the preconceptions of both liberals and conservatives, blacks and whites.

Moreover, if critics constantly harped on "solutions," Himes would, within the context of his narrative, proffer some that neither whites nor bourgeois blacks would like. *Lonely Crusade* might well be termed an "angry" novel, but more important, it would be something all too rare in American fiction, a novel of ideas.

In May 1946 Himes bought a six-year-old Mercury and a shotgun and headed west with Jean for Oakland, California. Jean's brother in the Navy, Hugo, had offered them the use of his ranch in northern California, parts of which he rented out to tenants. Here in the wilderness, Himes hoped he would be able to write his book with few distractions.

Along the way they stopped off in Cleveland, where they visited Himes's ailing father and afterward called on Ruth Seid, his old friend and colleague from WPA days. Himes had recommended Seid's novel *Wasteland* to Wright, who read it and reviewed it enthusiastically for the newspaper *PM*. Himes's reunion with Seid was amicable, though she told him she disliked his cursory dismissal of lesbians in *Hollers*.

The Himeses next drove on to Malabar Farm where they visited Louis Bromfield. Bromfield, according to Himes, was not exactly delighted to see them. He kept them standing, ushered them into the kitchen to meet the servants, and bade them farewell. Himes's devious, disagreeable capitalist in *Lonely Crusade* is based on Bromfield.

At their next stop, Columbus, the Himeses stayed overnight with Joseph and Estelle. Chester invited them to visit at the ranch later in the summer, and Joseph said they would. He had just won a faculty appointment at North

Carolina State College in Durham for the fall term, and this would be his opportunity to visit parts of the country he had never before seen.

The Himeses carried on west. Often enough they met with suspicion and hostility in small white communities, which inevitably meant that they had to drive into cities, where they were more likely to find food and lodging in Negro neighborhoods. In his autobiography, however, Himes did not dwell on these humiliations but instead lovingly recited the names of cities he drove through: Joliet, Des Moines, Davenport, Omaha, Denver, Salt Lake City, Reno, and finally San Francisco.

In San Francisco the Himeses met the O'Neills, friends of Jean's from Los Angeles. Martin O'Neill was the head of the San Francisco bureau of *Life* magazine, whose audience a budding novelist such as Himes could only wish for.

Afterward, the Himeses picked up Hugo in Oakland and rode back with him through Reno to his property, seventy-five miles to the north between Susanville and Milford in Lassen County. Hugo had leased his large ranchhouse to a Portuguese couple, the Mellos, but he had a three-room shack in a state of disrepair that he made available to his sister and her husband for the length of their stay. In no time at all Himes was busy applying the carpentry skills he had learned from his father, putting in a new door, strengthening the porch, and making other portions of the building habitable. He also had to kill nests of rats and the occasional rattlesnake. He recounted in his autobiography a particularly harrowing moment, when he had to shoot a rattlesnake slithering toward Jean as she languidly sat on the back steps, oblivious to her danger.

The shack served its purpose. Himes's chief task, of course, was to work on his novel, and he got right down to business. Once assured that the house was in shape, he hauled his typewriter out of the car, placed it on a table in the front room, and continued work on *Lonely Crusade*.

He wrote steadily, despite several visits from the Mellos' nonpaying sub-tenants, whom Himes recalled as a ninety-year-old Texan and his companion, a woman in her forties called Fertile Myrtle, so named because she had produced eight children by eight different fathers. A more welcome visitor was the local postmistress, who read and enjoyed Himes's manuscript. Hugo paid an occasional visit, and Joseph and Estelle came in July as planned. Even then Himes carried on working while the others scrupulously avoided the front room.

The summer was not, however, totally devoid of sociability. The brothers hiked and hunted in the mountains and made at least one more foray back to the Bay area, where they visited Hugo and the O'Neills. Martin O'Neill gave Himes (presumably as a joke) a *Life* magazine article on how to write a novel.

The brothers talked often about family, recollected their childhood, and worried about their father who was that summer undergoing liver surgery at a Cleveland hospital. To be sure, Joseph the sociologist and Chester the novelist also exchanged views about larger issues, which each in his own way addressed during his professional life. Among these issues was the lingering effect of slavery on the descendants of slaves (which became a theme of Himes's later novel, *The Third Generation*) and the character of the Negro woman (perhaps also a theme).

A sad portent for the future of Himes's marriage occurred some time after Joseph and Estelle's departure in August. Hugo, who was visiting at the time, went with Himes to Susanville to see about repairing Himes's car, which had been badly damaged in an accident. Upon their return in early evening, Jean was gone. They found her several hours later alone and weeping on the highway. During their absence she had read Himes's portrayal of Ruth, the black wife of Lee Gordon in the manuscript version of *Lonely Crusade*. Believing that she was the model for Ruth, she fled the house in tears. In the novel Ruth fears whites and thinks herself racially inferior. Himes wrote, "I spent many hours then and for years afterward trying to convince her I never thought of her as Ruth. But I'm afraid she never truly believed me; and I often wondered if I had drawn a true picture of which I was not consciously aware."[10]

In his autobiography Himes recalled that summer as the most pleasant of his life, but some of his correspondence belies the impression of contentment. At best his moods were mercurial. He was often torn with anxieties about the book he was writing. Was it any good? He knew the Communists would hate it. Was the interracial sex too graphic, too lurid? Was it unacceptable? And then there was his father dying in Cleveland. For emotional succor Himes turned to his friend Van Vechten in New York.

Van Vechten had read Himes's unpublished prison novel and wrote Himes in June to say that he liked it very much. But in August Himes wrote Van Vechten of his anguish. He was reaching a point of mental desperation, he said, nearing exhaustion. His father lay ill in a Cleveland hospital, and his puppy had just been run over by a car. "Out here in the lonely wilderness our puppy had assumed a place of tremendous emotional importance in our household and its death now seems a tragedy out of proportion with reality.

There are few things that ever happened to me to hurt me so, not even when I was sentenced twenty years in prison."[11]

Himes was aware that he had displaced his mounting anxieties on the death of his dog, but still, perhaps because he was childless, he invested great emotional value in his pets. In the two volumes of his autobiography, as well as in his unpublished letters, he devoted much space to the animals he cared for. They were his children and possibly also vulnerable extensions of himself.

Himes now asked Van Vechten to read his new manuscript, desiring reassurance that he was not embarked on a fruitless enterprise. Van Vechten responded almost at once that "it is quite tremendous and powerful; some of the scenes are as hard as nails . . . It may have too much sex for some, too much anti communism for others."[12] He also had some reservations about the plausibility of one of Himes's characters, Luther, a black murderer.

Himes was so glad to get an outsider's professional assessment that he wrote Van Vechten immediately to say that he was taking his advice. "I am going to de-sex it somewhat and straighten out the Lee-Luther relationship."[13] Soon after, he finished the draft of the novel, sold his irreparably damaged car, and returned by train with Jean to New York.

In mid-October the Himeses were living in a small flat above a garage on the Wading River, Long Island, estate of Frank Safford, a Columbia University neurologist. Himes probably became acquainted with Dr. Safford through the Wrights. His main responsibility, from Dr. Safford's point of view, seems to have been to take care of his prized Irish setter, which was pregnant. For Himes, Wading River made a peaceable setting in which to put the finishing touches on *Lonely Crusade* and to renew work on his prison novel (now tentatively called "Yesterday Will Make You Cry"). The little town stood seventy-five miles from the city, which meant that he was removed from the city's noise and distractions but still able to keep in touch with editors and publishers. The estate contained four or five summer cottages and a big house where the Saffords stayed on weekends. With the exception of a deaf caretaker in one of the cottages, the Himeses were the only tenants.

Their white neighbors in Wading River, Himes remarked, did not object to Negroes living nearby; indeed, the Himeses scarcely saw them. Thus the couple lived in virtual isolation, although Himes recorded one lovely weekend when the Ellisons visited. The men hunted cottontails in the woods, but the best they could come up with was a large male squirrel, which their wives served up as a tasty stew.

The Himeses remained in Wading River well past the new year, but in the second week of January they moved to Harlem's Theresa Hotel. Jean found work as a recreational director for delinquent girls in a program on Welfare Island, and Himes once more applied for funds from the Rosenwald Foundation for a proposed new book, "Immortal Mammy," relating his Hollywood experiences during the war. He had enlisted an impressive array of references: Van Vechten, Blanche Knopf, Carey McWilliams (a political and social commentator and author), Leonard Bloom (a sociology professor at the University of California at Los Angeles), Jack Aistrop (an English novelist who had written an introduction for the English edition for *Hollers*), and Billy Haygood, Vandi's husband. Later in the year Blassingame negotiated another $2,000 advance from Knopf, but for most of 1947 Himes found himself unhappily dependent on his wife's income.

Himes counted mainly on sales of *Lonely Crusade*, but for that he would have to wait. In the interim he continued rewriting, revising, editing, and condensing his prison book. His persistence after a decade seems unending, but for him, the dreadful years he passed in the Ohio penitentiary were the crucible on which his manhood was forged. The novel would be, among other things, emotional reassurance that he could survive.

Yet on a more down-to-earth level, Himes still needed to pay bills. When Wright returned that spring from a seven-month stay in Europe, Himes called at his Charles Street home to borrow $500. Wright, this time, put him off but arranged a loan via the Authors' League. The hand-to-mouth existence was again beginning to sap Himes's morale. He and Jean moved from the Theresa Hotel to a cheaper furnished room on West 147th Street. He would have liked to devote his entire time to writing, but barring that, he wanted the kind of job that would give him time to collect his thoughts and refresh his outlook.

In a poignant letter to Van Vechten Himes explained, "I have been out and around looking for work but without a union card, references, etc. About the only job I will be able to get is porter, handyman or dishwasher and while I don't mind any of them too much . . . [I] fear I might get sucked down into a lot of personal protests and humiliations which might stop the objective flow of my thoughts."[14] To add to his tribulations, he was sent a bill for his father's hospitalization.

Another thing that plagued Himes was the feeling that the gritty subject matter of his fiction embarrassed his friends. He believed nonetheless that to restrain himself would be doing an injustice to himself and his art. He was determined to tell about life as he experienced it. *Hollers*, he believed, was his breakthrough. Looming was *Lonely Crusade* with its challenging themes, and somewhere beyond that his prison book relating a homosexual love story.

> As I look back now I find that much of my retardation as a writer has been due to a subconscious (and conscious and deliberate) drive to escape my past. All mixed up no doubt with the Negro's desire for respectability . . . It brought a lot of confusion to my own mind added to which was a great deal of pressure of a thousand kinds being exerted by friends and relatives and loved ones who were half ashamed of what I wrote, forgetting that it was what I wrote that made me what I was.[15]

Langston Hughes and Van Vechten suggested that Himes apply to the writers' colony, Yaddo, in upstate New York. Himes did not want to go. He was fearful, he wrote Van Vechten, that he might be disturbed or distracted by other writers' viewpoints and that theirs might intrude upon his own writing. His art compelled him to be absolutely intolerant of opinions other than his own. He needed, he said, to be "apart from other writers" who might be dealing with the material he was using. "My own interpretations of my theme have to be absolute during the process of writing and I become confused and lose my point around other writers."[16] Himes's fears were well founded. The following year he did go to Yaddo, with disastrous consequences.

At this time Himes also was in touch with another writer friend, Bill Smith, a sometime journalist-screenwriter whom he had known in Los Angeles. Smith, a light-complexioned Negro, had moved his white wife and children east to escape the hostility of his Los Angeles neighbors. He now lived on a farm in northern Vermont and invited the Himeses up for visits. Jean, because of her job, was unable to come as often as she would have liked, but Chester appeared at the Smith doorstep several times during the spring and summer of 1947.

Smith, with memories of Los Angeles still in mind, had recently written a novel called *God Is for White Folks*. But he was much more at ease in his new environment, and Vermont intrigued Himes, too. Here, he felt, was a place truly free of racism. He even toyed with the idea of moving north himself, but he could not afford it. Still, he thought, Wright might be interested. Himes knew that Wright in Greenwich Village was subject to neighborhood prejudice similar to what Smith had experienced in Los Angeles. In a note to Wright, Himes said that a fine house could be had north of Burlington for $7,000. He and a friend would even drive him there, if he were interested. Wright did consider it but then decided to move to France instead.

Himes's dreams of Vermont were made more enticing by the dreariness of the furnished room he and Jean now lived in. In mid-June they left

Harlem for quarters on Welfare Island, where Jean worked. But Himes's main activities lay in Manhattan: dinner invitations here and there, as well as occasional business with the Knopfs, such as lining up prepublication support for *Lonely Crusade.*

The Knopfs approached Wright in Paris for a blurb, and he responded favorably, though he did not do exactly what they asked. They wanted him to say something about Himes's treatment of black-Jewish relations, but no such statement appears over Wright's name. Few other figures were willing to allow themselves to be quoted. Still, the Knopf publicity department seemed to be operating efficiently, preparing Himes for interviews and personal appearances. Assured that all was going well, the Himeses took ten days off in early August for another Vermont visit. They returned to a more spacious furnished room in Harlem, but at the start of September moved back again to Welfare Island, where they occupied the large apartment of Jean's supervisor, who had gone on vacation. As the official publication date of September 7 drew nearer, Himes invited his father, convalescing in Cleveland, to stay with them. He wanted Joseph Sandy to observe his triumph.

Publication day came, and yet again expectations were dashed. Himes was scheduled to address booksellers at Macy's and Bloomingdale's department stores, but both "events" were unaccountably canceled. Bloomingdale's did not even have copies of his book for sale. On the afternoon of the same day, he was to speak on the popular Mary Margaret McBride radio show, but Jean told him she had taken a call canceling his appearance. Were there conspiracies afoot to undermine him? He couldn't be sure.

*Lonely Crusade* is a somewhat sprawling novel whose main plot deals with the efforts of Lee Gordon, a college-educated Negro, to unionize the small Negro workforce at an aircraft factory during wartime. In the course of events, he discovers that he is being used or manipulated by white union officials, by Communists, by white women, and by his bosses. Racism may lie at the heart of their actions, but Lee is himself not without sin. He expresses anti-Semitic views, and at times he says he does not like Negroes. He treats his wife badly, betraying and beating her. Despite his intelligence, sensitivity, and self-awareness, he is deeply scarred. In time Lee clarifies his vision of American life, presumably overcoming his prejudices. With the aid of a kindly "defrocked" Jewish Communist, Abe Rosenberg, he decides to stick with the union, even at the risk of his life.

The most odious villains in the novel are the Communists who, for a while, seduce Lee with a white woman, and the capitalist boss Foster, who tries, first, to buy his loyalties. Himes also created a Negro monster in the person of Luther McGregor, a so-called Communist, who allows himself to be bribed by one and all, and who kills without compunction. Since everyone views him as a "nigger," Luther says, he may as well act like one. Conversely, Himes's most sympathetic character is Ruth, Lee's wife, stoic, loyal, and seemingly well adjusted, but not without racial anxieties.

No summary can do ample justice to this rich, complex, yet ultimately unsuccessful book, in which sensuous lyric passages may be followed by solecisms too embarrassing to repeat. Himes had attempted to write a novel of ideas, in which much of the dialectic is given over to communism, Negro anti-Semitism, black perceptions of organized labor, and black and white sexual attitudes. Unfortunately, the constraints and conventions of Himes's style at times render these discussions thin and insubstantial.

Yet as a love story between Lee and Ruth, and Lee and his white mistress Jackie Forks, the novel is convincing, and at times startling, for Himes saw sex and love as weapons in a kind of race war, not simply between blacks and whites, but between blacks and blacks. If Lee represents fragments of Himes's consciousness, the picture we see is not altogether flattering. Lee is honest with himself, but suicidally passive and fearful about his masculinity:

> But he had not told her about his fear. He had never told her how much he was afraid of going into the white world in quest of what he felt was rightfully his. Not always afraid of anything he could name, define, put his finger on. Afraid for the most part, of his own fear of his emotion that came unbidden to him and he had no power to dispel . . . During times such as this . . . he felt a sense of depression that reduced him to sterility as if castrated by it . . . She knew that he found relief in brutality . . . She had been absorbing Lee's brutality for six long years.[17]

For Lee, as for Himes, women who appear to be his equal or superior—which often simply means earning more money than he—threaten his manhood. In large part, this accounts for Lee's deteriorating marriage, because he has long had to depend on Ruth. Conversely, women who appear to him helpless or lost, appeal to his protective chivalric instincts. " 'I like women who are women,' Lee went on. 'I like to sleep with them and take care of them. I don't want any woman taking care of me or even competing with me.' "[18]

Lee's anxieties about competitive women contrast dramatically with the stereotype of the black male as exhibiting a kind of primitive virility. Indeed, Lee's fears contradict what he and other Negro figures in the novel view as their emasculation by white society. These men are nonetheless powerfully attracted to white women, despite or because of the taboo they represent.

White men's fears for the "purity" of their women "justify" black persecution. That white men may take black women with impunity signals the black man's impotence. Thus, possessing a white woman not only serves as clandestine revenge on white oppressors but also provides a sense of masculinity that a black man is unable to achieve with women of his own race. For Lee, however, respite is illusory. He can feel equal to Jackie only, he says, when he pities her vulnerability. In other words, for him she must become a symbolic Negro.

Jackie Forks is no less bound by racial fantasies. Unknown to her conscious self, there is a sense of noblesse oblige in giving herself to Lee. At critical moments she retreats behind caste barriers rather than risk social disapproval. Lee, for example, recognizes that she will not condescend to fight over him with his wife, not out of tender consideration for his marriage, but because it would offend her sense of racial superiority to squabble with a black woman. For Jackie, the black man simultaneously represents sexual fulfillment and social-sexual shame. As a Communist, she rationalizes her affair with Lee as a means to political ends. Thus does race consciousness cast a pall over these lovers.

Lee's anticommunism and anti-Semitism are largely motivated by his belief that Jews and Communists (all the Jews in the novel are Communists) regard him as a victim, as someone incapable of taking care of himself—in other words, as something less than a man. They pretend to know better than he what he truly needs and wants. This kind of paternalism—possibly a better term would be maternalism—is what rankles. Toward the end of the novel Lee seemingly overcomes his anti-Semitism when Abe Rosenberg counsels, comforts, and befriends him in his hours of dire crisis. But even here, Abe the Jew intriguingly plays the symbolic role of parent to the enfeebled Lee.

Needless to say, the Communist press savaged the novel in reviews, and the Jewish journal *Commentary* found it intellectually and aesthetically wanting. Nor were all black readers pleased with Himes's depiction of the "Negro problem." Nonetheless, Himes's book did air social issues and attitudes that had previously been left to smolder unrecognized by the public at large: blacks' resentment and suspicion of the motives of their Communist "champions" (a theme later developed in Ellison's celebrated novel *Invisible Man*); black anti-Semitism, a phenomenon more overt today; and a cultural and psychological defeatism that African Americans needed to overcome in order to fully partake of their citizenship.

At one point in the novel Lee Gordon suggests granting much of the submerged black population special privileges, on the grounds that they have so long been conditioned to thinking all gates closed to them that they are incapable of taking advantage of whatever chances they have. Some decades later such privileges came into being under the name of affirmative action, but in 1947 special privileges for any one group were generally regarded by civil rights advocates as anathema, an affront to democracy.

Shortly after the publication day fiasco, Himes repaired once again to Vermont to await responses to his book. He was obviously interested in what other blacks would say and especially disappointed that the novelist Willard Motley did not like his book.[19] Himes had met Motley at a dinner party at the Van Vechtens' and taken an immediate liking to him. When Himes read Motley's *Knock at Any Door,* the seventeen-year-old Italian American hero awakened in Himes memories of his own youth, so much so that he wrote Motley that he had felt exactly the same way at that age.[20]

What some of Himes's other black friends thought about the book is not clear. Hughes said nothing publicly, but later wrote Blanche Knopf that he disliked the book. He said he disapproved of fiction that portrayed pathological Negro characters. Horace Cayton liked it, but six years later wrote Himes that he believed that he and Himes and other blacks placed too much blame on society for their emotional ills. What Ellison told Himes is unknown, but he wrote Wright in Paris that he found Himes's book insufficiently political, and in some ways superficial and pseudo-intellectual. Wright himself liked Himes's treatment of the Negro's relationship with unions and the Communist Party, and he later wrote a laudatory introduction for a French edition of the work. A very young James Baldwin, whom Himes had not yet met, wrote in the *New Leader* that the novel was very poorly written but did convey how blacks viewed their American lives. As a kind of backhanded compliment, Baldwin noted that in its way *Lonely Crusade* was as important as *Uncle Tom's Cabin.*[21]

Afterward Himes used to say (and believe) that the reviews of *Lonely Crusade* were uniformly negative, but that was not the case. To be sure, some reviews were unkind, but prestigious publications, such as the *Atlantic Monthly,* the *New York Times Book Review,* and the *New York Herald Tribune Book Review,* reviewed the book favorably.[22] In addition, Himes received scattered favorable reviews in newspapers across the country, as well as in some of the Negro media, such as the *Amsterdam News* and the *Crisis.* He acknowledged these in some of his correspondence.[23] Still, he was devastated by what he regarded as unfair press coverage and seemed to dwell on the negative passages of the favorable reviews. He had poured his heart and mind into the book, he said, but people did not want to know the truth.

To those who argued that his characters and scenes were improbable, Himes responded that they were all taken from life. The wicked arch-conservative Foster was, as we have seen, based on Bromfield, whom Himes had once heard refer to President Roosevelt as "that crippled bastard." Luther was modeled on a pathological criminal Himes had known in prison. As previously noted, Dan Levin served as the model for Abe Rosenberg, and the Communist conclaves were not unlike the ones Himes had attended when he was living in Los Angeles. Jean, as we know, saw herself as Ruth, and Lee, Van Vechten observed, was not unlike the Himes-like protagonist of *Hollers*. Even Ellison saw himself as a minor character. But nothing Himes could say on his own behalf helped very much, and toward the end of his life he used to say that the poor reception of *Lonely Crusade* was the worst hurt he had suffered in his life.

Himes may have exaggerated reviewers' hostility, but he was right about one thing: The book sold poorly, probably not more than four thousand copies. Within a year it was withdrawn from bookstores. To add to his anguish, he remained in dire financial straits. At the start of 1948 he and Jean moved yet again, this time to a furnished room in the Bronx belonging to a black orchestra leader named Bonelli. Jean found another job as recreational director at a federal housing project, while Himes tried his hand at writing "commercial" short stories for the slicks, signing his name Jack O'Dell. Unsuccessful even in these efforts, he applied in February for admission to Yaddo for the May–June period. Here at least, he was accepted. The executive director informed him he would be welcome for the period requested. In the meantime, the Rosenwald Foundation, to which he had applied the previous year for a second fellowship, informed him it was ceasing operations.

Himes was not certain what he would write at Yaddo. "Immortal Mammy," the novel he had planned to write, no longer appealed to him. At one point he imagined it as a portrait of an "exceptional" Negro woman living in a white world, but this may also have been his Hollywood novel.[24]

Himes arrived at Yaddo in May and was much taken by its landscaped grounds, rose garden, and several splendid houses. He liked the room he was assigned, whose four windows overlooked a large expanse of lawn. There were six other guests at the house: two artists, a composer, and three writers (one of them Patricia Highsmith), but he had little contact with any of them.

The great question was what to write. Himes decided finally on a book that would complement his prison novel: "Stool Pigeon," a tentative title changed later in the year to "An Uncle Tom You Never Knew." It would deal with an ugly, deranged convict who informs on three other prisoners who are planning an escape. Their plans are foiled, but not before a fire intended to divert the attention of the authorities engulfs much of the prison. The enraged warden, whose reputation is sullied, lets the other prisoners know the name of the informer, and they set upon him with knives. Himes pondered whether anyone's freedom is worth the lives of others. He was unsure whether to make his prisoners white or black. He was afraid, he said, to play on racial themes for fear of the usual antagonistic reactions. As things turned out, he did not write very much of this novel at all. In the fall he applied for a Guggenheim fellowship to write the novel, but was turned down.[25]

Yaddo was not a happy experience for Himes. His isolation, rather than enhancing his creativity, exacerbated old anxieties and fears: about being an artist, about who he was, and whether he really belonged there. In his autobiography, he told of reading Joyce, Rimbaud, and Faulkner at Yaddo, but interestingly, the only specific title he cited was Faulkner's *Light in August,* whose central figure, Joe Christmas, does not know whether he is white or Negro. Himes drank a lot, and ironically one of his best stories came out of his Yaddo drinking. The piece, "Da-Da-Dee," depicts a writer's despairing consciousness as he wends his way back from a bar to his comfortable room at a writers' colony called Skidoo.

Not long after his arrival at Yaddo, Himes took temporary leave to address a writers' club at the University of Chicago. The invitation was arranged by his old friend Horace Cayton, acting as director of the South Side Community Center. Before a predominantly white audience, Himes spoke of the dilemma of the Negro writer. He tried to be politic, but his message was uncompromising. He said, in effect, that the Negro's life was degrading and that the Negro author could only write about life as he experienced it, but that most readers are incapable of empathizing with or imagining a black man's life. Thus, the Negro author's main dilemma resides in the reactions of his audience, in the intellectual limitations of readers, which so often confine people to habit and withhold from them the nobler instruments of reason and conscience. Whether or not he was speaking for all black authors is debatable, but surely Himes was expressing what he felt about himself. For him, fear lay at the bottom of the Negro psyche:

> There can be no understanding of Negro life, of Negroes' compulsions, reactions and actions; there can be no understanding of the sexual impulses, of Negro crime, of Negro marital relations, of our spiritual entreaties, our ambitions and our defeats until this fear has been revealed . . . If this plumbing for the truth reveals within the Negro personality homicidal mania, lust for white women, a pathetic sense of inferiority, paradoxical

anti-semitism, arrogance, Uncle Tomism, hate and fear of self-hate, this then is the effect of oppression on the human personality.[26]

As Himes recounted the event, nobody applauded, and he feared he had failed. Demoralized, he stayed in Chicago for the rest of the week, consoling himself with the equally unhappy Vandi Haygood. By mid-June he was back in New York. Jean was no longer working, and Himes asked Van Vechten for $100 to tide them over. He also borrowed money from his old friend Dan Levin, who was now living in lower Manhattan. Levin remembered Himes crossing town on foot to save himself a few cents. For a while the Himeses stayed with friends in Brooklyn, who recalled Himes getting very belligerent with men whom he thought were leering at his wife. But at last some good news came from France: A translation of *Hollers* was to be published there in October. Also, finally, Himes gained hope on the employment front.

Himes had evidently been advertising himself in the newspapers as an experienced caretaker, and in October he landed a job in a dormant summer resort on a lakefront in Newton, New Jersey. Here he hoped to settle in and write again. He and Jean lived in a three-room apartment above a disused tavern facing the road. Besides looking after the cottages on the property and the owner's three dogs, he was expected to do painting and plumbing and electrical repairs. Himes loved the work and the dogs (though one of them, aptly named Uncle Tom, seemed to prefer white people), as well as the chance to write uninterruptedly. But the Yaddo-Guggenheim proposals for his prison novel no longer worked for him, and he now conceived of writing an autobiographical novel that would portray his hero's life well into adolescence. Whether or not he began *The Third Generation* at this time is not certain; he was still deeply wounded by the reactions to *Lonely Crusade,* and what he wanted most was respite. He did, however, linger on the possibilities of his first novel and wrote a long two-act play based on *Hollers* that he mailed off to Van Vechten. All told, the quiet of the countryside suited him.

The Himeses were not alone in their retreat. The resort owners, Frank and Elinor Bucino, came up on weekends and socialized. Himes wrote Van Vechten that Bucino was a Little Caesar–type and that his bodyguard "Swede" looked as if he had come out of one of Himes's crime stories. Jean and Elinor hit it off. Elinor Bucino informed them that her husband was Frank Sinatra's godfather. In December Horace and Ruby Cayton came for a week's visit. There were long walks in the woods and probably unsuccessful hunting forays in the snow. Himes seemed to have recovered his spirits.

The new year of 1949 brought small disappointments. Van Vechten wrote in January that he did not like Himes's play, and the following month Himes learned that he had been turned down for a Guggenheim. For the length of his stay at the Bucinos', Himes determined he would not read any race literature, but in letters he mentioned some of the books he did read: *The Time Is Noon!* by Pierre Van Passen, John O'Hara's *Butterfield 8*, *What Makes Sammy Run* by Bud Schulberg, and Horace McCoy's *They Shoot Horses, Don't They*. By March the Himeses had returned to their furnished room in the Bronx.

It was still a hand-to-mouth existence. For a while in the summer, Himes worked as a bellhop at the New Prospects Hotel in the Catskills. He liked the owner, he said, but contracted ptomaine poisoning on July 4 and vowed he would not work there again. Later that summer he found another job as a warehouseman at the New York Museum of Science and Industry. Neither employment left him much time for writing, and in any case he was unsure if he was psychologically prepared to begin a new novel. In early October came another opportunity for employment as a caretaker, this time at a summer camp in Ware, Massachusetts. Himes's duties were presumably light, since he now found time to revise his prison novel once again, in hopes of finally getting the Knopfs' approval.

Back in New York a few months later, in February 1950, Himes mailed his rewritten prison manuscript to Blanche Knopf. She had read at least one of his earlier versions and disliked it. She did not like this one any better and returned it the following month.

The Himeses had been staying with friends in Brooklyn. The latest rejection from Knopf heightened their fears. Both Chester and Jean were edgy; each accused the other of infidelities. Both had begun drinking again. When Jean passed out from drink, Chester would carry her out of the room. Tensions abated somewhat in late spring when Himes found another job as caretaker at the Connecticut farm of a wealthy New York theatrical lawyer named Halperin. Here his tasks consisted mainly of mowing vast areas of lawn and preparing and serving meals with Jean when the Halperins and their guests came out on weekends.

Meanwhile, the prison novel passed from publisher to publisher, and for a time it looked as if Holt would take it. Buoyed by these hopes, the Himeses departed the Halperin farm (not without some unpleasantness from their employers) for Durham, North Carolina, where Chester's brother Joseph had arranged for him to conduct a two-week writers' seminar at his college.

Classes met for two hours a day, which gave Himes ample opportunity to expatiate on the dilemma of the Negro author that he had discussed in Chicago the previous year. This time, however, Himes felt his audience more appreciative, perhaps because they were black. Joseph, on the other hand, had his reservations about his brother's understanding of social causes. The brothers may have had some differences, but Chester was gratified that his classes were written up by the Durham newspaper, although he suspected that the favorable publicity was in part intended to deflect attention from a lawsuit brought against the city of Durham by the NAACP to demand equal school facilities for blacks. Himes attended one of the hearings, where he observed future Supreme Court justice Thurgood Marshall advising a couple of the NAACP Negro attorneys. Marshall's appearance in Durham, Himes wrote, produced so much media coverage that one would have thought Khrushchev had come to town. Himes also visited the prosperous black areas of the city and came away impressed by the successes of black-owned enterprises. Possibly he was reminded of his childhood visit to Mound Bayou, Mississippi, when he and his brother had looked with awe at other rich Negroes.

Upon his return to New York, Himes learned to his utter dismay that Holt had turned down "Black Sheep" (another of the tentative titles of his prison novel). Devastated, he left again for Vermont for another lengthy stay with the Smiths. He wrote Van Vechten that he hoped to work there on a structured first-person account of his experiences at Yaddo, "The End of a Primitive"—a title that, as it turned out, he used for an entirely different book years later. Yaddo may have been on his mind, but he found his autobiographical impulses reaching further back in time. Indeed, as we have seen, he had contemplated writing the book that would ultimately be called *The Third Generation* more than a year before in New Jersey.

The idea may have come from Himes's mother. Before she died, Estelle had wanted Chester to write a novel about their pre–Civil War ancestors, white and black. At the time, Himes believed that books about miscegenation would be too touchy for American readers. He said as much to Estelle, who instead started her own book (in longhand) about genteel southern post–Civil War Negroes. Himes did not use any of her material, but her attempts suggested to him that he might write something about his parents' tangled love-class-race relationship. His main emphasis, however, would be to tell about the "abnormal" relationship between a mother and her son. This work, tentatively titled "The Cord," would be psychological rather than "social," given the racial ambivalence of the hero's mother: what she gives in love she derives in large part from her social and cultural conditioning. Her son is never fully able to free himself of the peculiar racial attitudes she passes on to him. To some extent this also would be the subject of Himes's novel: the son's endeavors to come to grips with his identity.

In September 1950 Himes was back in Brooklyn. During the latter part of the year he and Jean accepted another caretaking job, this time at the sumptuous country-club estate of two brothers situated on an island on Lake Copake, New York. Here Himes acted mainly as a guard, with the aid of "brave dogs," but he was also expected to make repairs when needed. In early January a ferocious blizzard struck, but aside from these very difficult days, he and Jean were for the most part left to themselves.

Sometime in the spring of 1951, Himes bought a fifteen-year-old Plymouth, and he and Jean moved into a furnished room on Lenox Avenue in Bridgeport, Connecticut. There was no pressing reason for them to live in Bridgeport, but Himes had liked the look of the city during his drives to Vermont. Each day he used to take his car to Barnum Park near Long Island Sound and write on the back seat with his typewriter between his knees. "The sounds of the lapping waves and the cries of the sea gulls fishing on the rocky shoals were ineffably soothing and I was at peace with my work."[27] The peace lasted only until July, when time and money ran out. At one point the couple had planned to move back to California, but Himes's writing was going so well that he feared breaking his rhythm.

It was decided that Jean would take the train to New York to look for a welfare job, while Himes arranged to sell his car. On his way to see a buyer, he was sideswiped by another automobile passing the wrong way on a one-way street. As Himes told the story, the driver of the other car, a slightly intoxicated rich white woman, had him arrested—and since he had no money to bail himself out, he was jailed overnight with the probability of being sent off to the county prison for the week.

Unluckily, Jean was delayed in New York, and on her return the following day, she frantically sought her absent husband. She called hospitals, then the police. Finally, after several misunderstandings, husband and wife at last found each other. Their ordeal ended when Jean's chaplain brother, Andrew, wired her money from Washington. For Himes the whole episode left a bitter taste, and he rehearsed the events in some detail first in his 1955 novel, *The Primitive*, and then again in his autobiography. What rankled was not simply the injustice—that he was black and poor and his accuser white and rich—but also that jail awakened in him memories of the dreadful years in the Ohio penitentiary. He was now determined to leave America, if he could.

The Himeses were living in Harlem in the early fall. Himes found on-and-off work during the Jewish religious holidays as a doorman at Long Island hotels, but his pay was hardly enough to keep them alive. His new agent, Margot Johnson, had been unsuccessfully trying to sell his prison book, now called "Yesterday Will Make You Cry," and she had no better luck with a draft version of his autobiographical novel. The one bit of good news was that *Lonely Crusade* had been bought by a French publisher and that a translation would soon be undertaken.

This news did not alleviate their financial problems, so when Jean found work as a recreational director at the New York State Women's Reformatory at Mount Kisco, Himes followed her to a black middle-class neighborhood on the outskirts of White Plains. For the most part he lived alone, since Jean's job required her to stay overnight five nights a week. His morale picked up a bit in December when his French translator, Yves Malartic, wrote to say that he regarded Himes's political and trade union ideas as important and, above all, that he thought him a fine artist. An exchange of letters followed, resulting in an enduring friendship.

Meanwhile, Himes continued to seek jobs. He was offered employment as a clerk at the *Reader's Digest* offices in nearby Pleasantville, typing metal stencils for an Addressograph machine. He accepted, but made so many mistakes he was fired at the end of the first day. His main consolation, he wrote, was that his day's earnings enabled him to buy Jean a cheap Christmas present.[28]

In January 1952 Himes found more congenial work at the White Plains YMCA as a day porter cleaning and waxing floors and servicing the men's shower room. He was so good at it, he says, that the director hated for him to leave. But he needed more time to write. By mid-February he was back living alone on Convent Avenue in Harlem in yet another furnished room.

Seldom had Himes's morale sunk so low. Persuading himself that he was a failure, he felt ashamed to call on any of his old writer acquaintances, such as Hughes or Ellison, or any of his other New York friends. He did manage to make contact with his older brother, Edward, now living in Harlem, whom he had seen only once or twice since adolescence. Together, the brothers watched mindless television programs, played stud poker with Edward's friends, or sat down to his wife's delicious dinners.

But these were diversions. What Himes had to acknowledge to himself now was that his marriage had petered out. Jean came to stay with him one day a week, but by April 1952 they had decided on a permanent separation.

Afterward Himes wrote that "poverty and loneliness and our enforced separation convinced me I was a failure as a husband." And in a letter to Van Vechten later in the year, he observed: "We should have done it a long time ago, after *Lonely Crusade* was published, but for a long time we tried to overcome the break . . . Jean couldn't bear the things I wrote nor the processes of my thought which caused me to write them."[29]

It seemed that spring might begin a new phase of Himes's life. His income was still precarious, but he at least had the consolation of knowing that Johnson had finally sold his prison novel to Coward McCann.[30] Doubtless he received some advance payment, but not much, and in late spring he was taken on again as a bellhop at the New Prospects Hotel, where he had once suffered ptomaine poisoning. Substituting at the switchboard one night, Himes received a telegram that Bill Targ at World Publishing had bought "The Cord." He was overjoyed. With two new books in the works, it looked as if his career were at last about to take off.

With his boss's good wishes, Himes almost immediately departed the hotel to return to Harlem, where he still had his room on Convent Avenue. He collected an advance of $1,800 from Johnson and telephoned Vandi Haygood, who had moved to New York. Himes wrote that he wanted to sleep with a white woman, and "the only white woman in the city I knew at the time who was likely to sleep with me was Vandi Haygood."[31]

Thus began anew an intense, tempestuous, violent, and ultimately destructive relationship whose last New York days (the lovers met again in Paris) Himes later portrayed in vivid detail in the novel he believed his best, *The Primitive*. According to Himes, Haygood, now divorced, suffered from feelings of self-depreciation and rejection and took lovers—black and white, men and women—as a means both of reassuring herself that she was desirable and of punishing herself for what she regarded as her deplorable character. For Himes, sex with Vandi was at different times a weapon, an instrument for getting back at whites (she taunted him for this), and a means of enveloping and protecting a hurt, vulnerable white woman. In other words, he became her Lochinvar, but she was for him a symbolic Negro, the Negro he hated and loved in himself. He both loved and hated her.

The couple were both aware of what was happening to them, yet they were incapable of controlling their worst natures. They drank, popped pills to excess, and fought one another constantly. At one point Himes, in a drunken jealous rage, beat Vandi so savagely that she was unable to go to work.[32] Himes wrote that he stayed with her for two weeks after that and nursed her back to health.

At the end of *The Primitive* the black protagonist kills his white mistress. Himes said later that this was the only event in his novel that was untrue. Vandi survived her affair with Himes, but died a couple of years later, long after the two had parted company.

The ups and downs of their last seven months together can be only dimly charted. In May Himes was writing Malartic that he was hoping to come to Europe with a "friend" for July and August. Evidently the money he anticipated did not materialize, because the following month he wrote Malartic to expect him in Paris in the fall. Vandi was becoming restless, and Himes wrote that he was depressed, that this woman "now seems to be getting impatient for the money to start pouring in. These American women . . . for the most part they hate and envy writers and yet pursue them frantically, for one purpose it seems, to hurt them."[33] He apparently still expected to travel to Europe with Vandi, because he wrote his friend Levin, who was then living in Paris, to ask about accommodations. Despite their differences, as late as November Himes intended to marry Vandi if Jean would divorce him.[34] By now, Vandi, who may well have begun to tire of Himes, took occasional lovers, arousing Himes to predictable anger.

Occasionally Himes used to turn his fury on others. In one terrible scene that the Caytons and Ellisons witnessed at Vandi's, Himes taunted Ellison about his literary success in the white world, implying that Ellison had sold out.[35] The quarrel very nearly became violent, with Himes afterward telling friends that Ellison had drawn a knife on him. Himes and Vandi stayed more or less together through Christmas, at which time Himes introduced her to the Van Vechtens. At the start of the new year Himes departed alone for Vermont.

During the course of the affair with Vandi, Himes was also having disputes with his editors at Coward McCann. Perhaps because of their differences, the novel, originally slated for publication in October, was put off until January 1953. Himes later claimed that much of the heart of *Cast the First Stone* was excised. When the book finally appeared, few reviewers looked at it, causing Himes further pain.[36]

Despite the omissions and anachronisms of his work, Himes graphically described the gaunt, dreary, brutal rhythms of prison life as few other American authors have done. The point of view is confined to Jimmy Monroe, Himes's white alter ego, whose merciless self-portrayals are astonishing. He is at times narcissistic, self-pitying, self-delusory, paranoid, and fearful of his homosexual yearnings. In later life Himes rarely sustained such ferocious objectivity. Yet if Jimmy is not altogether admirable, he is capable of love, especially for his fellow convict, Dido (a character based on Himes's homosexual lover Prince Rico). Nowhere else did Himes write so tenderly of another human being as he did of Dido. *Cast the First Stone* concludes with Dido's suicide, which strangely liberates Jimmy. In his next autobiographical novel, *The Third Generation,* Himes would kill off his fictional father. Perhaps he was hoping to expel both these significant figures from his consciousness.

The rare notices *Cast the First Stone* did receive were largely positive, although Himes characteristically remembered mainly the unfavorable ones. There remained no reason to delay his European trip, and he was encouraged now by letters from his Paris friends Malartic and Levin, and also Wright, with whom he had been in correspondence for almost a year.

Himes's first letter to Wright thanked him for his introduction to the French edition of *Lonely Crusade.* In another letter, he told Wright that he was the only black author of stature capable of standing up to prejudiced reviewers. Wright's letters in return painted a rosy picture of life for Negroes in postwar France, though warning that some amenities, such as baths, might not be readily available.

Himes was not really convinced that better times lay ahead. What he wanted most was a change of pace. Moreover, he had the excuse that he had to revise the last chapter of his autobiographical novel. Both Van Vechten and Targ had thought it too tame. Of course, there were complications—mainly a lack of ready cash. In Vermont in January 1953, Himes learned that his father had died. He had to telephone Vandi for money to fly to Cleveland and was unable to take Jean.

When World gave Himes a further advance for the reprint rights of *The Third Generation,* he wasted no more time in making European plans. There were further snags, however: His passport did not come as quickly as he had hoped, arousing in him fears that his prison record or his past associations with Communists may have held things up. These were the days of the Red scare in America, and one never knew. He sent off to the State Department copies of the attacks on his books in the Communist press. Finally, the passport came. Himes was to leave for Europe on the *Ile de France* on April 3. Wright, Malartic, and Levin arranged to meet his train in Paris. Meanwhile, Himes would pick up good bond paper for Wright, as well as complimentary copies from Harper's of Wright's new novel, *The Outsider.* He stayed with Vandi one more night and told her he would meet her later that summer in Europe. What he felt at this moment about his estranged wife is not clear, but he dedicated *The Third Generation* "To Jean."

# 8

# INTERIM

IF HIMES LOOKED TO HIS journey as an adventure, he did not anticipate that the excitement would begin as soon as it did, nor would he have wanted to call it something as banal as a "shipboard romance"—which is what it was. Two or three days out to sea, he was introduced to Willa Thompson Trierweiler, who when she learned that he was an author, told him she was writing a novel herself with the paid assistance of Edwin Seaver, the publicity director at Little, Brown.

Himes was at first more impressed by Willa's social status than her literary aspirations, and by what seemed to him her lively, "innocent," but insecure personality. A Boston socialite in her late thirties whose father was the superintendent of schools, she was, she said, a direct descendant of John Hancock. At the time of their meeting, she was seeking a divorce from her husband, a Luxembourg dentist by whom she had four daughters. To Himes she appeared emotionally sick, but to Willa, Himes may have seemed wise and emotionally balanced. Running into him on a passageway, she proceeded to relate to him the "shocking" intimate details of her married life, including her husband's violent sexual aggression and infidelities. She had passed the war years in German-occupied Europe, during which time her husband had collaborated with the enemy. She spoke too of her own extramarital liaison with a student and a subsequent hospitalization for a nervous breakdown— all grist for an autobiographical novel.

Himes now saw possibilities of playing out his fantasies of an Arthurian knight galloping to the rescue of a damsel in distress. Simply listening to her endowed him with an exhilarating sense of power. He decided to help her write her novel (*The Silver Altar*), substituting himself for Seaver. Unlike

Seaver, he would not ask her for money, only for half the royalties after publication.

They danced, they drank, and Himes fell in love. Willa refused her sexual favors but promised to join him on the Continent after visiting her daughters. They made plans to meet in Paris and to leave afterward for Mallorca, where they would work on her novel. Himes's plans to remain in Europe no more than six months, to deny himself women, and to work exclusively on his own fiction were now laid aside.

The ship docked in Southampton, where Himes disembarked to confer with his English publisher. He met Victor Weybright of Falcon Press in London, and together they decided to change the name of his forthcoming novel from "The Cord" to *The Third Generation*. On April 10, 1953, he arrived in Paris, unable to find his friends Richard Wright, Yves Malartic, and Dan Levin, who had come earlier to the Gare Saint Lazare to meet his boat train. Himes took a cab to Wright's place, but there the concierge, thinking him an intruder, threw him out. Panicky, he returned to the station and found a cab driver who understood his French and his predicament and drove him to the Hôtel Delavigne, where coincidentally Wright had already booked him a room. At length all parties found each other, to Himes's great relief, and Wright immediately took him under his wing.

The Malartics invited him two or three times to dine with them, and soon Himes encountered other American race "brothers": Ollie Harrington, the cartoonist of "Bootsie," whom he had met years before at the Moons'; William Gardner Smith, the novelist; Bill Coleman, the jazz trumpeter; Mercer Cook, an academic; and Leroy Haynes, an ex-GI who ran a soul food restaurant on the rue Manuel. At the time they looked to him a "lost and unhappy lot."[1]

One afternoon Wright asked Himes to accompany him to a café to meet James Baldwin. No sooner were the three men seated than Wright took Baldwin to task for writing an essay critical of Wright's committed social fiction. Baldwin, who believed that literature had to avoid open social comment, responded that "the sons had to kill the fathers." Wright was incensed, for he had not only loaned the hard-pressed Baldwin money but also helped him get a grant. From Himes's point of view, neither Wright nor Baldwin emerged from the dispute looking particularly noble. Baldwin appeared cowed, and Wright, something of a bully.[2] Later, at a gathering of white European literati, Himes found himself stoutly defending Wright as a "great man and a great writer."

On the whole, Himes's initial impressions of Paris were not favorable. This was not the tourist city he had imagined. He didn't like the bistros, the good restaurants were too expensive, the sexuality of Pigalle was dull, the nightclubs were tourist traps, he was overcharged everywhere, and the French girls apparently did not succumb to his charms.

He also hated the "US Go Home" graffiti he saw scribbled everywhere in chalk on the walls of the Latin Quarter: "although the French whom I met swore it was the 'other' Americans they hated because I wasn't an American. I didn't particularly like the connotation, nor the exclusion. If I'm not an American, what am I?"[3]

To be sure, there were saving graces. He enjoyed the Seine, Notre Dame, the Louvre, and the sidewalk cafés, Les Deux Magots being his favorite. Moreover, he transacted business of a sort in Paris. Ellen Wright, who had become a literary agent (representing Simone de Beauvoir, among others), told him she would represent the novel he was writing about his affair with Vandi. And he was delighted to learn that *La Croisade de Lee Gordon* (*Lonely Crusade*), with Wright's introduction, had come out in his publisher's prestigious collection called "Le chemin de la vie" (The Path of Life). The French could at least judge good literature.

Vandi Haygood arrived on April 22, and the "brothers" were duly impressed by her looks and her flair. Before her departure for other parts, she and Himes passed a riotous night together requiring the manager of the Hôtel de Scandinavie to relegate them to a back room.

Willa arrived later that month. Himes introduced her to the Wrights, but he felt that Richard behaved boorishly, condescendingly in her presence, as if she were some kind of "cheap" white woman.

Himes and Willa left Paris in early May for Arcachon in the southwest, where the Malartics had lent them their summer home. Himes thrived in the new environment. In letters to friends he wrote of "the quiet exquisite enchantment of the shore and the fishing boats and the busy fishermen repairing and painting their boats."[4] The weather was fine, and the lovers liked to drink champagne and walk to the church or out along the pier or shore. Neighbors were kind and helpful. "It is so different from the hard hurried contest and sexuality of Paris. It is peaceful and warm and friendly— the way one hopes the world would be."[5] They swam, they ate oysters, they painted the Malartics' boat a bright yellow and learned to sail it. Himes later recalled this period as one of the happiest of his life.

On May 25 Himes mailed Bill Targ of World Publishing the revised final chapter of *The Third Generation*. He was glad to get it out of the way but lamented his lack of progress on his Vandi novel. He was just reading and rereading *The Brothers Karamazov,* he wrote to Wright in June. He later submitted a section of Willa's novel to Targ, saying that it might have women's magazine appeal or movie potential. Willa, he wrote, was "a good money writer staying temporarily in Arcachon."[6] He did not say that he was living with her or that he was helping her write the book.

In the interim Vandi had discovered that she was the subject of Himes's next novel, and she demanded that Ellen Wright let her see what he had written. In high dudgeon Himes wrote Ellen that "the courts are the resource of those who feel they have been libeled in published works."[7] Soon after, he severed his contract with Ellen. He did not trust her.

Himes had at first planned to leave Arcachon for the writers' colony of the journalist-historian Daniel Guérin in La Ciotat. The Wrights had sponsored him, but at the last minute he and Willa decided to go to London instead, where they hoped to devote themselves entirely to Willa's novel. Wright's treatment of Willa still rankled, but Himes was also anxious to dissociate himself from Wright professionally. "Unfortunately," he wrote Targ,

> Wright's works over here are being exploited as anti American propaganda; and his prestige is based on the proposition that here is a great man who was forced to flee his native land because of racial prejudice. On the basis of the merit of his work he is not too well liked or too well admired—which is doubly unfortunate. I don't want to get caught within the limited evaluation of racial protest writing and have my work used exclusively as ammunition in a propaganda campaign.[8]

Like Baldwin, Himes felt he had to carve a space for himself as a writer apart from Wright.

On July 7 Himes and Willa arrived in London, where Himes learned quickly that another color bar awaited him. They resided first in a cold basement flat on Randolph Crescent, whose landlady complained that Himes looked "slightly colored." In August they settled in an old house within walking distance of Keats's home in Hampstead, where the Jewish refugee proprietors were far more welcoming. There Chester and Willa worked assiduously on Willa's manuscript, taking time off occasionally to visit the Regent's Park Zoo, go to the movies, or take sight-seeing trips along the Thames.

Willa thought their London days constituted the happiest moments of her life. Two years later she wrote Himes that the only time in life one is happy is during acts of creation. Remembering fondly the writing they had done together, she invested the ambience of their neighborhood—the streets, the nearby liquor store, and Sainsbury's—with an aura of romance.

Himes was less taken with London but agreed that their surroundings were appropriate for what they had set out to do. "We have been living cheaply and quietly in this big ugly and dismal city. But it is a good place for work," he wrote to Malartic.[9] He told Willa he did not want his name to appear as coauthor on their novel, believing that her race and social status would hold more appeal for readers. As regards his contribution, Himes seems to have been responsible for shifting the narrative from the first person to the third and for inserting long passages dealing with the young American's painful sexual initiation as a bride in Luxembourg. In essence, he was recasting Willa's experience into a kind of psychosexual study.

During September Himes sent drafts of two sections of the manuscript to Targ at World requesting a large advance and asking that the book be copyrighted in Willa's name. Both he and Willa were convinced of its commercial possibilities and looked forward to their long delayed escape to Mallorca. But Targ did not like the book and returned the manuscript a few weeks later. The lovers were devastated.

Himes could at least hope for better news about *The Third Generation*. It was due out December 13, and an advance review from *Kirkus* was encouraging.[10] Yet as the raw, damp London winter crept into their apartment, he and Willa became more anxious. Money was running out, and they saw little likelihood of gaining more in the immediate future. Himes's appeals for an additional advance from World lay unanswered. He pawned his typewriter, and Willa pawned her wedding ring. Finally, Targ came through in January, wiring Chester $500. The couple promptly departed for Mallorca.

Himes's hopes that *The Third Generation* would represent a financial breakthrough were not met, despite favorable reviews during the first months of 1954. Several critics thought the novel too contrived, while others complained of its loose structure and "lack of animal fun." Perhaps Himes was too close to his material. Still, more reviewers spoke admiringly of the book's prose style, its "searing pathos," and "tragic power."[11] In hindsight, the more positive responses appear justified.

The autobiographical Charles Taylor's struggle to free himself of his possessive mother, Lillian, constitutes the thematic center around which much of the narrative revolves. External events in the main follow the descending fortunes of the Taylor (Himes) family from Charles's early childhood in the South to his eighteenth year. Himes's portrait of his light-complexioned mother (if not quite biographically accurate) recalls her as a strong-minded, self-possessed woman whose many racial and emotional inner conflicts eventually destroy her—and very nearly her husband and youngest son as well.

Fess, the dark-skinned husband and father, is proud but deceptively servile, affable, extroverted, yet silently brooding over hidden anger and hurts. Born and bred a southerner, he is defeated partly because of his inability to adapt to the anarchy and indifference of northern cities. Lastly, the tormented and self-absorbed Charles, a product of the psychology and values of his parents, endeavors to discover his true self among the cultures of the South and North, rural and urban. Taken together, Himes's family portrayals suggest the variety of psychological stresses of the Great Migration.

But *The Third Generation* is ultimately a saga of a family's decline. Near the start of the novel, Professor Fess Taylor takes his wife and three young sons on a mule-drawn journey to an obscure Mississippi backwoods college where he has found work. Their journey anticipates metaphorically the family's life journey through the years:

> The road turned, crossed the stream, the iron tires rattling the loose boards. Then slowly, at first imperceptibly, the road began to sink, the countryside rose higher, corn gave way to green rows of cotton; the banks closed in and the road became narrower. Soon the bank was as high as their heads and then it was over the top of the hack, cutting off the light. They moved like a boat down a shallow river of darkness beneath a narrow roof of fading twilight. As the road deepened, roots of huge trees sprang naked from the bank like horrible reptilian monsters. Now overhead, the narrow strip of purple sky turned slowly black, and it became black-dark in the deep sunken road.[12]

Unhappily for Himes, the book found few buyers. World sold its reprint rights for $10,000 to New American Library, whose editors may have thought the novel commercially viable. If so, they were wrong. Himes himself was uncharacteristically ambivalent about what he had written. He told Wright (inaccurately) that the reviews were poor, and described the book as "sort of a fictional autobiography of my childhood . . . a rather strange and different book, but at least it's honest."[13] A few years later he confided to novelist John A. Williams that it was a "subtly dishonest book, made dishonest deliberately for the purpose of making money. Strangely enough it didn't live up to expectations."[14]

What Himes meant by "dishonest" is not clear. Later he dismissed the remark by saying he had meant that the idea for the book came from his mother, though this would hardly make it dishonest. His brothers, as noted earlier, felt he grossly exaggerated their mother's racism,[15] and his mother was never the militant Himes made her out to be. Very possibly Himes felt that he had overemphasized the oedipal ties between mother and son. Freudianism and psychoanalysis were very much in the air in the 1950s, and Himes may well have thought he could exploit what was then fashionable. Possibly he acted on Targ's and Van Vechten's advice that he should revise his final chapter to make it more dramatic and by so doing made it melodramatic and unfaithful to his own life. The book ends with Fess, the hero's father, being stabbed to death in the dissolute hero's presence, thereby shocking him into a new sense of responsibility. This curiously upbeat but ultimately unsatisfactory ending may well have left Himes uneasy.

An endless train trip behind frosty windows and a nightlong boat crossing from Barcelona took the lovers to Mallorca. The weather belied Spain's sunny promise: A cold snow fell on their arrival. The modest Residencia Tanger they had booked in Palma proved too expensive, prompting them to move further along the coast to Puerto de Pollensa, but their new quarters on the Cala San Vincente remained uncomfortably cold despite blazing fires. Willa fell ill with nervous fits, and they lived for several weeks in seclusion.

Himes again began to work on his Vandi novel, now called "The End of a Primitive," while Willa did the cooking and managed the house. Demoralized by her failure to find a publisher, she became fascinated with Himes's fictional account of his affair with Vandi (Himes became Jesse, and Vandi, Kriss, in the novel). It was as if she had begun to identify with Vandi and feared that Himes was verging on pornography. Himes disagreed, claiming that this was the best writing he had done yet.

Some weeks into their stay at Puerto de Pollensa, they found themselves drawn into a circle of English and American expatriates who, Himes believed, viewed them as interracial curiosities. Despite misgivings, he was at once intrigued with the social centerpiece of the group, an attractive blonde woman named Kathy King. At one point Willa, fearing for her man, forbade him to see her. Nonetheless, they joined in a great deal of drinking and socializing, which on one occasion resulted in Willa falling and dislocating her shoulder. This incident formed the basis of Himes's story, "Spanish Gin," which he later expanded into an unfinished novel, "The Lunatic Fringe." On reflection, Himes despised the whole expatriate colony. He wrote Willa the following year, "The whole fucking lot of assholes thought of me as some kind of sex animal you had picked up somewhere."[16]

Roch Minué, a talented local painter who befriended the couple, advised them to rent a house in the picturesque (and cheaper) pink-stone village of Deya. In Deya they moved into a ground-floor apartment where Himes passed his days typing his Vandi novel at the kitchen table or, on glorious afternoons, outside under a fig tree. Several of their neighbors invited them to their homes, among them the English poet Robert Graves. Graves did not endear himself to Himes by presuming him to be a black musician. More infuriating was Graves's mild flirtation with Willa. At one point Himes became so violently jealous that Willa thought he would smash her. She was ironing at the time she sensed Himes about to strike. She wrote to him afterward that she had been prepared to "wallop" him with the iron if he tried.[17]

Himes later endeavored to make literary use of their relationship in a fragment of the novel he never completed. He wrote of Willa:

> She was descended from one of the most aristocratic families in America. In a direct line from the Mayflower. He'd wanted her to look the part always. Inside, he was very proud of her tradition. It was like an honor that had been bestowed upon him; the greatest of all honors that could be given him; and also the greatest of all trusts. It was as if he had been given the exclusive charge of something infinitely precious to be guarded with his life. But sometimes he felt trapped by the responsibility and hated the very preciousness.[18]

Himes thus pinpointed his own dilemma, which elsewhere he cast in wider terms as typical of relationships between white women and black men. He passionately believed that black men had the ability to heal white women because both were oppressed and humiliated by white males. Unhappily, Himes was unable to heal himself. Willa was important to him not because she was a beautiful woman ("not in the sexy way of a woman men desired"),[19] but because she symbolized for him vulnerable white America. Being responsible for her gave him unexpected strength. Doubtless his view of their relationship bolstered his faltering ego. Yet by the same token his inability to provide for her infuriated him since he could not always fulfill his self-appointed role of being the sole source of her happiness.

The couple's money troubles eased somewhat when Chester managed to garner an advance of $800 from World for a collection of his short stories, "Black Boogie Woogie." Life for a while became idyllic. The lovers passed whole days shopping in Palma or lingering sensually on the beach. The one catch was Himes's dispute with his landlord. The cause of the dispute was an apartment toilet that also served as a garbage disposal for an upstairs tenant. A trapdoor on the ceiling above the commode would occasionally open, and trash would suddenly descend chutelike. Outraged, Himes refused to pay his rent until the situation was corrected. His landlord threatened to cut off their electricity. Himes threatened the landlord. Now the entire village took sides, including the *guardia civil*. Himes and Willa celebrated his forty-fifth birthday with cognac under the stars and then departed.

The couple next moved to Terreno, a district southwest of Palma where they shared an apartment with a large family named Sureda. His Vandi novel completed, Himes thought he should be able to relax. He enjoyed the company of the Sureda women, observed with curiosity and wonder the U.S. Sixth Fleet docked at Palma and even attended a corrida whose pageantry impressed him as being equal to a Catholic mass. Later Willa recalled, "I was happiest with you . . . typing your manuscript in Terreno. Remember how good we felt when both manuscripts were done, one evening. That was the evening you gave me my 'complete compliment.' "[20]

But Himes was incapable of sustained serenity. He accused Willa of flirting with a young German and complained later of hating the autumn rains. Above all, he felt frustrated that he had not achieved literary success. When Donald Friede at World sent Himes the short stories he had selected for "Black Boogie Woogie," he threw the package into the sea. He hated what he had written and told the editors he did not want the book published. Once more money ran low, and now Willa began to loathe Palma. Brother Edward in New York sent Chester fifty dollars but wrote that it was time he stood on his own feet. Chester did not take the advice kindly. He needed to get away, but how?

In despair, Himes at last resorted to borrowing money with a bogus check as security, and he and Willa fled to Arcachon where they hoped to take refuge at Malartic's house. Unknown to them, however, Malartic had sold the house. They would have to move on. Willa again pawned her ring, and Himes pawned his typewriter. They took the train to Paris where Willa eventually found part-time work as a copy editor. They stayed in a cheap hotel on the rue de Buci. Willa cried and drank.

After several infuriating rejections, Himes at last sold "The End of a Primitive" to New American Library and determined to use his advance of $1,000 to return Willa to America. She was not sure she wanted to go, but he feared for her equanimity. She was not suited, he believed, for the hand-to-mouth existence he lived, and he felt himself no longer able to bear the strain of her gloom. He told her that the separation would be only temporary and that their chances of selling her book in America would be better if she were there. Meanwhile, he would try to get on a better financial footing and join her later on. Malartic's wife Yvonne, who met them at this time, thought that Himes was deeply in love. About Willa, she was not so sure.[21]

Willa sailed on the *Ryndam* on November 30, 1954, weeping profusely. She feared that Himes wanted to get rid of her. Disembarking in New York, she decided at the last minute not to go to a hotel near Gramercy Park because she remembered that in his novel Himes had described the character Kriss (Vandi) as living nearby. She looked up Vandi in the telephone directory and noted also a Mrs. Chester Himes living on West Twenty-second Street. Willa wondered if Chester was really divorced.

Willa went to live with an aunt in Boston and later found work as a dental assistant. She tried without success to place her book and then began revising it drastically. In large part she returned it to what it had been before she met Himes.

With Willa's departure, Himes drifted into melancholy. "I missed her. We had already had everything there was for us but I convinced myself there was more. I persuaded myself to believe what I had told her was a lie; that I had sent her back to sell our book."[22] Inadvertently he discovered that his French publisher Albin Michel had printed ten thousand copies of the translation of *If He Hollers Let Him Go* but had paid him for only a fraction of that number. Frustrated without Willa as his interpreter, he was unable to collect. Suddenly Paris had become hateful to him, and he decided to return to London.

The friendly attentions of a lovely East Indian woman in a London roominghouse were not enough to prevent Himes from having an emotional collapse—not unlike the one he had had at Yaddo. He took to wailing so irrepressibly to the tune of "I'll Get By" that his landlady called in Scotland Yard. He visited Wright's Trinidadian friend, the historian George Padmore, but found their discussion about Wright's recent visit to the Gold Coast somewhat tedious. He grew even more restless and irritated because Willa's letters suggested that he was losing her to the middle-class values of her family.

Himes returned to New York in early February 1955, taking up residence at the Albert Hotel in Greenwich Village. His story "Spanish Gin" was turning into a novel. He visited Willa in Boston, but their reunion was short-lived. Willa told him she had to attend to some business at her aunt's. Himes felt, not without justification, that Boston was hostile to blacks, and he went back to New York. Willa wrote him afterward that she doubted that they were capable of understanding each other or living peaceably together. Earlier she had come to New York and observed Jean leaving his room. Chester, she said, thought nothing of spending a few hours in a hotel room with his wife. How did Jean know he was in New York or where he lived? Chester explained he had been asking Jean for a divorce but that Jean was reluctant to give him up. In fact, she had earlier gone to Europe to get him back. Willa found it hard to believe that they were no longer lovers. Moreover, she was suspicious of Himes's efforts to reach Vandi and did not believe him when he told her he simply wanted to get back some family silver and a scrapbook he had left with her. He was unable to speak to Vandi the first time he phoned. On his next call he was told she had died the night before of a drug overdose. He wept uncontrollably.

Willa wrote Himes that she was ready to give him up if that was what he wanted, but also said that she was prepared to come to New York to be near him. She asked not for fidelity but for honesty. Otherwise there was no point in carrying on. The end of the affair was at hand. During several of their meetings he was impotent. He did not want to admit that his feelings had changed, but Willa reminded him of what he had written her in one of his first letters:

> Darling, we are at an age when life has one last flickering chance of running uphill. Then its downhill to the end; *a portioned distance from the dead.* We are lucky. It rarely comes to anyone but once—to most, never. What do you do with a peak but mount it, climb it? What if it fails? What if it all crumbles into dust? The dream is only true while you are dreaming it. Always only true. Never true otherwise.[23]

Now Himes began rationalizing. He wrote to Willa that her family's objections were a handicap he could not overcome, though in another letter he said, "You must never consider yourself alone. I will always be with you in love, always somewhere in the world loving you." But his words sounded desultory, and there was bad faith in a letter of June 28 claiming that they had not given themselves completely to love. Here Himes sentimentalized, quoting lines from one of his old stories: "All of his life he had wanted to experience it—just this one, simple emotion—just to be in love. He'd searched for it; he'd been everywhere looking for it." He was deluding himself when he told her she was the love he had always sought and that he would not let her get away.

During these months of unceasing correspondence, emotional self-flagellation, and unrewarding sex, Himes kept trying futilely to place his stories. He saw few friends in New York and felt ashamed of his failure to achieve literary recognition. Once at a dinner at Van Vechten's he met the Jamaican novelist George Lamming. Afterward they passed the night in Harlem, an experience that awakened in Himes another view of the black heart of the city. He began returning to Harlem, viewing with fascination the low life, the gamblers, the pimps, and the prostitutes, and gathering material for a kind of fiction he did not yet know he was going to write.

Several editors at the New American Library diligently applied themselves to making the final version of *The Primitive* (the new title of "The End of a Primitive") "palatable to the general reader" by omitting not only "gross" references to sex but also several of Himes's surrealistic and grotesque images. Regarding the latter, Himes quite rightly felt that the editors had damaged his aesthetic project. Furious, he went over the whole text again, restoring what he could, mindful not to ruin his chances of making money by delaying publication.

Himes managed also at the time to see Arnold Gingrich at *Esquire,* who bought the story "The Snake," a fictional account of Jean's near escape from death at her brother's California ranch. But he was unsuccessful at selling some of his other stories, especially the one he liked best, based on an episode Willa had told him about a confrontation with her husband.

In August Willa went to the Belgian seaside to spend time with her children. By the end of the month she was back in Paris, working as a medical secretary. Meanwhile, Himes in New York had taken a job as a night porter at a Horn & Hardart restaurant on Fifth Avenue and Thirty-seventh Street. He did not get along especially well with his white boss, but he could not afford to quit. Besides, he wrote, he was eating better than he had in some time.

Several years later Himes used the restaurant as a setting for his novel *Run Man Run.* The idea for the novel came on his last day at work, when a drunken disruptive police officer intruded on the premises. Himes tried to imagine how the policeman would try to cover his tracks if he had killed someone. Would he try to pursue and kill witnesses? The possibilities percolated in his mind for some time.

Earlier in the summer Himes had enlisted the legal assistance of the Authors Guild to require Berkley Books to pay him for the reprint rights of *Hollers.* He won his suit with a settlement of $1,000 and booked immediate passage for Europe, taking with him recently printed copies of *The Primitive.* An unpublished autobiographical fragment reads:

> When I was forty-five years old, I made the biggest mistake of my life. It had taken me 44 years to get away from the U.S. And less than two years later I went back. And that was the mistake I had never gotten over. When I had left NY in the spring of '53 I felt at least a few people wished me well . . . But when I left the second time at the end of December 1955, I knew I had had it. I had blown it. Killed all respect. Everything. Blacks and whites alike. Get a white woman and go from Cadillacs to cotton sacks.[24]

Further setbacks and white women awaited Himes. Oddly, the literary popularity he had sought came at last from a direction he had not anticipated. For the time being, however, he was certain of only one thing: that he did not want to live in the United States.

# 9

# CELEBRITY

BACK IN PARIS ON DECEMBER 26, 1955, Himes invited Willa to join him at the Malartics', but he failed to show up and she left after an hour. He spent his first night near the Gare Saint Lazare allegedly renewing his virility with prostitutes. Shortly thereafter he moved briefly to Levallois-Perret, near where Willa was employed, and later to the Hôtel Royer-Collard in the Latin Quarter. He had spent so much money in nine days that he had only a couple of hundred dollars left out of his Berkley Books settlement.

*The Third Generation* was about to be published in France by Plon in its Feux Croisés (Cross Fire) series, which Malartic considered the most prestigious collection in France. This prompted Himes to request double the $150 advance he was offered. It diminished him as an author, he wrote his publisher, to be paid so little: "I can't accept any privilege or any honor, however great, on any terms less than those which are offered as a matter of practice to other U.S. writers, so many of whom are far less successful, far less talented, and far less important than myself."[1]

Himes's notes for his autobiography start 1956 with a listing of his extensive wardrobe and go on to mention his "wild skyrocketing temper" due in part to frustrations in the United States and his resentment of Willa. Elsewhere he notes: "Remember being drunk first six months—drunk and defeated . . . I drank so much half of the time I was sexually impotent and in a rage at my incapacity." Without Willa he felt lonely and insecure. "I needed my own woman around me all the time, to make love to, to keep house for me and not least of which to translate for me in a country where I couldn't speak the language." He seldom saw Willa now; she called on him once at his hotel, after which she refused to visit him again. Infuriated, he accused her of being a lesbian and next wrote her apologizing and asking for mercy. In Willa's last letter to Himes she responded that she would never remember him with mercy: "What a word! I'll remember you with love."[2]

Himes liked to say that he desired black women but found none willing to consort with him because he was poor. But poverty affected more than sexual conquests, it was a matter of survival. Himes complained bitterly to others that his publishers were cheating him or sending him insufficient funds. From time to time Van Vechten and Walter Freeman, a New American Library editor in New York, mailed him small checks. Often Himes imagined that attackers lurked everywhere, and he began to carry a hunting knife and wrench to protect himself. "But no one in Paris was uptight enough to challenge me. I was as dangerous and violent and undiscriminating as a blind rattler."[3]

By mid-March Himes was cooking in his new fourth-floor room in order to save money on restaurants. "So I buy my bottle of red wine (about 20 cents) and some stew meat and leeks and carrots and potatoes and a loaf of bread and scoff [sic] away."[4]

He had planned to begin again his aborted Spanish manuscript, now called "It Rained Five Days," but instead he began a new novel, "Mamie Mason" (whose American title became *Pinktoes*), a thinly disguised satire about Molly Moon's "brotherhood" parties. The writing went quickly, and in March 1956 he sent off the first two chapters to Freeman at New American Library. Freeman thought the work better suited for another publisher and forwarded the sample to James Silberman at Dial Press. Silberman returned them to Himes, saying that what he had written so far was mainly a series of set pieces, lacking plot and full-blown characters.

Caricature was what Himes had aimed for, but he nonetheless took Silberman's criticisms seriously. For most of the wintry month of April he reworked the novel (often at the Café Au Départ, where he completed 120 pages of text, including a 20-page introduction). "Mamie Mason" would be a different kind of Negro novel. Readers, he said, were tired of protest fiction arousing pity for poor downtrodden Negroes.[5]

"From here the 'Negro problem' in America seems very strange," Himes wrote Van Vechten, "and I don't think I'll ever be able to write about it seriously. It doesn't make sense any more on either side."[6] Racism was absurd, and from now on absurdity would inform his fiction. Years afterward he recalled how the writing of *The Primitive* opened his eyes to the absurdity of racism for both perpetrators and victims. But absurdity as a theme was implicit in *The Third Generation*, where the light-complexioned Negro mother of the protagonist turns on her husband in large part because he is dark-skinned.

"Mamie Mason," like *The Third Generation*, proposed characters different from the usual "downtrodden" Negro peasant and proletarian types. The characters were middle-class, Himes wrote Freeman, not unlike the kinds of families that produced the Ralph Bunches and Walter Whites. He noted that when he first arrived in Paris, his "thinking was confused. I had the creative urge but the old tired forms for the American black writer did not fit . . . I wanted to break through the barriers that kept them labelled as protestors."[7]

That spring Himes was very much alone. He wrote mornings, and passed afternoons and evenings at the Café Tournon, where the circle surrounding novelist William Gardner Smith and cartoonist Ollie Harrington had grown larger than the Richard Wright entourage at the Monaco. Himes and Harrington became close friends, and their good-natured banter drew customers' attention to Himes's presence. Despite his rage and paranoia about racial slights, he was, as always, able to project warmth, humor, and charm.

Himes's popularity, or more accurately his prestige, was enhanced by news of the impending publication in France of *The Primitive*, under the French title *La Fin d'un primitif*. It did not matter at the time that the book would draw scarcely any media attention. It was triumph enough that the "brothers" in the café saw it.

To the end, Himes viewed *The Primitive* as his best book despite its few readers. It is undoubtedly his best structured work, positing in alternate beginning chapters the seemingly dreary and prosaic daytime lives of his lovers. Exposition of their private and social histories is seamlessly integrated into the greater part of the narrative relating their explosive affair. Himes always preferred *his* title "The End of a Primitive" because "end" ironically indicated the protagonist's ultimate induction into and destruction by "civilized" society.

What Himes had produced was not a "shocking" interracial romance to get back at Vandi, as some have argued, but an intense, incisive, psychological portrayal of tormented lovers. His understanding of and compassion for the seemingly worldly-wise Kriss (Vandi) is as remarkable as his picture of her bitter, angry, self-pitying black lover. Both in their different ways are lost and alienated from a popular culture depicted as being somehow the moral equivalent of the society at large. The novel is also a kind of roman à clef in which Himes paints some not very flattering portraits of colleagues.[8] Toward the end of the novel Himes projects a vision of American life in terms of a surreal, "cute" talking monkey on television that predicts both domestic crimes, like the murder of Kriss, and world events. On a more subjective plane, the actual process of writing *The Primitive* helped clarify Himes's sense of what had attracted him to Vandi and the forces that drove them apart.

Just as Himes perceived the absurdity of American racism, he was not blind to its manifestations in France. Paris in 1956 was astir with anxieties about the Algerian uprising, and while the procolonialist Organisation de l'Armée Secrète planted bombs and fired shots at the police, many of the French professed fears of Arabs and Arab terrorism. French anti-Americanism also struck Himes as hypocritical and self-congratulatory: "The French don't have too much liking for that type of propaganda which involves cases of actual Negro advancement. The Emmett Till case [where a young black boy in Mississippi was killed for speaking "impudently" to a white woman] is more to their liking, something 'bloody . . . terrible . . . inhuman' that brings out all the good grim grisly adjectives."9

Soon Himes interrupted his account of Mamie Mason to begin a new novel about how the French viewed American Negroes. Racial problems in France, he believed, were compounded by blacks' misconceptions of Europe. He then began to focus on the psychological baggage blacks brought with them from America.

Himes viewed racism as grounded in unconscious sexual fears and guilt. He was aware too of how sex and racism fed his own neurotic impulses. "I needed sex as much as I needed food. Without sex my mind would get stuffed . . . and I would lose myself in the contemplation."10 Afternoons he would pick up American or Scandinavian girls at cafés, and evenings he would go with his Tournon friends to the nightclub where Art Simmons played the piano at the Hôtel des Etats-Unis, a veritable hive of interracial couples. In late May he met a German drama student, Regine Fischer, who agreed to accompany him to a party. Himes did not know at the time that she was one of Harrington's several girlfriends, a factor that afterward strained their relationship.

Himes and Regine became lovers. Regine did not at first wholly give up Harrington, much to Himes's dismay. But in a frank admission of his own shortcomings, he related that Regine had to instruct her much older lover that there was more to sex than his immediate physical satisfaction. In the course of events Himes also learned that she was far less promiscuous than she liked to give the impression of being. In his autobiography he occasionally disparaged her, but his letters at the time suggest that he was strongly drawn to her and felt great affection for her.

Meanwhile, Himes was finding it difficult to keep "Mamie Mason" as funny as he wanted it to be, and he began a synopsis for what he hoped would be his contemplated novel about American black expatriates and their "place" in French society. An unpublished fragment of his autobiography, however, indicates that the racial situation in Paris and Himes's memories of Molly Moon's Harlem parties were linked in his mind: "All the sex surrounding me was interracial, bizarre, side-splittingly funny."[11] Yet somewhere along the way the humor was lost. The work published as *A Case of Rape* turned out to be a much more somber treatment of white-black race relations in France.

One reason that Himes could not sustain the high jinks of his satire was his financial outlook. Money was forever scarce; the seventy-five dollars he received from Plon for *The Third Generation* was scarcely enough to keep him alive. And his books were not earning royalties. As usual Himes resorted to asking friends for money. In a letter to Freeman dated May 22 Himes thanked him for the five dollars he sent, acknowledging again his "desperate" straits.

Regine saw Himes off in early June as he headed south for Daniel Guérin's writers' colony to finish "Mamie Mason." He had deposited most of his belongings in a trunk at the Malartics' and borrowed money for his train fare. "I'm still trying," he wrote Freeman. "There is a line in *Lonely Crusade* that reads: 'In this world men never do give up.' Bastards don't have any choice, that's the only reason."[12] He did not even have enough money for cigarettes and stamps, he wrote Van Vechten.

Himes had the run of Guérin's large house in La Ciotat. There were five other authors on the beautiful estate overlooking the bay, but he had little to do with them, fearing French intellectual condescension. His writing came quickly. By mid-June he had nearly a complete draft. He summed up his novel for Silberman as "a very simple plot, telling how Mamie Mason tries to force Juanita Wright, the wife of the great race leader, Wallace Wright, to come voluntarily to her parties and how, in so doing, Mamie fouls up the lives of many people and has to set them to right again."[13]

In a much later account for his publisher, Himes described his book as

> a Rabelaisian treatment of the sex motivation of New York City's inter-racial set by a member of long standing. The author reveals some of the backstage and bedroom scenes in the great struggle of Negro equality in a graphic detail seldom found outside psychiatric case histories. Underlining the depiction of the Negro people's illimitable faith in a just solution of their dilemma is a hilarious account of the aphrodisiacal compulsions of the "Negro Problem" in which the dedicated crusaders against racial bias are shown more often falling in bed than in battle. The story is authentic and many of the scenes and characters are drawn so closely to life as to be recognizable.[14]

Himes wrote Van Vechten that same June: "The end is terrific . . . Some of it is funny, none of it is bitter . . . I call it, for my own personal satisfaction, an experiment in good will." Then, rather unexpectedly, he added: "I have a great feeling now that I am going to be free forever. It is such a very strange feeling it makes me want to cry. But even if I am disappointed, even if I am never free, I will never quit."[15]

Himes truly felt he was turning over a new leaf. In the same letter to Van Vechten he acknowledged that he had come to the end of his three-year love affair with Willa, whom he described as "a very nice person, democratic, non-chauvinistic, compassionate, intelligent, interesting, and very good and yet there was an area in [her] mind that retained values of a sort as essential to maintaining a certain reserved position in this world and . . . these values would destroy the world." He rationalized their failure as a consequence of racial and cultural differences. "I didn't have a chance but it took me three years to discover it. What saved . . . me I suppose is that my own acceptance of myself in an emergency gives me an equal indestructibility."[16] He said nothing about Regine.

Back in Paris in mid-July, he settled in with Regine on rue Mazarine. Willa may have been on his mind because he now intended writing his Spanish novel, "It Rained Five Days," but inspiration eluded him. One unexpected joy was a chance encounter with his brother Joseph and Joseph's wife Estelle at the American Express offices. Joseph was by now an established sociologist who had come to Europe to attend a conference. The brothers and Estelle dined together, and afterward Chester took them to meet the Malartics. Joseph's success very nearly made Chester forget his own troubles. But the euphoria did not last.

Himes was still waiting to learn the fate of "Mamie Mason" and said he felt as if he were serving time. When Dial turned him down, he desperately sought money from Willa's publisher. She had at last sold her novel (now called *Garden without Flowers*) to Beacon Press, but no money was immediately forthcoming. For the next several months Himes had to live on the goodwill of friends, among them Wright, on whom he still occasionally called.

Ralph Ellison, visiting Paris during the summer of 1956, met Himes briefly at Wright's. Ellison's impression was that Himes seemed as "tortured" as ever. He wrote Cayton that although he had not read the Vandi book he thought Himes a cad for exploiting white women while hating them for being white.[17]

Ellison's views notwithstanding, Himes did not live off white women. To be sure he was flattered that Regine liked him, but he also felt responsible for her. When he did receive money for his books, he turned much of it over to her to buy clothes. Indeed he gave serious thought to marrying her.

But first Himes had to deal with Jean. He needed her consent for a divorce, although he did not know how he could get together $1,500 for legal fees. "I am in such a hole now I might never get out and I would like to have this one freedom at least," he wrote Jean on his birthday. But in Jean's mind he was still very much her husband. In October he wrote Van Vechten, "I am living more or less on faith and the love of a beautiful young German girl."[18] A few days later he sent Jean another letter saying that she could get a divorce routinely on grounds of desertion for only court costs (about a hundred dollars). He continued: "I want to marry a young woman from Germany who is now two months pregnant with my child and I want with all my heart to have this child in marriage." This was untrue, but he did add truthfully: "I would like to give you a settlement of some kind, but I owe everyone whom I know here in Paris, and if it weren't for the help of the woman I love I couldn't exist."[19] Jean did not respond, and on December 4 Himes wrote the attorney Grant Reynolds that he could prove Jean had deserted him in 1952. He asked if he would have to appear in court in New York if he filed suit for divorce.

Himes and Regine spent the summer of 1956 at the Hôtel de Buci close to the lively market on the rue de Seine and then in September moved to the cheaper Hôtel Rachou.[20] He described their room at the latter as pleasant with white walls, a tiled floor, and a two-burner gas hot plate. The amiable hotel proprietors gave Himes a better feeling about Paris, although now he got about much less. If he could stay in this room until Christmas, he wrote Van Vechten, he might be able to write a very good novel.

Wright, who was spending much of the summer on his farm in Normandy, had become an isolated "middle class French-type political analyst" trying to escape his "aloneness," Himes observed in another letter.[21] Himes was apparently projecting Wright as a model for Roger Garrison, the out-of-touch, long-time black expatriate in his novel about American blacks in Paris. At the same time he thought of reworking his Spanish novel about Willa, but hesitated because he was afraid no U.S. publisher would take that story from him. To compound matters, he was struggling with his feelings about Regine. One draft for his autobiography reads: "Here I am with that unripe *Fraulein* and thinking it was the greatest because it was young and available and the best I could do."[22] His dehumanizing of her as an "it" betrays Himes as jealous because further on he alludes to sharing her with another black. And yet he was "thriving on it" and "still getting inspired and even writing masterpieces."

Elsewhere Himes wrote that living with a twenty-year-old West German girl from a bourgeois family turned out to be one of the best things he ever did. She came to love him, she was loyal, and she could speak French. "I had been . . . running around and drinking so much I was becoming impotent again and headed for a nervous breakdown."[23] Another page notes reactions: "sweet affair—exciting—made me feel important." Regine liked Harrington better "sexually at first, but then she came to own me—German women are very brave in their sex if they like a man sexually and don't give a damn if he is red white or black."[24] Often Himes looked at Regine in terms of what she could do for him rather than recognizing her as a deeply troubled young woman. He admired her courage in having taken a succession of lovers, white and black, but failed to perceive such behavior as potentially self-destructive. He flew into rages when he suspected she still desired Harrington and awoke one morning astonished to find that she had attempted suicide with sleeping pills. Did it make him think of Vandi's death? She had learned that she had failed her examinations at the Vieux Colombier drama school the day before. Fortunately, Himes was able to take her to the hospital to have her stomach pumped out.

Himes was perhaps more engrossed with his personal well-being than with racial problems when he attended the First Conference of Negro Writers and Intellectuals organized by the Société de Culture Africaine at the Sorbonne in late September 1956. Although not a delegate, he conversed with Wright, Baldwin, educator Mercer Cook, and civil rights advocate James Ivy, among others, remarking blandly that he found the proceedings "quite interesting in a way." His main concern remained getting on with *A Case of Rape,* since he was in such urgent need of money. Even before its completion, he sent off a seventy-page synopsis to New American Library in hopes of getting a paperback contract.

*A Case of Rape* deals with four U.S. blacks convicted of raping a white American woman, and "a U.S. Negro writer, living in Paris since the war who sets out to investigate the lives of the defendants with a view to proving that all convictions of Negro men for raping white women are political," that is, designed to continue Negro oppression. The expatriate writer character was obviously based on Wright. Himes described the novel to Van Vechten as a sort of condensed detective story, "like one might do of the whole murder story in *The Brothers Karamazov.*"[25] Yet he had trouble giving the novel the attention it deserved.

Plagued by debts, Himes had begun sending off a flood of letters to his various American and French publishers demanding the return of unfinished manuscripts, requesting further advances, and questioning the accuracy and honesty of their royalty statements. He even sought legal assistance where he thought he was being cheated. The tone of these letters became increasingly querulous, acerbic, angry, panicky. Strangely, even his friend Malartic was suspect because he seems not to have liked Chester's criticism of French justice in *A Case of Rape.*

"I can't help getting pushed around by everybody," he wrote Freeman on December 5. "Someday I'll jump out of the goddam window." And again to Freeman a week later: "At this time I have no other publisher but New American Library. You control my destiny. I owe 38,500f in back rent. That is for 11 weeks. Cooking my own food it costs me $4 per day to exist." Van Vechten received similar letters. "I am living on a prayer . . . I don't have a job. I don't have an income. I don't have a salary. I have to live."[26]

Finally, fearing Willa's betrayal, Himes wrote again to the director of Beacon Press, claiming that he owned one-half of *Garden without Flowers* and threatening to sue for an injunction to prohibit its sale if it appeared in print without his consent. "I wrote it on my typewriter and my paper. I spent 18 months working on it. I have already lost a $500 (cash) option on it out of my own pocket."[27] Still he had to wait.

There remained one other possibility. On his return from New York in January, Himes had gone to see Marcel Duhamel who some years before had translated *Hollers* for the French edition. Duhamel was now editor of a series of police thrillers (La Série Noire, or "The Black Series") for the prestigious French publishing house Gallimard. He suggested that Himes try writing crime fiction. Himes protested that he didn't know how. It might not be that difficult, Duhamel said. Start with a bizarre incident, any bizarre incident, and see where it takes you. As for style, follow the example of Hammett and Chandler: avoid excessive exposition, avoid introspective characters, and employ dialogue to convey movement. Above all, include action. From time to time Duhamel reiterated his advice, and on October 16 Himes wrote him to say that he was prepared to submit a synopsis and produce the kind of material Duhamel needed. "As you know this plot is flexible and I will follow your suggestions in all aspects."

A month later Himes was struggling with a detective story, but having reached page sixty, he doubted he could finish it.[28] He regarded his efforts as demeaning. He felt he was hustling to keep alive, and hoped soon to get back to serious writing.

Himes's difficulties were not exclusively confined to literary matters. His relationship to Regine continued volatile. Torn between Himes and her family, she craved mutual acceptance. Early in December Himes reluctantly agreed to go with her to Bielefeld, Westphalia, where her father, Otto Fischer, owned a bookstore–art gallery. The family greeted Himes cordially, but Herr Fischer understandably balked at the age difference between him and Regine. Himes was almost forty-eight, more than twice as old as Regine. Couldn't they wait a year before making a decision? Regine meanwhile could take a secretarial course in Germany.

Himes agreed, feeling somehow cheated, and returned to Paris without Regine. He found Herr Fischer overwhelming. Himes now wrote Regine that they would never be able to live together or marry. Regine telephoned him a few days later, complaining that he had left her with her family against her will and that he ought to assume his responsibility. She felt terribly isolated, her family was cold, and she feared a nervous breakdown. Only when "Chet" helped her did she feel secure. He offered to marry her, but Regine said he wouldn't have to.

Regine did come back to Paris for a short stay, but Himes sent her back alone to Germany for the Christmas holidays. Herr Fischer, fearing for his daughter's mental health, begged him not to join the family at this time. Himes replied that he believed that Regine's emotional troubles were the result of her feeling rejected by her mother and that she would go to any extreme to win her father's sympathy. But "she must feel needed by one whom she loves or she will destroy herself. I am the only person who ever needed her. I sincerely believe, before God, that her only chance of happiness is with me." Regine could have a purpose with Himes because she could share completely in building their lives together. Possibly Himes was reading Regine's reactions in the light of Willa's when he added: "Our own personal problem, from the beginning, has been her doubt of my need, the fear that I would pass on to another woman."[29]

Himes liked to share his literary enthusiasms and misgivings with Regine, who wrote to reassure him:

> How it [the detective novel] is, it is no great book, but it isn't bad or cheap. Why should it be cheap? Just because these people don't have great social ambitions? Jackson certainly takes his Imabelle for as important as Lee Gordon his place in the world. The world is full of people and they are different. Your job is to make them convincing and true. In one of your letters you wrote that you would cut throats, eat spit, and live in sewers for the one you love. Make it the same for Jackson.[30]

Regine's advice was sound. On December 26 Duhamel wrote Himes that he had read his new sequences and found them better, except that Himes, as narrator, had too much to say. "I would like you to put most of these happenings into dialogue, which is a much straighter way to tell a story. But then, I suppose, it would be too crowded . . . From now on, try and use more dialogue, please, even if you have to cut down on events. Apart from a few details what you have done so far is all right."[31]

Himes struggled with his book more than he cared to admit. He thought of it initially as a potboiler and longed to return to "serious" writing. Afterward, however, in a discarded autobiographical fragment, Himes declared: "I have no doubt that my book, *La Reine des pommes*, the first book of the series of Harlem detective stories, is a masterpiece and will some day be acclaimed alongside *War and Peace* and *Mrs. [sic] Chatterley's Lover*."

*La Reine des pommes* ( *For Love of Imabelle*, later called *A Rage in Harlem*) was not strictly speaking a detective story or even a mystery, since the reader watches the machinations of the crooks as well as the actions of their victims and the police. Moreover, the role of the colorful detectives, Grave Digger Jones and Coffin Ed Johnson, is somewhat limited. But Himes's low-life dialogue, characters, and background offset his lack of expertise in creating thrillers. The twists and turns of the narrative are so convoluted, funny, and violent that they make up for the occasional lack of suspense.

Himes had an eye for the grotesque and slapstick of the kind associated with silent movies, Keystone cops, and animated cartoons. His thrillers feature runaway hearses, headless motorcyclists, exploding houses, brotherhood street fights, men walking the streets of Harlem with daggers through their foreheads, bodies tumbling from tenement windows, corpses in breadbaskets, and bodies soaring through the air after being hit from behind by trucks. His Harlem demimonde consists of juvenile delinquents, pimps, pansies, political hacks, quacks, femmes fatales, addicts, pushers, numbers racketeers, black "nationalists," prostitutes, stool pigeons, and bizarrely costumed religious charlatans of every ilk. Several sport comic names, such as Sugartit, Ready Belcher, Uncle Saint, Sister Heavenly, Sweet Prophet, Sassafras, or H. Exodus Clay. Himes even made use of the underworld monikers of his pre–prison days Cleveland associates. Some of his characters are throttled, mauled, sliced, stabbed, shot, or garroted, and they themselves commit similar kinds of violence against others.

Himes initially wrote with an awareness of a French readership for whom denizens of Harlem were exotic jazzy creatures who sometimes blustered in stereotypical dialect. Frequently these characters first appear before the reader amost as cartoon figures: "From the darkened squares of tenement windows . . . crescent-shaped whites of eyes and quarter-moons of yellow teeth bloomed like Halloween pumpkins."[32] Yet these caricatures often turn out to be wise, bawdy, earthy, and hip. Of course, some are gullible, and they are the ones the cop heroes try hardest to protect.

The most startlingly original element of Himes's thrillers is his use of Harlem as a funny mirror, as a metaphor, as a conflation of the self-delusions, corruption, and venality of the larger America:

> in the murky water of fetid tenements, a city of black people . . . are convulsed in desperate living, like the voracious churning of millions of hungry cannibal fish. Blind mouths eating their own guts. Stick in a hand and draw back a nub.
> That is Harlem.[33]

Himes signed his contract for "The Five Cornered Square" (his working title) and got the remainder of his advance. As usual on such occasions, he rushed to take his belongings out of pawn and bought expensive clothes, this time at an exclusive New England men's clothier near the Opéra. His contract called for eight more books of a similar type, each with a Harlem locale, to be turned out at a rate of one every two months.

Thanks to Regine, Himes now attempted to settle into more regular life habits. At the start of February 1957 he reluctantly began taking French lessons at the Alliance Française, urged on by Regine, on whom he had to depend for daily communication. His classes, attended in the main by English-speaking teenagers, took all morning, thus requiring him to write in the afternoons, often on the heated terrace of the Café Select. But Himes's French never improved much, and he was discouraged by the attitude of Parisians who, he said, were more interested in correcting foreigners' mistakes than in trying to understand them. "Looking back, I am certain if someone had said to me: 'You are an ass,' I would have smilingly conceded: 'Ah, wee,' no doubt startling him in my comprehension of the language."[34] Doubtless, too, he felt embarrassed that his fellow students were so much younger than he and perhaps making greater progress. After a month, he dropped the courses, saying they interfered with his writing.

By late April he had nearly completed his second thriller, "A Jealous Man Can't Win" (later published as *The Crazy Kill*), its working title an inside joke about himself. He prepared to write this book, he said, by rereading his battered copy of Faulkner's *Sanctuary* in order to re-create in his mind an atmosphere of violence. Later he said that Faulkner's absurdist view of the world was not unlike his own.

Himes also often looked to his friends for ideas. Walter Coleman, the painter and a member of the Tournon crowd, told him about a notorious Harlem con game, called "the blow," whose practitioners persuaded their naive victims that they could multiply their dollars by placing them in a complicated contraption. Needless to say, the money and the alchemists disappeared soon after the money was surrendered. Himes used this device in the first of his thrillers, *For Love of Imabelle,* where his hero (of sorts), the hapless lovesick Jackson, is led into a den of thieves by the alluring Imabelle.

On another occasion Harrington told Himes a story "about a man in Harlem falling out of a window in the early morning during a wake and landing unhurt in a basket of bread." Hence the French title for *The Crazy Kill,* "Couché dans le pain," or "Lying in Bread" (*pain* is French slang for "money," like *bread* in English). *The Crazy Kill* was a simple "domestic" story, Himes told his friends, in which his pair of black detectives, Coffin Ed Johnson and Grave Digger Jones, played a more active role than in his first novel. Himes jotted down the plot of this story one evening, and Duhamel approved it the next day.

Duhamel may also have suggested that Himes allow his two black detectives to play a greater role in the mysteries.[35] In any case, Coffin Ed and Grave Digger take charge in later books. They are heroic in their fashion, though not without sin. In the course of their investigations, they appear to take for granted violence, cupidity, betrayal, and brutality, and they rarely delude themselves about the true nature of their jobs.

> They took their tribute, like all real cops, from the established underworld catering to the essential needs of the people—gamekeepers, madams, streetwalkers, numbers writers, numbers bankers. But they were rough on purse-snatchers, muggers, burglars, conmen and all strangers working any racket. And they didn't like rough stuff from anybody else but themselves. "Keep it cool," they warned. "Don't make graves."[36]

Like other cops, these Harlem detectives have their own peculiar code of honor: They are fiercely loyal to each other (indeed, in the first couple of books their personalities are barely distinguishable); they have their own personal interpretation of law enforcement; and they possess a high-minded zeal, not unmixed with brutality, to protect the downtrodden poor of Harlem from their worst exploiters, black and white.

Coffin Ed and Grave Digger are nonetheless ambivalent about the roles they play. They recognize that the police department that employs them is an extension of the larger society that has brutalized and exploited their community. This may in part explain the excesses of violence they commit against persons (almost always black) whom they suspect of wrongdoing. Are they directing their rage away from themselves for serving an oppressive society, are they expressing subconscious hostility toward their own people (as Himes himself sometimes did), or is their brutality a justified means of saving Harlem from even worse violence? By the time Himes wrote his ninth thriller in the series, he himself could not quite resolve their ambivalence and made the once inseparable partners bitter enemies.

But for now Himes was beginning to enjoy his "cheap" fiction. He claimed, not quite accurately, that he was no longer ashamed of this type of writing. " 'The Five Cornered Square' is the bloodiest book I have written by far," he wrote Van Vechten in April, "and one of the bloodiest I have read this side of Hamlet. I kill off six people in the bloodiest manner of homicide yet recorded and still most of the book is considered funny. It is a simple story about a Harlem square and his high yellah girl."[37] At the time Himes was still hoping for an American publisher, but he found no takers.

Himes's contract with Gallimard seems to have kept him safe from harassment by the U.S. embassy. Agnes Schneider, the consul in charge of passports, was holding up renewals of passports of U.S. blacks openly opposed to U.S. policies. Himes had no problem, perhaps because he was under the wing of the respectable house of Gallimard. In fact, Himes was not publicly critical of his country, and in his personal life he appeared to be thoroughly domesticated. Regine used to take him to movies and plays in the (mostly vain) hope that he would become better acquainted with French culture; he did, however, see much less of the Tournon crowd and only occasionally encountered Wright and Smith.

In early March 1957, when Plon published *La Troisième génération*, Himes felt that he was beginning to gain recognition as a serious, rather than popular, writer. He remained, however, a bit envious of Wright, all of whose books were regarded as "legitimate literature."

Himes now actively enjoyed writing his thrillers. He recalled in his autobiography that "the only time I was happy was while writing these strange, violent unreal stories. I accepted them to myself as true. I believed them to be true. As soon as they sprang out from my thoughts . . . I loved black people, felt sorry for them, which meant I was sorry for myself. *The Harlem of my books was never meant to be real; I never called it real; I just wanted to take it away from the white man if only in my books.*"[38] Paradoxically the most popular white author to "use" Harlem as a setting was Himes's good friend Van Vechten, who had published *Nigger Heaven* in 1926.

One sign of Himes's new affluence was his acquisition of a car. He was, he noted, the only black writer in Paris other than Wright to own one. At Regine's suggestion he settled for a used Volkswagen. In early July the two set out for Germany to visit Himes's agent, Ruth Lippman, in Stuttgart and to call once more on Regine's family.

The German trip was uneventful, and the Fischers proved cordial, but Himes wasted a prodigious amount of time and energy getting the Volkswagen roadworthy. This was the start of a three-year struggle with his wayward, leprous Beetle, the account of which assumed epic proportions in the second volume of his autobiography. In his notes he remarked, "The car became a challenge. I had to steal the time from this obsession to write my books." He advised Van Vechten, "Never buy a German car in France."[39]

Earlier in the spring Himes had become friends with Baron Timme Rosenkrantz, a Danish jazz authority married to the black entertainer and Latin Quarter star Inez Cavanaugh. The baron invited Regine and Himes to visit the couple in Hellerup, an invitation they took up after paying their obligatory respects to the Fischers. Afterward they passed the greater part of the summer nearby in Seeland, about halfway between Copenhagen and Helsingor, in the lovely village of Hoersholm, surrounded by woods and lakes. Their house was inexpensive and tastefully furnished and had a small garden for privacy. Here Himes wrote the third of his thrillers, challenging himself to produce at least ten pages a day. By September he had nearly finished his book. But still he was unhappy.

Himes seldom socialized—the Rosenkrantzes excepted—and he did not cultivate new friends. He wrote to the Malartics in July that he didn't like clean, polite Denmark any more than regimented Germany and added— perhaps remembering his days with Willa—that he preferred the madness and inefficiency of Spain.[40] A month later he told Van Vechten he had never before encountered so much rain and wind: "I'd go crazy with this weather over a period of time but now I'm working so hard [on] my book that it doesn't matter."[41]

During the summer months Himes was especially piqued that his Danish hairdresser had misunderstood his instructions and cropped his hair too short in the middle. He was so annoyed that he shaved his head. Given his vanity there is little wonder then that he socialized so infrequently. He later said the whole summer was a waste of time, but he did complete his book. Its tentative title, "If Trouble Was Money" was inspired by a Bessie Smith lyric; it was later published as *The Real Cool Killers*.

On October 1 Himes and Regine were back at the Hôtel Rachou, where they learned that their friendly hotelkeeper had just died in an automobile accident. But there was also good news: High praise awaited Himes for his as yet unpublished first thriller. He had gone to Gallimard to complain about the delay in publication and learned that Duhamel was gathering testimonials from literary "greats" like Jean Cocteau and Jean Giono. Indeed, the latter had already written that he would "give all of Dos Passos and Fitzgerald for a few pages of Himes." Duhamel was thus handling things masterfully. He did not want word to get around that the intelligentsia was enthusiastic about Himes's first book until the fall season, the season of literary awards. Moreover, he wanted to make Himes's swift-paced, humorous literary style characteristic of the entire series—a style his other authors might wish to emulate.

When publication day arrived the "Himeses," the Duhamels, the Colemans, and Harrington celebrated at Leroy Haynes's soul food restaurant. Begun as a refuge for impecunious "brothers," the restaurant had since become a popular rendezvous for sophisticated French writers and artists. Haynes still kept in touch with his fellow expatriates and was a well-known mediator of their disputes. His talents were put to the test at Himes's publication party when Himes suddenly became enraged. Everyone was speaking French and ignoring him. The dinner was in his honor, was it not? Haynes managed to pacify him. English would be the language of choice. In the end the dinner was deemed a success.[42]

Himes also attended the thirtieth-anniversary celebration of Plon's Feux Croisés series. The publisher had asked him to represent its English-speaking authors, and Himes delivered a brief speech eulogizing some of the other writers in the collection, among them Tennessee Williams and Merle Miller. Other literary figures who spoke at the event were Nikos Kazantzakis and Rebecca West. At last, Himes believed, his prestige equaled that of Wright among the Tournon crowd, who were as important for his self-esteem as the French intelligentsia.

On October 8 and 10 Himes signed contracts with Gallimard for two new thrillers, *Tout pour plaire* and *Il pleut des coups durs* ("Anything to Please" and "Rain of Blows," later published in English as *The Big Gold Dream* and *The Real Cool Killers*). He was not altogether clear what these French titles meant, but he was confident of his ability to handle the Harlem locale and the exploits of his two black detectives. His business arrangements settled, he told Regine he wanted to write in Spain or, as he put it, "go to grass" in Mallorca.

Why he chose to return to Mallorca is unclear. Was it because the island was inexpensive and he felt he would be able to work better in warm weather, or was he motivated by the half-conscious wish to repeat with Regine the idyll he believed he had lived with Willa?

On the drive south the couple stopped for a few days in Perpignan, a city whose ambience enticed Himes into remarking that he wished he had enough money to live there. After arriving in Mallorca, in a kind of repatterning of his earlier journey with Willa, he elected not to stay in Palma and instead took an apartment in Puerto de Pollensa. The house sat among the pines, away from the traffic and the main quay. There on the terrace Himes began again to write about his love affair with Willa. An unpublished fragment of his autobiography noted the repetition of his experiences. "In 1954 while living with Alva [Willa] in Mallorca I had written a book about Vandi . . . And in 1957 I tried to write a book about Alva while living with Marlene [Regine] . . . but it never jelled. Marlene and my Volkswagen caused too many distractions: Marlene was too young and my Volkswagen was too old."[43]

In reality, neither Himes's car nor his companion was the cause of his frustration. As we have seen, fragments and drafts indicate that he had begun writing about Willa as early as the winter of 1954. As always, writing for Himes was a kind of expurgation. He could rid himself of his feelings for Vandi while he was with Willa, but while he was with Regine he remained unsure of what he truly felt about Willa. He tried assimilating a couple of unpublished stories, "Spanish Gin" and "The Pink Dress," into his novel with mixed results. The "Willa" manuscript contained passages of fine lyric prose, purple prose, and prose that smacked of "confessional" magazine fiction. Clearly, Himes was still trying to come to terms with his feelings, and the medley of styles suggests his own confusion. At one point his hero cannot bear the sight of his beloved in a pink dress because it gives away so much of her voluptuous figure; at the same time he is proud of her distinction "befitting a descendant from one of the most aristocratic families in America in a direct line from the Mayflower."

Now Himes planned to transform the love story into a detective novel by subordinating the romantic element to a mystery. When he informed Duhamel he was thinking of writing a "white thriller" with a Spanish locale, Duhamel responded skeptically. Himes's two black detectives constituted a successful recipe. Why tinker with it?

Late in November the American publisher Fawcett copyrighted *La Reine des pommes* under the title *For Love of Imabelle*. To celebrate, Himes bought his first European dog, Mikey, an Irish setter puppy. He hoped the puppy would release him from his tensions, but not so: He still could not get on with his novel. In a letter to Van Vechten he blamed his failures on the approach of cold weather; of course, the house was hard to heat. On some days the electricity was cut off, requiring him to write by the window. The trees outside tossed so violently in the wind, he complained, that they cast shadows on the table. Frustrated, demoralized, he was inclined "to get drunk off the cheap Spanish gin and go to bed."[44]

The truth of the matter was that thoughts of Willa continued to haunt him. He revisited Roch Minué and other old acquaintances, reawakening in him memories of Willa's upper-class manners. To his mind, Regine suffered by comparison. At the same time he was groundlessly jealous of Regine's social ease with the people he introduced her to. Whether he knew it or not, he was reacting to her social skills in much the same way he had reacted to Willa's. To exorcise his demons he wrote a piece he called "Regine" and sent it off to Van Vechten in January of the new year. Until then Van Vechten had known very little about her.

In an earlier response to a letter from Van Vechten, Himes had surprisingly declared: "Please forgive me for not having written about my wife . . . I thought I had done so. We were married . . . in Germany. She is German Lutheran, her name Regina comes from 'Das Sinngedicht' by Gottfried Keller . . . We have some awful fights at times but get along on the whole quite well. She is only twenty two years old and has all the intolerance of the very young." His statement about the marriage was an outright lie, but it probably expressed Himes's desire for respectability. Equally interesting, his letter revealed a continuing uneasiness about writing popular fiction. He told Van Vechten that should his present books become popular in France, he would again write different kinds of material. As regards his other prospects, he had had bad news from New American Library. His contract for *Cast the First Stone* had been rescinded, and he was having trouble placing *A Case of Rape*. Other than that, he was happier than he had been in a long time. And his health was fine "as long as I don't think about my native land."[45]

Himes and Regine spent the Christmas holidays with her family in Germany, and during the first few months of 1958 they took short trips to Barcelona and France to change money. Yet Himes was growing more and more testy. Although he had settled into a kind of conjugal life, he could not repeat with Regine his passion for Willa. He drank more and began to drive recklessly.

To add to Himes's instability, Duhamel rejected his "white" detective novel and suggested he rewrite it. Himes thought himself incapable of doing so. He had already drawn an advance of 200,000 francs on the title, and when

Regine suddenly required an emergency appendix operation, he spent what he had left on her. At least, this is what he wrote Malartic, but in fact Herr Fischer had wired money to cover Regine's hospital costs. Regine recuperated, and she and Chester passed a few days in a farm south of Pollensa. Not long afterward the two headed back to Paris, smuggling their Irish setter across the border under a blanket.

The couple's luck changed. Duhamel suggested that Himes try another New York novel, this time without his black detectives, and he advanced him half-payment on his next book. Soon after, Plon bought "Mamie Mason," offering him an advance of 50,000 francs. Within a week Himes and Regine were driving south again, this time to the Côte d'Azur. On their way they visited the spectacular Verdon canyon and called on Himes's new great admirer, the novelist Giono, at Manosque.

Himes so liked the Riviera that he said he wanted to live there for the next several months. In June they rented the basement of a large villa in Vence. The house stood high on a hill above the sea with views extending from the suburbs of Nice to the lighthouse at Antibes. Now Chester began *Run Man Run*, his thriller about a black man in constant flight from his white demon, a policeman who wants to kill him. The writing went quickly, perhaps because the plot had been hatching in his mind since his last stay in New York. He remembered the coarse white police officer who had barged into the Horn & Hardart restaurant where Himes worked, and he transfigured him into a killer.

The easy flow of writing relieved Himes of his usual tensions, and he began to enjoy the sunny, picturesque setting of his new home. He made friends, appeared more relaxed, and generally came to regard his neighbors as more lively and intelligent than Spaniards. In unpublished fragments of his autobiography, he noted, not for the first time: "I can truthfully say those were the happiest days of my life . . . people liked me. I could have lived there forever." In fact, he lived there fifteen months.[46]

*Il pleut des coups durs (The Real Cool Killers)* was published in August 1958. Although it was the third of his thrillers (written in Denmark), it was published second. Its not very original plot tells of Galen "the Greek," a sexual pervert who exploits the black community. A subplot deals with adolescent street gangs. The novel's main strength lies in its vivid portrayals of some of Harlem's death-laden streets.

By now Himes had already signed another contract with Gallimard for three more novels. He had finished *Run Man Run* in Vence in record time and looked to be well under way on *The Big Gold Dream* in September.

The latter reintroduces one of Himes's favorite themes: the crooked street preacher who manages to charm a fortune out of the desperate religious-minded poor. Characters not unlike Sweet Prophet had appeared in Himes's early stories of the 1930s and 1940s, but now he fleshed out his charlatan in more grotesque detail:

> Sweet Prophet sat on a throne of red roses on a flower-draped float . . . Over his head was a sun-shade of gold tinsel made in the shape of a halo . . . His tremendous bulk was impressive in a bright purple robe lined with yellow silk and trimmed with mink. Beneath it he wore a black taffeta suit with white piping and silver buttons. His fingernails untrimmed since he first claimed to have spoken with God, were more than three inches in length. They curled like strange talons, and were painted different colors. On each finger he wore a diamond ring. His smooth black face with its big buck teeth and popping eyes was ageless; but his grizzly hair, on which he wore a black silk cap, was snow-white.[47]

As depicted by Himes, black religion, whose believers respond with something akin to sexual ecstasy, is corrupt and self-serving. The narration conveys a kind of burlesque symbolism (one of the main characters, Alberta, is "resurrected" in a parody of God's seven-day creation), and the plot is possibly Himes's most exciting.

In October, after another visit to Bielefeld, Himes and Regine stopped off in Paris to see Duhamel, who showed Himes a bound copy of *La Reine des pommes,* disclosing as well the complimentary quotes he had been gathering for its promotion. The critic for *Mystère-Magazine* in an advance review said of the book that it was "destined to become a classic."[48] Cocteau called it a "prodigious masterpiece," and the critic Jean Cau declared, "It requires a white stone to mark this achievement in the black series." Giono's comment about Himes's superiority to Hemingway and Fitzgerald was also quoted, as well as praise from other notable figures.

In Vence in November Himes learned that he was to be awarded the Grand Prix de la Littérature Policière. A distinguished jury that included the writers Boileau and Narcejac, over which Maurice Endrèbe presided, had selected an American—and a black American at that—as the winner of the 1957 prize for detective fiction published in France. This was a double first.

Himes returned to Paris in triumph, where he was met by a team of *Paris-Match* photographers—an indication, he hoped, of extensive publicity and future sales. Enthusiastic reviews did indeed follow in daily newspapers and the prestigious magazine *L'Observateur;* others appeared in French-language newspapers outside the country, such as *Le Soir* in Brussels and *La Tribune de Genève.* Back again in Vence, Himes was besieged by local journalists. Overnight he had become a celebrity.

Soon Himes was recalled to Paris for publicity pictures and an interview with the *Time* magazine reporter, Geoffrey Blunden. The *Time* article, "Amid the Alien Corn," published in the November 17, 1958, issue, dwelled more on the comparative lack of racism in France than on Himes's books. Yet the award did wonders for Himes's self-esteem. "I became a person in Vence not to be thrown away," he wrote in his autobiography. "I became a person comparable to Richard Wright."[49]

For the next couple of months Himes enjoyed being sought out by journalists for interviews and articles, but then old anxieties crept back to haunt him. Could his success be really lasting? He could not bring himself to trust publishers. In November he complained to Van Vechten that the Fawcett series Gold Medal Books had so cut and distorted *For Love of Imabelle* that it bore little resemblance to the original. As an addendum to a 1959 New Year's greeting to Malartic, he wrote: "I live here in my little house in the pitch black dark . . . As my fame increases, my fate remains the same—broke, desperate, urgent and trying to work beyond the capabilities of my poor brain."[50]

Himes exaggerated. January 1959 was a productive month, during which he wrote most of *Imbroglio négro (All Shot Up)* and began again "It Rained Five Days" (later called "The Lunatic Fringe"). But there were unhappy portents. In a four-month period Himes crashed his automobile in several accidents. Although he was uninjured, the accidents betrayed a reckless impatience with his life.

A brief trip to northern Italy in March served as a prelude to a lengthy visit by Regine's mother, who joined them in Vence. Regine, who had been keeping house for Himes and acting as his interpreter and secretary, now had to cope with occasional flare-ups between her mother and Himes. When Frau Fischer persuaded her daughter to go to Hamburg for the next several months to complete her secretarial studies, Himes did not object. It would give him an opportunity to return to Paris, he told Van Vechten, to study French. Since he was now a famous author in France, he said, it was incumbent on him to be able to communicate better. A more likely explanation was that he felt bored in Vence.

Frau Fischer's visit ended on a disquieting note when Himes accused her of plotting with her daughter against him. He stalked out of the house one day to vent his fury on Mikey, who was misbehaving. In an attempt to whip the dog, he struck his own right eye with a switch. Regine, who had never driven a car before, took him in second gear all the way to Guérin's writers' colony in La Ciotat. Two weeks later Himes removed his bandages. He was ready for Paris.

Soon Himes's newly painted blue Volkswagen zoomed to a screeching halt in front of the Café Tournon. Lesley Packard, a thirty-year-old English-woman who worked for the Paris *Herald Tribune*, was sitting on the terrace with Himes's friend William Gardner Smith. A new phase of Himes's life was about to begin.

# 10

# THREE WOMEN

LESLEY PACKARD LIVED IN PARIS on the rue Grégoire-de-Tours, renting an apartment from Edouard Roditi, an American literary expatriate who had been expelled from France for associating with an Algerian terrorist. Upon Himes's return in April 1959, he stayed first at the Hôtel Welcome nearby, but after his novel *Dare Dare (Run Man Run)* was published, he settled for a sublet Lesley had found him on the Boulevard Brune on the southern edge of the city. Before long Lesley and Himes became lovers. At first they passed their days taking long walks along the Seine, visiting galleries, or seeking out "undiscovered" cafés. On occasion they would motor to the forests of Rambouillet or Fontainebleau with Himes's dog Mikey and Lesley's blue-point Siamese cat, Griot. Chester was happy and inspired, and work on his new thriller, *Imbroglio négro (All Shot Up)*, was going well.

Like its predecessor, *Imbroglio* unfolds at a fast clip, in a plot replete with slapstick, macabre murders, and familiar stock types (e.g., the seductive high yellow and the black "square"). In this work Himes drew one of his most intriguingly controversial characters, a rather smug, corrupt (but courageous), secretly homosexual Harlem political leader, Casper Holmes. Perhaps he was thinking of one of Molly Moon's guests. Moreover, the French title accurately describes Himes's own situation, caught as he was between two women.[1]

In late June Himes left for England on business. Abroad, he said he longed for Lesley but still felt responsible for Regine. On his return he drove to Hamburg to bring Regine back. Apparently he had told Lesley he was married, because on July 28 he wrote her, "My wife is going to finish courses on Sept 1st and take a job and my great hope is that we'll be able to effect a

Joseph Sandy and Estelle Himes with sons Joseph, Jr., Edward, and Chester

Joseph, Jr., Chester, and Edward, c. 1943

Prison sketch by Chester
Himes from the early 1940s.
Yale Collection of American
Literature, Beinecke Rare
Book and Manuscript
Library, Yale University

Chester Himes by Carl Van
Vechten. Yale Collection of
American Literature,
Beinecke Rare Book and
Manuscript Library, Yale
University

Wife Jean Himes with Sterling Brown, Chester, and Bucklin Moon

Himes with Sterling Brown, Bucklin Moon, Owen Dodson, and John Bright

Vandi Haygood, c. 1947

Willa Thompson Trierweiler

Regine and Chester at Antibes

Himes with Fred Kassak, receiving the Grand Prix de la Litterature Policiere, 1958.
© Universal Photo 23039 Edimedia

Himes at bookstand in Paris, 1958. Photo Tesseyre

Himes with Fiat roadster, 1963

Himes with Picasso and Marcel Duhamel, c. 1960

Marianne Greenwood by
Carl Van Vechten, 1962.
Yale Collection of American
Literature, Beinecke Rare
Book and Manuscript
Library, Yale University

Himes with James Baldwin

Chester and Lesley Himes with Clarence Major, Ishmael Reed, Joe Johnson, and Quincy Troupe, 1973

Chester and Lesley on the terrace at Casa Griot

Chester and Lesley in Hyde
Park

Himes in Moraira, 1978.
© Editions des Autres

permanent cancellation of this business." To further reassure her, he added, "I confess it is a relationship that is absolutely dead."[2]

Nonetheless, a few days later Himes and Regine moved into the house of the literary editor of *Die Welt*, Dr. Ramseger, who wanted a caretaker for his Hungarian shepherd dog while he took his family on vacation. The new situation did not suit Himes. He said he was unable to work well in Hamburg, blaming the stifling atmosphere of the city. Then too there were endless quarrels with Regine, who accused him of excessive drinking, not to mention perilous driving. Tensions rose to such a pitch that Himes required treatment for ulcers. When Regine repaired to Bielefeld for a home visit in September, Himes hastened back to the Boulevard Brune and Lesley.

In mid-October Himes in Paris was putting the finishing touches on *Imbroglio*, while Regine in Hamburg was preparing to come back to Paris. Himes dreaded her return. How would he be able to juggle two women? He much preferred the company of the down-to-earth, stylish Lesley, but he was fearful of upsetting Regine. Of all the women he had known, she was the most unstable.

Himes put his dilemma aside for the moment when two journalists from *Paris-Match* approached him about writing a script with a Harlem locale for a film to be directed by Louis Dolivet. The movie-loving Himes was delighted. He quickly sketched out a fifty-four-page scenario entitled "Blow Gabriel Blow," which instead of focusing on crime and violence (as was expected of him), dwelt on another of his favorite themes: the religious charlatan. Its script tells of a preacher on a white horse who performs "miracles" for the gullible black masses. Dolivet liked it and confidently predicted financial backing. For Himes, who had yearned to write for Hollywood in the 1940s, it was a dream come true. To celebrate he gave himself a party at which Lesley presided, but he got so drunk on the potent punch he had prepared that he and Lesley departed the premises leaving behind several of their guests. His destination was the exclusive Mars jazz club. As he tells the story in his autobiography, he aimed their 1937 roadster in the right direction but scraped an entire row of parked cars along the way. What really mattered, however, was that he was admitted to the club despite his disreputable state—clear proof, he believed, that he was indeed famous, a national celebrity.[3] Always insecure, Himes needed such reassurances.

"Blow Gabriel Blow" was not produced. Dolivet could not come up with the necessary financing, and Himes was paid only $100 for his efforts. But his interest in scriptwriting was revived by Pierre Lazareff of *Paris-Soir*, who requested he write a script for a documentary about Harlem. This time he would place greater emphasis on Harlem's social ills. A French movie crew planned to travel to New York in the spring, and Himes contacted the executive director of the National Urban League for permission to film scenes at the Beaux Arts ball. Several misunderstandings about dates and schedules ensued, the cameramen were unable to get to New York in time, and the project was indefinitely abandoned. At bottom Himes believed Lazareff did not like his somber portrayal of Harlem. "He wanted all singing and dancing," he told an acquaintance.[4]

In December 1959 Regine rejoined Himes, having finally found secretarial work in Paris. Fearing her volatility, Himes did not tell her about Lesley. Instead he used to arrange to meet Lesley secretly, sometimes under the pretext of walking the dog. Regine was not long deceived, and one day she kicked violently at Lesley's door, screaming abuse. On another occasion she called Lesley at her office warning that she was about to kill herself. By chance Himes arrived home at the moment she had turned on the kitchen gas. Their most melodramatic scene came when Himes surreptitiously left to meet Lesley at her office at the *Herald Tribune*. Regine appeared suddenly on the street and began assaulting Himes with her fists. Lesley hailed a passing cab, while Himes picked up his glasses, shoved Regine into his car, and drove her home. He went back to Lesley, but returned later to find Regine with her wrists slashed.

Himes arranged for Regine to be taken to a hospital, after which she was transferred to a psychiatric clinic in Vincennes. Yet even from her sickbed she persisted in deluging him with letters, decrying his treachery. Possibly to quiet his own roiling emotions, Himes got right down to work on his next thriller, which he called "Be Calm" (published later in America as *The Heat's On*).

Himes was unsure about his feelings for Regine. His autobiography and manuscripts reveal his ambivalence. On the one hand, she irritated him to the point of fury; on the other hand, when she was not about, he missed her and wanted her. A discarded autobiographical fragment relates his reason for journeying to Hamburg after his return from England: "I missed Marlene [Regine] so much I went to Hamburg to take her back." To be sure, she was useful to him in retyping his manuscripts, but he did not think he was exploiting her. In his fashion he loved her, and now that she lay helpless in the hospital, he had begun again thinking of "rescuing" her. An outraged letter from her father, Otto Fischer, written in January 1960, warned him not to. The day would come, he wrote, when he would have to leave her, "if not by God's judgement, then as a result of your distinct instinct for self-preservation." By then she might be a broken creature, and he would be morally responsible.[5]

Himes could not commit himself one way or the other. He felt enormously responsible because of their age difference, but he clearly resented Herr Fischer's implication that he was the cause of her illness. Nor did he take kindly to Fischer's view that he was neurotic, and responded: "The trouble with [Regine] is you've never been kind to her. Neither have I. She may be hurt but she must do the right thing and eventually she'll get over her hurt . . . You said to her once, your Chester is the most mixed up man I ever saw . . . So you must know I don't know what the right thing is. What is the right thing . . . For me to let your daughter die?"[6]

For the time being at least, Herr Fischer had his way. Regine was removed to another clinic at Nogent-sur-Marne and then to Giesherslag for further treatment—which meant that Himes now had a clear field for his affair with Lesley.

To give the affair a boost, Himes decided to rent a house at Cagnes-sur-Mer near Biot, where his friend Walter Coleman and his Swedish wife Torun were now living. Lesley was due for a vacation that spring, and it would be their first long trip together away from Paris. It very nearly ended in disaster. Soon after their arrival they had gone to call on the Colemans; Walter's brother Emmet was also visiting. Lesley remembers innocently chatting with Emmet when Himes suddenly struck her. She was his woman, he said, and had no business enjoying the company of another man. Lesley related:

> We went straight back home. Emmet was furious and so was I. I told Chester, "You know I'll leave in the morning. I won't accept to be treated this way."
> "You should know better."
> "Know better? I am sure he is your friend as much as mine."
> "It was not his fault, it was *your* fault. You're my woman."[7]

Perhaps to make amends, Himes took Lesley to Milan, where the publisher Longanesi had expressed an interest in doing an Italian edition of *La Reine des pommes*. They quite enjoyed their Italian journey, especially the Milanese cuisine, which Himes afterward said made him appreciate the phrase *la dolce vita*. But their return to Paris was marred by Himes's fear of Regine. She had come back to work at her old job and phoned Lesley to find out Himes's whereabouts. Himes, who by now had moved in with Lesley, fled to Biot to take refuge with the Colemans.

Regine prevailed. Three months later, in the summer of 1960, Himes was again living with her in Austria. She had lost her position in Paris and had been stopping with her sister in Munich when Himes picked her up to drive her to Kitzbühel. Whether he was primarily motivated by her plight or whether he needed someone to translate and type his novel is uncertain.

Possibly he feared committing himself to Lesley—who was herself in no hurry to make decisions. In any case he managed to finish his book.

"Be Calm," Himes wrote Van Vechten, "is about Sister Heavenly, Uncle Saint, Pinky (a giant Negro half wit), a three million dollar bundle of dope [that] mysteriously disappears and my two hard shooting detectives."[8] Some of the action takes place outside Harlem, which distressed Duhamel a bit, but the novel was Himes's most entertaining to date and its mystery certainly the most engrossing. Included was the by now almost obligatory amoral light-skinned femme fatale and the usual macabre, slapstick violence. For example, Uncle Saint grapples with a stubborn goat and inadvertently kicks over a bottle of nitroglycerine, blowing himself up along with his house and his animal. There is also humor of a more melancholy sort, as when a black fugitive refuses to take his son with him to Africa because the son is fair-complexioned. Here too, Grave Digger and Coffin Ed, Himes's two flamboyant detective heroes, begin to take on greater differences. Ever since Coffin Ed's trauma in an earlier book, when a young thug splashed him with acid, he has not been the same. His fear and fury make him impulsive and near paranoid. By contrast, Grave Digger is a model of restraint and fair-mindedness. In a curious way, the two assume the opposing sides of Himes's character.

The unpredictability of Himes's characters in a fashion corresponds to Himes's own behavior with Regine. Just as suddenly as he seems to have resumed his relationship with her, he left her. In a letter from Paris dated September 8, 1960, he told Van Vechten, "My wife and I have parted ways and I am engaged to an English lady with a sense of humor . . . I still have my dog Mikey, and now I have a 1934 Fiat roadster [his Volkswagen had not survived an early morning crash on the Place Maubert earlier in the year] which I now drive about Paris with great pleasure." For her part, Lesley gave up her job at the *Herald Tribune* to live with him, and in September they inaugurated their new life together with an auto trip to Italy in Himes's other car, a secondhand Hillman.

One of the couple's destinations was the western Italian shore village of Acciarola below Salerno. Miles of deserted beach were theirs alone to enjoy, although from time to time a local priest trotted after them, whom Himes believed lusted after Lesley. Himes liked to think he had gone to Italy to write another detective novel, after which time he might journey to Africa to write nonfiction. Perhaps he imagined himself appropriating Wright's mantle of authority on rising Third World countries. In August he had written Van Vechten: "The Negro is also a big topic of discussion and debate over here and I feel now is the time to go and live among them and learn and write about their private lives and loves." A month later, however, he was not so sure and told Van Vechten that he hoped to get to Tunis around the middle of December and then begin an extemporaneous journey through the more settled parts of the new African countries. "However from here I can't say and may end up in a pot of cannibal stew." Insecure as always about his "importance," he sought to reassure himself: "I know a great number of Africans and they have been interested in my books for a long time. *Lonely Crusade* is a sort of classic among the intellectual Africans and they are showing great interest in French translations of my detective stories."[9]

But such talk was desultory. The couple drove only as far as Naples, catching glimpses of Capri from the heights before descending to the brightly lit city. On their approach Himes began expressing fears about the drinking water and the scarcity of food. It was as if he were already imagining himself in the Third World. The journey cost more than they had anticipated, and they returned to Rome in mid-November, where Himes expected to find royalty checks awaiting him, but in vain. He drove back to Mougins to borrow money from Duhamel. Since he did not really know how much he needed, Duhamel advanced him just enough to settle his debts in Rome and return to France. Back once more on the Riviera, Himes and Lesley discovered an inexpensive off-season rental in Saint-Tropez, but they were still short of funds. Himes again had to borrow money, this time from a friendly pharmacist—an admirer, as it happened, of his thrillers.

The couple's stay in Saint-Tropez was interrupted in late November 1960 by news of Wright's sudden death. They rushed back to Paris, where Himes endeavored to comfort Ellen Wright and help with the funeral arrangements. Ellen had planned for a closed private funeral, but Himes and others persuaded her to enlarge the ceremony as befitting her husband's stature. The cremation took place at the Père-Lachaise cemetery. Himes and Ollie Harrington sat in the rear of the chapel barely able to restrain their laughter as they imagined the earthy Wright's voice mocking the dreary solemn eulogies of a succession of speakers. Wright's death was traced to an amoebic illness he had contracted years before on the Gold Coast while investigating his African roots. From Himes's point of view, Wright's fate was but another example of the absurdity of black lives.

The death was so unexpected that it aroused a host of rumors in the black expatriate community: among the more bizarre was that Wright had been murdered, either by the U.S. Central Intelligence Agency for his frequent public denunciations of American racism, or by the KGB for his anti-Soviet views, or by African nationalists for his skepticism about aspects of African independence movements. Himes did not give much credence to any conspiracy theory, though in the past he had regarded Wright as a pawn of anti-American propagandists. (See his portrayal of Roger Garrison in *A Case of Rape*.) Yet Wright still remained his lodestar, the greatest black novelist in the world, and his passing truly saddened Himes. Later he commented, "I had never realized before how much influence Dick had on me. Faulkner had the utter influence over my writing, but Dick had influence over my life. I didn't consider anyone else."[10] He would always remember Wright as a champion of the oppressed. When Herbert Hill of the NAACP wrote Himes a few months later, asking for suggestions for an anthology dedicated to Wright, Himes suggested the inclusion of a thirty-eight-page letter Wright had sent to one of his editors: "Everyone who reads [it] would understand Dick's basic attitude toward life and the reasons for his hatred of the oppression of *all* people . . . [In] the final analysis, he speaks for us all."[11]

Himes returned with Lesley to the Riviera in early December and made preparations to join the Colemans at Biot for Christmas. The holiday season, however, was complicated by renewed anxieties about Regine. In Kitzbühel and still ailing, she continued bombarding Himes with letters. On December 21 she wrote that she could not believe he wanted to leave her and accused him of being afraid to face loneliness, which was why he was living with Lesley. Himes kept up the correspondence, perhaps out of guilt, but his letters could be cruel. One of his responses was that although he still loved her, he intended remaining with Lesley. Regine answered that he should understand that it was not simply the privileged sensitive artists who suffer; ordinary mortals suffer as well. For the time being, Himes hardened himself to her entreaties.

In mid-March 1961 Himes and Lesley drove back from Saint-Tropez to attend the Paris opening of an exhibition of Coleman's portraits of jazz artists. The following month he was apparently living alone in a studio across the street from the picturesque park of Les Buttes-Chaumont, which he considered "the outskirts of Paris." There for the next two months he rewrote "Mamie Mason" for Maurice Girodias's "erotic" Olympia Press, presumably spicing it up with more titillating scenes. His original manuscript had been lost at Plon and he had to request a duplicate copy that he had earlier sent to the James Weldon Johnson Collection at Yale. By May he was giving out his address as the rue Botzaris, where Regine now lived. In all probability she was typing his revisions. The following month he and Regine departed for Hamburg, where Himes determined to demand money from his agent because, as he put it in a July 7 letter to Malartic, he was still living "on the edge of a precipice." Lesley took Himes's latest defection with outward equanimity.

Himes and Regine spent the summer again in the home of Dr. Ramseger, taking care of his dog. Himes's previous objections to Hamburg appear to have been forgotten, and he hoped to continue work now on his next thriller. His account with Gallimard was as usual overdrawn, and he had fallen six months behind on his new manuscript, for which he had not yet found a title. Progress was slow. The weather was rainy, and visitors distracted him—among them Ellen Wright and her daughter Rachel, who stayed two weeks, and Regine's teenage brother, who stayed the entire time. A letter to Van Vechten on Himes's fifty-second birthday discovers him feeling lost and morally disoriented. He had not, he said, found a country, a work, even a destiny. He believed he could not experience stability without happiness. He needed answers to his discontent. "I have been tramping over Europe with one companion or another . . . I have not greatly liked any place but now I am coming closer; Regine is back with me; I doubt if she is the answer, but I am coming closer at any rate."[12]

As regards his work, Himes felt like someone skating from one extreme to another. He considered *Pinktoes* (the American title of *Mamie Mason*) the best thing he had written since *The Primitive*. At first his detective stories had been amusements, "fillers," beside being a source of essential income, and he had enjoyed "creating the grisly fantasy." But he felt he could not count on U.S. editors to take them, and he imagined (wrongly) that Gallimard had restrained sales to keep his mysteries from overshadowing the other novels in the Série Noire. Gallimard simply wanted to keep him "at the grindstone turning out one after another. So the idea has soured and the fun of writing those books has gone and now it is hard—hard work, and I don't want to do them anymore . . . But I must until something better comes along. So I will." He was also feeling homesick: "America is home; the only home I know, and I always think wistfully it would be wonderful to go back. But I don't believe I can . . . Dreams bloom fuller in America but so far I have very few people, you most of all, who love me. And I would be a burden. I do not feel despondent; up to a point I enjoy Europe but basically I am a stranger and always will be a stranger."[13]

Van Vechten responded encouragingly: "You are, I believe, at last growing up and beginning to understand . . . the mysteries, and agonies and wonders of life . . . I have wanted you to write a book to top *Lonely Crusade* and I think you can, a book about loneliness and sorrow and every kind of torture flesh is heir to."[14]

On the Ramsegers' return, Regine and Himes moved to Darmstadt as guests of his publisher, Ullstein Verlag, and afterward rented a house in dreary Wiederstadt. They had been so long alone together that they had again begun irritating one another. Himes claimed it was because Regine wanted to live somewhere in Germany where she could find work, while he needed to get out of Germany.

Himes drank. One evening driving back with Regine from Frankfurt after visiting Dean Dixon (who was then director of the Frankfurt radio symphony), police officers arrested him for drunken driving. He was jailed overnight and the next day fined with a suspended sentence and forbidden to drive in Germany. His German publisher bailed him out. Disgusted, Regine packed her things and left for home, while Himes managed to hire a driver to return him to Paris. There he found Lesley half-waiting for him. She was now supporting herself at Time-Life and was probably the only person capable of giving him the security and reassurance he needed.

In early August Himes left again for Biot, where he stayed with the Colemans before finding an apartment in Mougins-Village, not far from the Duhamels' country place. Once established, he wrote Lesley: "I am lonely as hell with the slight disgust I feel when I am not occupied with my work and living with the person I love."[15] His loneliness, however, was allayed by fame: Total strangers in bars and cafés stopped to talk to him and plied him with drinks. To enjoy his peace, he wrote Lesley, he had to stay indoors or take walks in the woods.

A more significant sign of Himes's celebrity was an invitation to visit with Picasso. Duhamel, who arranged their meeting, wanted Picasso to produce a comic strip of *La Reine des pommes;* although nothing came of the proposal, Picasso did consider it. Reporting on his visit, Himes wrote Lesley, "Duhamel and Germaine took me to a place in Cannes to have lunch with Picasso and all the little Picassos (two are his and two are his wife's) and then afterwards we had to go to Picasso's 'castle' and all this lasted from 12.30 until almost 8 p.m. and then my nerves were jumping out of my skin."[16] Picasso's collections and works were splendid, and he was an exciting host, but Himes was irritated by what he considered the painter's spectacular egotism and by the sycophants around him.

At the start Himes hated being alone and often called Lesley, demanding that she too phone him daily. In the seclusion of Mougins, he wrote: "I'll try to be as honest with you as I can ever be . . . You are one of the two women in my life of 52 years that I know that I have loved. Of the two, I still love you as completely and as absolutely as ever. The other, by the way, was Willa

Thompson. Both of you, I suppose, had the absolute appeal to me—and that is simply femininity in the highest of all possible meanings." No woman could guess "how absolutely incomplete [he felt] inside, how hurt, how lonely, how insecure." It was essential that Lesley should know this, otherwise she would be loving a fantasy Chester. He admitted that he was a liar and generally despicable, that he drank to deaden his emotions, and that he had lived in "a veritable ocean of self-torture" all his life. He had tried to give Regine the security he thought she needed, and it had been a mistake; to Lesley, he offered his love but warned of the dangers:

> Just for my love you must be willing to starve, be maligned, abused, spat on, live in material insecurity and have hope of only one security, one compensation, one reward, and that is . . . all the evil and all the good things of me . . . There isn't any other way—I may run but I cannot hide. I am in for it. The only thing that is going to let me out is death . . . You should have known. Can you and I change this old and terrible world? The only lines that Hemingway ever wrote that sounded true to me were: "If you are strong and brave, this world will break you. If you are very strong the break may heal and perhaps be stronger than before. But it will break you anyway" . . . so if you want me, darling, this world is going to crucify you. But you may have me, all of me.[17]

The letter, not very different in tone and rhetoric from the kind Himes had written Willa, stressed that "the only thing that could save [them] for a short time [was his] work." Yes, material survival was important, and especially his ability to provide for Lesley so that she could be completely his, but writing was the aim and justification of his life, and Lesley must understand this. Indeed *her* devotion to his writing was indispensable. One way or another she had to be part of it—not as material to be resurrected imaginatively, as Willa had been, but rather as a muse, an inspiring presence. "Even if you were the richest woman in the world," he concluded, "you would have to live inside of me, with my hopes and fulfillments, my ambitions and despairs, the evil and the good. With your eyes open as your heart."[18]

Lesley could hardly resist. Himes was an exacting companion who could not bear sharing her with others, even when she was at work, yet he could not be expected to provide for her when it was all he could do to support himself. At the moment he felt unable to carry on work on his next detective novel, although Gallimard had already advanced him $2,000. To make matters worse, Avon Books had announced that it was discontinuing his paperback detective series after the reprint of *A Rage in Harlem* (the new title of *For Love of Imabelle*). His other books remained out of print in his native country.

Himes hated being alone and often dined with the Colemans, who enjoyed entertaining and would frequently invite up to a dozen people for dinner. It was at one of these gatherings that Himes met Nicole Barclay, who suggested that he write blurbs for her record company. Himes responded enthusiastically, submitting an outline for a complete history of jazz to be presented in a series of albums, along with iconographic material. In the end the bookkeeping department of Barclay's Records rejected the proposal as too expensive.

Another of the Colemans' guests was Swedish photographer Marianne Greenwood, whom Himes first met in mid-October 1961. She was a friend of Torun, living in Antibes, whose pictures had been published in a book called *Picasso in Antibes*. At the time of their encounter, she had accepted an assignment to do a book on Latin America with the Swedish writer Ernest Taube.

Himes was smitten. Marianne was a tall, slim, attractive blonde and possibly flattered by Himes's interest in her. He had been wavering between Regine and Lesley and had chosen the latter. Now he had an opportunity to choose yet another. Unsure about finding happiness even with Lesley, he decided to risk a new adventure with another woman.

Himes and Marianne became lovers at her studio home in Antibes. They tried to keep their romance a secret, but Lesley and the Colemans guessed the truth almost from the start. To assuage Lesley, Himes wrote her a cock-and-bull account to the effect that he was acting as Marianne's bodyguard because she was being pursued by a gangster who had once been her lover. Even when telling deliberate lies, Himes liked to fancy himself a protector of damsels in distress.

The day neared when Marianne would have to leave France for Sweden before venturing on to Guatemala. Himes took Mikey his dog along with him and drove Marianne in the ancient Hillman to Paris. They arrived late at night, and Himes determined to drive back almost immediately rather than spend these last hours with her, because, he said, it was difficult to say good-bye and staying over would only make it worse. He departed Paris at three in the morning but after sixty miles fell asleep at the wheel. The Hillman smashed into a tree. Himes managed to extricate himself and flag down a passing car, whose driver took him to a hospital in Sens. Mikey was picked up by another motorist who later adopted him.

The Sens police called Lesley at Time-Life later in the morning, inform-ing her that a brown-skinned man with a large red dog had been taken to the hospital after a serious automobile accident. He had given them her office phone number, requesting that she come to him. Lesley rushed to Sens but at once realized that Himes had changed his mind and did not want her around. Days later the doctors discharged him, concluding that his cuts and bruises were mainly superficial. Ollie Harrington paid his hospital expenses and drove him to the Hôtel Aviatic, where Lesley stayed with him. Clearly he was not yet fully recovered. Suddenly, he collapsed. Doctors at the American Hospital in Neuilly diagnosed acute anemia and a broken pelvis, requiring him to spend the next week or so on crutches. Meanwhile, he passed his days in the hospital jotting down notes for a new film script. The producer, Pierre-Dominique Gaisseau, who had filmed the successful documentary *The Sky Above, the Mud Below* in New Guinea, had long been trying to get in touch with Himes and was finally able to do so because his automobile accident was reported in the newspapers. Gaisseau was convinced that Himes could produce a better story than *A Raisin in the Sun* and managed to persuade the president of Michael Arthur Film Productions, Arthur Cohn, to undertake a Harlem movie. A tentative agreement was reached stipulating that Himes would receive $1,200 to write the outline of a screenplay. Upon the acceptance of the outline, the producers would pay him $1,000 monthly to complete it. Thus was begun "Baby Sister," a far grimmer vision of Harlem than the one in his previously rejected script, "Blow Gabriel Blow." As Himes depicted it, the entire rotting atmosphere of Harlem conspires to violate and destroy the heroine and her family. He later called it his Greek tragedy in blackface. In his autobiography Himes told of some of his influences: "memories of Faulkner, the writings of slaves, the novel of a black woman writer [Ann Petry?] and the title *Baby Sister* evoked by Tennessee Williams' title, *Baby Doll,* and the way I looked at Harlem."[19]

Himes's accident caused Marianne to postpone her trip long enough to make sure he was in good hands. As soon as he emerged from the hospital in Neuilly, he flew to Stockholm to spend a week with her before her planned December sailing for Central America.

On his return, Chester rented Marianne's second-story studio in Antibes, situated in an old house only two doors from the Picasso museum. One wall, an extended window, faced the sea, allowing Himes clear views of his beloved Nice. Here he put the finishing touches on "Baby Sister." He wrote Van Vechten about his new romance: "I am very much in love with this woman who is in her late 40s and she is very much in love with me." He was working very hard on "Baby Sister" because he wanted to be in New York for the filming. If all went well, the couple would rendezvous there. Marianne, he confided, would come to New York as the still photographer for the company, and the two of them would produce a book with pictures from the screenplay. "If we make this movie, I feel certain that my life will become stabilized. Marianne and I will marry; and I am certain this time it will work out and that she is right for me and me for her."[20]

Who would it be now, Marianne or Lesley? With Marianne away, Himes endeavored to win back Lesley, and together they passed Christmas and New Year's Day in Paris. Around this time Gaisseau thought he had found a backer for Chester's screenplay, and he took the couple out to celebrate in grand style at the Arlequin. Later they left for the Blue Note to listen to Bud Powell, and danced and drank at a Saint-Germain-des-Prés cabaret where Himes passed out smoking a reefer.

In February 1962 Cohn departed for the United States to seek a financial guarantee of completion of Himes's "Baby Sister" from a major film studio. Meanwhile, Himes tried his hand at another script (since lost), called "An American Negro in Black Africa." The story apparently dealt with a well-known black writer, Edward Brown, who visits the country of his ancestors. Possibly the plot was patterned after Wright's ambivalent reactions to his Gold Coast visit in 1952. Himes, as we have seen, also contemplated making such a trip. Whatever the case, he seems to have anticipated by fifteen years the "return home" theme that later made Alex Haley's television series *Roots* an international success.

A half-dozen U.S. studios rejected the script for "Baby Sister" before Cohn decided to become sole producer of the film. Contracts were signed, and Himes was paid 6,000 francs, but a long-standing dispute between Gaisseau and Cohn on an unrelated matter halted progress. Then in April a new obstacle to production appeared when Herbert Hill of the NAACP wrote Cohn that he considered "Baby Sister" a "travesty of life in Harlem" consisting "almost entirely of banal caricature, unrelieved violence and endlessly repeated eroticism."[21] Years later Himes told his friend John A. Williams that Hill's objections were self-serving because he had become aware of Himes's ridicule of NAACP-types in his forthcoming *Pinktoes*. Whether or not Hill's letter caused Cohn to change his mind is uncertain, but Cohn held up production, whereupon a frustrated Himes wrote Cohn asking for the return of all the production rights assigned for his scenario, agreeing to pay back the sums he had received if he succeeded in disposing of the screenplay himself. Himes hoped that Joseph Levin of Embassy Films might do the film, although Hill may also have contacted Levin to make him aware of the NAACP's opposition. In any case, Himes believed that one of America's major civil rights organizations was doing all it could to censor his work.

Understandably dismayed, Himes persuaded himself that he had to become his own business agent. As early as March he had traveled to Darmstadt to contract with Ullstein for publication of *The Third Generation.* But usually personal management of his affairs got him in trouble. Among other things, he had sold *Mamie Mason* to Plon, and by so doing he had broken his contract with Girodias of Olympia, since *Mamie Mason* was in all particulars identical to *Pinktoes* (published in English by Girodias in 1961). The imbroglio was finally resolved when Girodias agreed not to claim his share for the French rights and Plon agreed to leave Olympia Press translation rights in other languages. At long last *Mamie Mason* would be published in French.

On March 10, 1962, Himes moved into Lesley's new apartment on rue de la Harpe in the Latin Quarter. If Lesley entertained misgivings about their renewed relationship, she would not have been unjustified. Months earlier, Gaisseau had approached Pierre Lazareff of *France-Soir,* who still wanted to make a documentary on Harlem, this time for the French popular news program "Cinq colonnes à la une" (Front-Page Headlines). Gaisseau suggested that Himes be recruited as an interpreter and contact man during the on-site filming. Himes would also write an article or essay about Harlem for Lazareff's newspaper. Remembering his earlier disappointments with Lazareff, Himes reluctantly agreed to sign with him, even accepting a meager salary of $500 because working in New York might be a way of meeting Marianne. On July 1 he flew to New York.

The French crew began shooting scenes in Spanish Harlem while Himes reconnoitered other spots: Rosa Meta's beauty parlor, Daddy Grace's old temple, the Afro-American Bank on 125th Street, Adam Clayton Powell's Abyssinian Baptist Church, and the upper end of Central Park. He also wanted to contrast the images of upper-class Harlem—Sugar Hill, for example— with junkies' bars on Eighth Avenue. He helped the crew establish their headquarters for a time at Lewis Micheaux's famous bookstore across the street from the Theresa Hotel, where Micheaux, a good friend of Malcolm X, helped provide the crew with footage of Malcolm. (Unfortunately, much of this footage was later lost for lack of a competent translation.) What Himes later called his "Harlem gig" turned out to be a pleasant experience. After the crew returned to France, Himes and Gaisseau tried to prepare a realistic budget for "Baby Sister" to give to Joseph Levin who had tentatively agreed to make the movie. They wanted to recruit a black crew, but few black technicians belonged to the union. Meanwhile, the NAACP continued to voice objections. Plans for casting had not even begun when Gaisseau suffered a nervous breakdown and had to be put on a plane to Paris. With nothing left to do, Himes followed in mid-August.

It is not clear whether Himes actually saw Marianne during his months in New York—he certainly intended to—but for the most part he attended to business. The civil rights struggles roiling America at the time did not much impress him. At best, he felt, peaceful protests were doomed to fail. Whites, he believed, would never passively surrender their dominance. Now he met Malcolm X and got to know him quite well. Malcolm "did not have to indoctrinate me into distrusting white people; I had distrusted them all along."[22] Some years later, in *Blind Man with a Pistol*, Himes portrayed protesters, black and white, as ludicrous. One good thing that came of Himes's visit to New York, however, was that he met the African American novelist John A. Williams. They became good friends, and an extensive correspondence between them followed.

After getting back to Paris Himes went with Lesley to Corsica for the duration of her vacation. On the way they stopped in Marseilles to visit an old acquaintance, Roger Luccioni, a heart specialist (as well as a first-rate jazz drummer). Luccioni must have made it known that Himes was in town because the local Communist Party newspaper, *La Marseillaise,* played up his arrival. Given Himes's anticommunist views, he may have been puzzled but professed himself elated. He was delighted too with Corsica's sunny empty beaches, a welcome respite after the bustle of New York. But back in Paris he expressed disappointment. He did not like the Harlem documentary he had seen previewed on September 7, pronouncing it superficial and verging on the exotic. In addition, the reportage he had written for *France-Soir* was not published because, he believed, it seemed too bitter and full of protest.[23]

All this took place against the increasing tensions of the French-Algerian war. In letters Himes tells of being shocked by the brutality of the Paris police, who seemed forever bashing demonstrators' heads and beating up Arab carpet vendors. He observed Paris cops smashing the plate-glass window of a café and arresting a couple of Algerians for having committed the vandalism. For years the native Algerian liberation organization, the Front de Libération Nationale (FLN), had been conducting a campaign of terrorism, but now Himes saw the FLN being outdone by the bombings of the white nationalist Organisation de l'Armée Secrète (OAS). Himes wrote a short piece on blacks in America for the weekly *Candide,* comparing the racists in Mississippi to the OAS. Warned by friends that it might arouse OAS anger and that it would be wise for him to leave Paris, he prudently took cover on the Riviera but returned a couple of weeks later to Lesley's apartment on rue de la Harpe.

Antibes, Himes wrote his new friend, novelist John A. Williams, was in fact a hotbed of OAS activity.

Himes had first encountered Williams earlier in the year at a dinner party at Van Vechten's. An admirer of Himes's writings, Williams contacted Van Vechten, who told him where to write to Himes in Europe. "Chester likes you too," Van Vechten wrote Williams. "People say bad things about him because he doesn't like most people and shows it . . . I admire his books: 'Yesterday will make you cry' [an early version of *Cast the First Stone*] is probably his best but it was so cut for publication that in that form it is worthless."[24] Thus was begun a regular correspondence between Himes and Williams. Williams told Himes of a project he wanted to undertake, an essay dealing critically with five or six Negro writers, Himes among them, and he asked Himes to write him about his life. Himes got around to doing this in November, at the same time waxing enthusiastic about Williams's *Sissie*, for which he wrote a blurb calling it the "greatest novel written about an American Negro family and certainly one of the best books written about any family." Did he regard *Sissie* as superior to his own *Third Generation*? A note he wrote Williams at the same time is revealing: "You come pretty damn close to answering the eternal question: what is a woman?"[25] In view of Himes's endless search for the ideal mate, no encomium could have been greater.

Although he was living with Lesley, Himes still fancied Marianne and yearned to return to her. She had been wandering about Central America seeking material for a new book, and Himes hoped they would be able to meet in New York. He also imagined that a trip to New York would expedite business matters. Among other things, he felt that his American agent, the Samuel French Literary Agency, was not sufficiently aggressive, and he sought out Carl Brandt, who was Williams's agent. Himes wrote Brandt that he was contemplating a new book about "a strange love affair between an American Negro and an American white woman in Europe (France, England, Mallorca)."[26] He apparently had not given up the idea of writing about his affair with Willa as "legitimate" fiction rather than as a thriller. A variation of this idea, he told Van Vechten, was an autobiographical novel, or better still a straight autobiography, in three books, "each book about my life with a woman, all three completely different; the first an American socialite (Boston, Smith College, etc.) married, divorced, three daughters, the second an infantile, immature, very crazy German in her twenties; the third English, good family, in her thirties, a member of the right people." He added that he did not know how American readers would react "and that is what I must come to New York to talk about."[27]

Finally, Himes believed that he might be able on his own to resell *The Primitive* and *Cast the First Stone* to paperback publishers. Unhappily, his business hopes were dashed somewhat by James Reach of the Samuel French Agency who refused to release Himes from his contract unless Himes paid back the $504 he claimed Himes owed.

Reach was not alone in claiming that Himes was indebted to him. In 1961 Himes had drawn several advances from Gallimard on two books he never completed. His royalty statement in December 1962 reflected these monies. Himes was furious. He asserted that he had put out much of his own money for publicity appearances for which he was never compensated. He also disputed an advance for "The Lunatic Fringe," which Gallimard failed to publish. There were other items too for which he was being unfairly billed.[28] He threatened to walk out on Gallimard, upsetting Duhamel, to whom Himes addressed these complaints. Duhamel liked Himes and had put himself out for him on more than one occasion. If Himes were to walk out on Gallimard, Duhamel wrote him, "I am going to have a lot of explaining to do for I shall be personally responsible for those 13,000 new francs which they claim you owe them."[29]

In truth, Himes's differences with Gallimard may not have been uppermost in his mind because he was still trying to figure out a way to see Marianne. She was now in Mexico suffering from anemia and also troubled by lack of money. Her writing was going badly, she wrote Himes, something he could perhaps help her with. Himes would have loved to travel to Mexico, but he had little money to spare. It was all he could do to pay his dentist, he told her. But Plon suddenly came through, providing him with an advance for a new detective book. On January 3, 1963, Himes flew to New York, ostensibly to clear up business with Samuel French. Two weeks later he was in Mexico, writing Lesley that he hoped to begin work there on a new thriller. He said nothing about joining Marianne.[30]

Marianne at the time was living in Sisal, a primitive fishing village in the Yucatán, taking photographs and writing about the local folk. Her home was a large thatched structure whose terrace fronted an immense sandy shore. "I burst in on Marianne taking a shower and everything is all right," Himes wrote Williams. "If I can clear my mind of all guilt, trepidation, anxieties, etc., I will be able to write because if I can't write here, I can't write anywhere."[31]

Life should have been easy. A Mayan family who lived next door cooked and did the couple's household chores. Himes claimed he enjoyed the little neighborhood children who ran barefoot through the house. But by early February he was complaining. The high winds of winter prevented fishermen from sailing, which meant that food was dull and scarce—mainly beans, fish, tortillas, chili, and a few vegetables. For drinking water the village depended on rain. He was also bothered by a week of seemingly endless noisy celebrations of the Virgin Mary. There was too much dancing and drinking of fermented cactus juice. Despite all, he wrote Williams, he did manage to produce a first draft of seventy-five pages of his "exercise with Grave Digger and Coffin Ed" and hoped to complete the story in ten days.[32]

Himes awoke one morning to discover he had lost his voice and could not move one side of his body. His Indian neighbors thought he had been stung by a scorpion. A few days later he recovered somewhat in a hospital in Mérida, ascribing the experience to a "brain spasm." (Neurologists in Manhattan afterward termed the event a "thrombotic cardio-vascular accident.") On February 25 he wrote Williams that he expected to come to New York the following week. He had no money and owed some to Sisal fishermen, but Plon had agreed to send him a ticket on the balance due for his book. In the same letter he mentioned almost casually, "Marianne and I have discovered that we can't possibly live together with our separate careers and our egos, and without money; so we have come to a parting of the ways." What he did not tell Williams was that Marianne demanded her sexual freedom—something Himes could not tolerate—and that he believed she had liaisons with Mayan fishermen. His violent jealousy may well have aggravated his hypertension.[33]

In the meantime, Lesley, who had been receiving tender letters twice weekly from Himes (none of which alluded to Marianne), was becoming worried. She had not heard from him for a while until one day she opened a letter in very strange handwriting saying he had been bitten by a scorpion. He was in the hospital in Mérida, he wrote, but without enough money to get out. Lesley tried sending him money, but exchange regulations made it impossible to cable funds from France and money that she sent via a Swiss bank never reached him. Fortunately, in March one of Himes's German publishers managed to wire him $250, which allowed him to pay his bills and fly to New York. After about a week Marianne joined him—but too late.

Himes's infatuation with Marianne had come to an end. Realizing that Himes no longer wanted her, Marianne telephoned Lesley in Paris telling her to get in touch with Himes—that he still loved her and wanted to speak to her. Years later he not very gallantly called Marianne a nymphomaniac who tried to cash in on his writing ability. But Van Vechten, who met her around this time, believed she was "enchanting and completely unselfconscious in her passion for Chester."[34] Whatever the truth, Marianne departed, and Van Vechten and Williams looked out for Himes for the next several weeks. His doctors at the Presbyterian Hospital advised rest, which for Himes meant another stay at the Albert Hotel. To help him pay his bills, Van Vechten lent him more money, as did Williams, who visited him daily. During this period he finished his new book for Plon—tentatively called "Back to Africa" (later published as *Cotton Comes to Harlem*)—and made plans with Bucklin Moon, his very first book editor, to write a novel for Pocket Books with an African background. Now he had good news from Europe: A small French publishing firm agreed to publish *A Case of Rape,* and a German publisher wanted to do another of his detective books. Life was looking up. In late March 1963 a battery of tests at Presbyterian Hospital reassured him. He suffered from hypertension, but at the moment nothing else appeared to be wrong with his health. He could return now to the Continent.

Some weeks later Himes moved in with Lesley. His affairs with other women were a thing of the past. From now on it would be Lesley.

# 11

# LESLEY

LESLEY'S PLACE ON RUE DE LA HARPE was a ground-floor, two-room apartment near the Saint-Severin church. She had spent much time making it cozy, which Himes appreciated, having come to view his "stroke" as a warning. In the spring of 1963 he was determined to settle down and find quiet happiness in Europe. These days he was regarded as an oldtimer in the Latin Quarter, and some of the younger "brothers" would call on him. Among them were Melvin Van Peebles, who shared Himes's interest in scriptwriting, and Ted Joans, the "surrealist griot" poet who read his works at the Mistral Bookshop. Another admirer was the expatriate Cuban Carlos Moore, who angrily denounced race discrimination in Castro's Cuba. Moore, a former minor government official, was utterly persuaded that Castro loathed black people, and Himes listened attentively, more convinced than ever that racism was endemic to Western civilization. His new novel, *A Case of Rape* (published in France as *Une Affaire de viol*), conveyed much the same message.

Although *A Case of Rape* may not have garnered Himes much money, it did win him favorable attention, especially among feminists such as Christiane Rochefort, who in an afterword stressed the similarities between the oppression of black Americans and the plight of women in modern society. Theirs was an odd juxtaposition, given Himes's occasional violent responses to women—not to mention his insistence that "his women" be dependent on him. Although one would hardly categorize him as a champion of feminism, the novel and his thwarted screenplay "Baby Sister" do depict women as being exploited, violated, and brutally misused by men.

*A Case of Rape* (Himes's first published novel with a European setting) tells of four black Americans in Paris who have been tried and convicted of the rape and murder of an American white woman. Although the actual causes of her death could be traced to her husband's brutality, the central black protagonist refuses to reveal what he knows for reasons of honor and racial pride. The novel, besides being an indictment of French and American racism (with which the dead woman was herself contaminated), also tells something of the components that constituted the expatriate black community. Each of the convicted characters, as well as an outsider (a famous novelist and black American expatriate who sadly misunderstands the case and tries to reopen it), is examined by Himes for his reasons for coming to Paris as well as for his reactions to the events portrayed. Whatever else the novel does, it gives the lie to the image of a monolithic African American expatriate community, mirroring instead diverse backgrounds, subjective cultural motivations, and complicated psychologies. As Himes later acknowledged, the characters are modeled on Richard Wright, James Baldwin, Ollie Harrington, and William Gardner Smith, and there is a Himes-like figure who has had a love affair with the deceased woman, remarkably like Willa. By killing her off, Himes may have hoped he was ridding himself of memories of Willa, but, as we shall see, she kept returning in his other writings.[1]

Despite its possibilities, *A Case of Rape* fails to develop into a major work largely because the difficult issues Himes raises demand more illustrative treatment. Himes seemed to tire of his themes once they were imagined, though at conception he envisioned the work in several volumes. What is printed reads rather like a long synopsis, and Himes acknowledged as much in his autobiography. What saves the book from being mere summary is the seemingly deadpan "objective" tone, which paradoxically evokes the reader's indignation. As one French critic put it, "his writing is terse and powerful; within the closed intimacy of each sentence one feels that a spring uncoils in order to deal a powerful blow."[2]

Himes's publisher, Les Yeux Ouverts, advanced him 1,500 francs for the novel, part of which he used to spend a few days in May with the Colemans in Biot. He attended the Cannes film festival that year and passed much of July with Lesley in Antibes. Here Chester worked on revisions of his "Back to Africa," while Lesley spent much of her time at the beach.

Himes worked extensively on revisions for most of the remainder of the year in Paris, but still managed to fit considerable socializing into his schedule. The Dixons visited in early November when Dean came from Frankfurt to direct a concert at the Théâtre des Champs-Elysées. Chester introduced him to the blind saxophonist Roland Kirk and afterward to his brother Joseph, who appeared in Paris at about this time on his way back from a Fulbright teaching appointment at the University of Helsinki. Although Himes always enjoyed his guests and friends—he was a generous host—he felt he needed more time for his novel. Accordingly, in mid-December he departed Paris for Saint-Laurent-du-Var to work on another revision of *Cotton Comes to Harlem*, which he later called "the best of my detective stories."[3]

*Cotton* is surely one of Himes's most satisfying works and may well be his funniest. Perhaps because he thought then of his Harlem series as potboilers rather than as "literature," he allowed his imagination fuller rein than he might otherwise have done. But he could not quite overcome the feeling that these works were artistically inferior; only in his later years did he call them major contributions. Still, by now he felt confident enough to play deliberately with social themes without fear of bogging down his narrative. *Cotton* satirizes white supremacists, jabs at black nationalist movements like that of Marcus Garvey, pokes fun again at black religion (emphasizing again the link between spiritual ecstasy and sexual climax), and bravely depicts Negroes who hate whites. The device of the missing treasure (used in so many of his other thrillers) is reintroduced, but this time it is the real thing—somebody gets away with it. Finally, *Cotton* is far less violent than many of his other Harlem books. Possibly he was more at peace with himself when he wrote it.

In mid-January Gallimard staged a week-long publicity campaign for its Série Noire, which required Himes's presence in Paris as a star attraction. He and Lesley had to return from the south, this time settling in what he considered his first real apartment, at 3, rue Bourbon-le-Château. It was ideally located, close to the familiar Buci market and only a stone's throw away from Gordon Heath's Club de l'Abbaye. One of the couple's neighbors was the abstract painter Jean Miotte, who over the course of years became a good friend. Some of Himes's other callers at this time were photographers Emile Cadoo and John Taylor, pianist Art Simmons, painter Herb Gentry, and writers Melvin Van Peebles and John A. Williams (the latter on his way to Rome). One afternoon Malcolm X climbed the seven flights of stairs for a long private colloquy. He had come to Paris by way of a return trip from Mecca and told Himes he had read *Hollers* when he was twenty and that it had deeply moved him. Himes said later the two mainly agreed on the politics of the black struggle in America, although Himes was not particularly attracted to Islam. Shortly after Malcolm's departure, two men came up the stairs looking for him and hammered violently on their door. Lesley refused to open it. She and Himes thought they were perhaps killers or CIA operatives. That evening Himes attended a huge rally at the Mutualité, where Malcolm addressed an enthusiastic overflow crowd. Not many weeks later he was assassinated in New York.

The start of 1964 looked brighter for Himes financially, with half a dozen U.S. publishers contracting to print his novels. *For Love of Imabelle* soon came out in America as *A Rage in Harlem,* and Putnam promised to print *Cotton Comes to Harlem* in a hardcover edition. There was talk as well of screen adaptations of some of Himes's books. Yet Himes himself remained somewhat sour during this period, still unsure about his real importance. "I am well but almost always in bad temper," he wrote Van Vechten. "The news from the U.S. do not seem very good and the French are having a bad spell of anti-Americanism and I am beginning to feel trapped . . . now I want to do something definite—write a good book, I suppose."[4]

From Himes's point of view, *A Case of Rape* was "legitimate" fiction. Van Vechten thought so too, telling him he believed it to be one of his more serious books, carefully written, and perhaps his masterpiece to date. Himes was pleased, though he doubtless exaggerated its message, claiming that he had become notorious for denouncing racism in France.[5] The novel did attract some media attention: *Le Figaro* had an editorial about it, and the ultra right-wing weekly *Candide* ran a half-page interview alongside a photograph of Himes with a white woman incorrectly identified as his wife. "At first the French were indignant," Himes wrote Van Vechten, "then the French press had a sort of soul searching and recently there has been a number of articles about the growing racism in France (and how un-French it is), so at least it stirred up some attention and also made the people who read only my detective novels begin to take them more seriously, which is a good thing."[6] He liked shocking Europeans, he continued, and was anxious to get on with the book about his life and loves in Europe, which would "shock EVERYBODY."

At about this time Himes was approached by a French filmmaker named Panijel, who wanted to do a movie version of *Une Affaire de viol.* Both men tried to prepare a French script with the assistance of Himes's friends. But Cadoo wanted to make Himes's characters homosexuals, and Van Peebles, who was also enlisted, did not really know enough French. Even Lesley's help did not suffice, and the project was eventually dropped.

In May 1964 Himes's plans changed again. He wrote Van Vechten that he had "found the handle" to his new book, which he wanted to call "The God in Me." He had gone to see the film *Dr. Strangelove* and had had a dream about a little boy's pet ducks who were towing all the world's warships out to sea and exploding them. That dream had triggered the story, he explained:

everything fell into shape from beginning to end—the absurdity of it, I
suppose—for my book is about a Negro man who falls in love with an
American white woman on the way to Europe—the love goes into pity,
the pity into sacrifice; all of it takes place in Europe; and there will be no
melodrama, no purple passages, just the bare necessary minimum of violent
action for the motivation of emotion; in fact, it will be a book almost entirely
on emotion—love, pity and sacrifice. I am sure it will take me on a long
journey, for how long I do not know: two years, three years I can't say. But
I feel very good about it because I think this book I want to write won't be
affected by time or change unless the human soul changes. Somehow all
my other ventures have become unimportant. And I start on this journey
unafraid.[7]

Of course, Himes was going back once again to his projected autobiographical novel dealing with Willa. That he was still thinking of her
suggests something of his melancholy. Telling about his love was a way of
understanding himself. The writing acted as catharsis. There is no way of
determining whether his project ever really got under way. Late in May a
second cardiovascular "accident" (a stroke) sent him for seven days to the
American Hospital in Neuilly. On his release he said he didn't feel well, nor
did he feel much better for the next five or six months. Since a new thriller
was still required of him, he probably put his autobiographical novel aside.

Meanwhile, Himes saw his reputation as a sage growing. He told an
interviewer for the Jewish review *L'Arche* that the underlying causes of
black anti-Semitism in the United States were economic: competition between blacks and Jews for jobs and Jewish ownership of businesses in black
neighborhoods. The Black Muslims, he said, should not be regarded as a
predominantly negative influence, since they often channeled latent hostility
into nonviolent constructive achievements. Himes made clear that he was
aware of the historic persecution of Jews, but that he felt the situation of
blacks in America to be far more critical.[8] In a July 13 vignette for the *Nouvel
Observateur,* Himes gave further expression to his views: Black Americans,
he stated, were torn between integration into a "burning house" and race
nationalism.[9] Later in the month he undertook an outline of a report on
Harlem for *Paris-Match*. One section, "The Revolution of the Mind," raises
the issue: "Not *how* to fight but *who* to fight."[10] In a sense, this was Himes's
dilemma too. Like Malcolm X, he understood that in part the enemy lay
within the stricken black psyche. The project was eventually forgotten.

Himes's first trip to Africa took place in September when he and Lesley
flew to Cairo. He envisioned this visit as a prelude to a lengthier African
sojourn, but after a week in Alexandria he said he hated the poverty and

lack of facilities, and after several days in Cairo he declared he was utterly sick of Egypt. Later he conceded that he might have reacted precipitously, but he based his revulsion on grounds that black Africans were still being treated as slaves in Egypt. On September 12, 1964, he and Lesley were back on the Riviera with the Colemans. Himes and his host may have had words, because Himes afterward wrote Van Vechten that he could no longer stand Coleman, who had become "a French Uncle Tom for free." Himes and Lesley went next to "racist" London, which Himes wrote was like jumping from the frying pan into the fire. "So I went to bed; at least for most of the day I was safe in bed."[11]

Although Himes often accused the French of racism, the French usually preferred to ask him about American race relations "to avoid [their] Algerian problem no doubt."[12] He was not, however, averse to speaking of race relations in the United States. In a long interview in the November 1964 issue of *Adam* (the French counterpart of *Playboy*), he expatiated on American race violence and riots: They would continue so long as poverty persisted in the ghetto, he said. This was an unoriginal insight but, more interestingly, he quoted his cousin Henry Lee Moon as saying that though Himes's bitter first novel, *If He Hollers Let Him Go,* told the truth, such truths were better off not told. Here possibly lay another source of the acrimony between the cousins. Perhaps Himes's most interesting comments concerned black men's compulsion to have sex with white women: It was, he said, a neurosis engendered by racism, a drug like whiskey and jazz, assuaging a need to prove that the black was the equal of the white. He assured his interviewer, however, that in Europe blacks felt no such need to prove themselves.

The year ended with Himes once more embroiled in a dispute with a publisher—this time, Olympia. Himes had finally managed to sell *Pinktoes* to the American publisher Putnam, but Maurice Girodias of Olympia claimed that Himes had signed over the foreign contract rights to him. Girodias had already sold the book to another American publisher, Stein & Day. Himes was adamant, claiming he did not know that his signature with Girodias made the contract legal; moreover, Girodias had cheated him on his royalties, and hence he believed he had not acted immorally.[13] The issue was left unresolved, and Himes departed for the new year to Cannes, where he rented a studio in the antiquated Palais Rouaze to begin work on a new thriller. The lease on the Paris apartment had expired, and Lesley, whose job at Time-Life required that she stay in Paris, settled into a new flat on the rue d'Assas.

Himes wrote Lesley about his new book. It was something of "a cross between *La Reine des pommes* and *Pinktoes.*"[14] After a month in Cannes, he came back to Paris in early 1965 to help Lesley furnish their new apartment but returned two days later to his Cannes studio, wondering what strange new turns the plot of his thriller might take. About these books, he told an acquaintance, he never knew how or where they might end. He was most concerned with style and pacing.[15] "I like to both read and write novels that swing," he wrote Lesley. "In writing there is only one reader I must please and that is me (that is the only thing I ever liked about Hemingway)."[16] What bothered him most at the start was that this novel "moves all right but it is not swinging." Nonetheless, work was progressing, and this, after all, was his aim in a first draft.

Those were lonely months on the Riviera. Himes wanted to marry Lesley and jokingly wrote her that if she kept on putting him off, he would allow one of his other many female admirers to do the honors. He wanted Lesley to inherit his books and keep them in print; he didn't want Jean to have them. Lesley had told him she and a friend were contemplating going into the travel business, to which Himes replied that he would gladly send her three or four thousand dollars to start up, if ever he had that much money to send. He was famous, yes—but he was still convinced that his publishers (especially his French publishers) were cheating him of his royalties.[17]

Himes's longings for stability were doubtless exacerbated by what he saw happening to the Colemans. Their marriage was breaking up, and each was trying to enlist Himes's sympathy. Although he was by now fonder of Torun, who had become a successful businesswoman, he refused to tell her the whereabouts of Walter's mistress. Among other things, he did not want to make matters worse for Walter, who was about to go to trial for possession of heroin. To compound matters, Himes believed Torun wanted to take him as a lover. To extricate himself, he returned to Paris a few weeks before the lease to his studio expired.

Himes was in Paris for about a month before flying to New York. It was strictly business this time. The imbroglio between Putnam and Stein & Day regarding *Pinktoes* had been resolved. Both houses would participate as co-publishers. Girodias received his due, and Himes netted $10,000. Although the reviews were mixed, *Pinktoes* sold well in America, surpassing by far sales of Hime's other books. Perhaps equally important was the reconfirmation of his friendship with Bill Targ, at present an editor at Putnam. Targ's fiancée Roslyn Siegel, a literary agent, introduced herself to Himes later that fall in Paris, and Himes let her represent him with publishers. Indeed, Himes quite enjoyed her ebullience and told Lesley she was the ideal person to sell his works. It was the beginning of a long friendship.

Earlier in the year, Himes and Lesley spent the first half of May in Greece, during which time Himes hoped to read and edit for publication his original manuscript of *Cotton Comes to Harlem*. Unfortunately, he left it behind on his return journey at the Athens airport. From France the distressed author made frantic efforts to recover the manuscript, but no one reported it found, though some time later, another copy of the original was found at Yale University.

The brief vacation in Greece further persuaded Himes to make Lesley his wife. He now pressed his suit with renewed vigor, while enthusiastically helping to furnish their new apartment on rue d'Assas. In his fashion, he was becoming domesticated. That he was not yet legally divorced from Jean did not seem to him an insuperable obstacle. For the time being, at least they could live as man and wife. Indeed, later on Lesley legally changed her last name to Himes. His anxieties about reputation, finances, and celebrity seemed in abeyance. To signal to himself and the great world beyond the fact of his success, he decided to buy himself a new Jaguar—something rarely seen on the streets of Paris at this time.

The plan was this: Lesley had to go into the hospital for treatment of varicose veins. In her absence Himes would cross to England, acquire the car in its Coventry factory, and drive it back to Paris. The mechanically oriented Himes had always loved the fine craftsmanship and looks of Jaguars, as well as their possibilities for great speed. (In his memoirs Himes devotes more space to the car than to Lesley's veins.) To prove his devotion to Lesley, however, Himes would not remove the car from its Paris garage until Lesley emerged from the hospital. It was his way of telling her she was the only one he wanted to share it with.

At last Himes managed to persuade the somewhat skeptical Lesley that he could support her. She quit her job at Time-Life as well as the Paris apartment they had both worked so hard to decorate, and in late October the couple left for Denmark, where Chester intended writing a new Série Noire thriller. His differences with Gallimard were now presumably resolved. That Himes chose Denmark is perplexing, given his expressed disgust with the Danes and the Danish climate after his stay there with Regine. It did not seem to bother him that he chose to live in Holte, not far from where he had stayed with Regine. Himes did manage to get some writing done in Denmark, socializing chiefly with his Paris painter friend Gentry, who had recently gone to Sweden to live with his Swedish wife, and Torun, now divorced from Coleman and living with a musician. The one Danish contact Himes mentioned in his autobiography was Birgit Rasmussen, a journalist who had written about Himes for her newspaper and helped the couple find a house.

Besides his Série Noire novel, as yet untitled, Himes began writing about his early days in Europe. He mailed to Bill Targ an episode dealing with his arrival in Paris and liaison with Willa, along with several short stories. His Willa piece, he told Targ, would not be part of his autobiography, which in any case would name names (Willa is here referred to as "the dutiful wife") and would deal chiefly with his "Negro compatriots" who would be "the feature of the book along with some very amusing Europeans."[18]

Until now, Himes had often misrepresented the events in his life for publicity purposes. One instance is an autobiographical sketch he wrote for *Cotton Comes to Harlem* in July 1964, in which he said he attended Ohio State University "for two years but withdrew because of failing health" and that his accident in a Cleveland hotel "invalided me for ten years during which time I turned to writing to relieve the boredom." He said nothing about the years he passed in the Ohio penitentiary for armed robbery.

Now Himes endeavored to produce a more honest account of his years. "My First Months Abroad," a fifty-page-long piece, was such an effort. An introductory note later deleted from his memoirs tells how he perceived himself:

> There can be no doubt that I am a new man; I am the product of the amalgamation of white and black races resulting from the enslavement of blacks by whites in the United States of America during the seventeenth, eighteenth, and nineteenth centuries when most of the world had been so long formed as to be approaching decadence . . . I am a new man in thought, outlook and principle as well as in physiognomy; my color is brown, my features are nordic, my hair is kinky; I believe I am the human equal, in the sight of God . . . of whites along with non-whites in all circumstances of human existence; I become infuriated when others, whether whites or non-whites, reject my conviction of equality . . . I am as opposed to the criteria of caste, class and race in the determination of human worth as I am to the criteria of wealth, position and previous condition of servitude. I am unimpressed by rank and title; the phrase "noble blood" has no more meaning to me than the word "black blood," blood being neither noble nor black; I am ignorant of the meaning of tradition.[19]

Predictably, Himes soon began to tire of Denmark. In February 1966 he wrote Malartic that he would gladly return to the south of France if he could find a house large enough, cheap enough, and sufficiently isolated to permit him to continue writing.[20] The cold was intense, and he was beginning to suffer again from arthritis. He was also irked that he was not invited to the funeral of Larry Potter, a popular African American painter in Paris. That told him "more than anything else that I was not popular with the black community in France."[21] He was getting testy. Another reason he wanted to escape Denmark, he wrote Williams, was that despite their availability, Danish "chicks" were "not all beautiful," in addition to which he found "the Danes [were] egocentric, stupid and over-sensitive about their little country."[22]

Himes managed his getaway with Lesley in mid-February, driving across Germany to La Ciotat as a guest of Daniel Guérin at Rustique Olivette. No longer a writers' colony, the house had reverted to living quarters for its owner. Himes was of two minds about his host. He described Guérin to Williams as "the rich leftist authority on the brother here"[23] but nevertheless appreciated his generosity, since it allowed him to proceed with his autobiography. He had reached his Arcachon period with Willa, which he remembered as "two months [that] were the happiest I spent during my 13 years in Europe."[24] In point of fact, however, he was very much enjoying his life with Lesley now, and Lesley herself wrote: "I . . . remember having such a wonderful time. The weather was dreamlike, the house was comfortable and we had wonderful friends . . . and the best food in France."[25] When Himes was not plugging away at his autobiography, he socialized with Guérin and friends who came down from Paris. On occasion he and Lesley used to drive along the Riviera, sightseeing, visiting, and looking for a place they could call their own home.

In July the couple moved to Aix-en-Provence and rented a renovated farm near Saint-Hypolite, at Venelles. With the passing months Himes grew more and more to love their new home and the magnificent Cézanne-like views. The house and surrounding property were vast, consisting of outbuildings, barns, and open fields, as well as a garden and swimming pool. Himes spoke of it as his dream house. Perhaps understandably, his desire to write abated. He spent endless hours fixing up the place, tending the garden, cutting wood, clearing the ground, or taking long walks in the countryside with Lesley. There were visitors, of course—one favorite of Himes's being Jay Clifford, an eighty-year-old former New York customs official who told colorful stories of his misadventures in America and Europe dating back to World War I. Himes liked to drive down to Monte Carlo, where Clifford lived, to take him back. Another favorite was Nicole Toutain, the companion of the late Larry Potter. Toutain worked on films in Nice and often came weekends. Then there were Lesley's Paris friends who stopped with them frequently.

But however genuinely pleased Himes was to see all his callers, he tired easily. With the approach of cooler weather, his arthritis worsened, and it was not unusual for him to go to bed after an evening meal. At Christmas time he and Lesley gave a huge dinner party, after which Himes simply excused himself to retire. His lack of energy was not confined to day-to-day activities; his writing also suffered. He had begun several detective stories but then abandoned them for lack of interest. One piece he worked at on and off, which he called "Tang," dealt with a black terrorist organization that tries to foment a revolution—but even this he put aside. Another story, which he called "Regina," had a plot that was "strange and fuzzy," he wrote Targ. "It might very well impress one as gratuitous vulgarity, pornography and vituperation," he said, but it was beginning to take shape, somewhat in the fashion of Faulkner's *Light in August* when Joe Christmas lands in Jefferson. Characteristically, he had trouble separating fact from fiction, which prevented him from getting back to his autobiography because Regine (Regina) was also part of it. "But I had to make it fiction for every reason."[26] In addition to his fiction, his other main trouble was the Jaguar, which did not idle properly. Himes took it to Marseilles for repairs and finally had to resort to a lawyer to extricate it from the garage, whose owner tried to charge him while his warranty remained in effect. The trauma of the Jaguar loomed large, a threat and a challenge to his dignity.

Himes could not shake what he assumed was a general malaise. In February 1967 he consulted Paris specialists, who diagnosed him as having osteoarthritis and radiculitis. Suddenly he felt restless again. In March he and Lesley crossed into Spain at Port-Bou and drove all the way to Gibraltar. He could not seem to stay put. "I'm getting pissed off with France," he wrote his friend Williams, "and I think we might go to Amsterdam."[27] But instead he left for America in early May. A local dentist had damaged a cap in his mouth and Himes, annoyed and believing the French could not be trusted, sought out a Dr. Platt in New York whom he had visited years before. Himes decided he did not want to bother any longer with ailing teeth and asked Dr. Platt to produce a set of permanent dentures for him. This required a longer stay in New York than he had planned. Lesley joined him in mid-June while Himes got accustomed to his new teeth. Meanwhile, he became involved in a new project.

A year before, Samuel Goldwyn, Jr. had bought the film rights to *Cotton Comes to Harlem* and wanted Himes to write the script. Chester advised him to try Claude Brown, but Goldwyn persisted. He suggested that Himes pare the complex plot and sharpen the differences between the two detectives, perhaps even reduce his two heroes to one as a way of adding more suspense. As an inducement, he offered Himes $750 a week, a secretary, and expenses, hinting that he might drop the option unless Himes agreed. Himes thought he could do the work in a week, but whatever he submitted failed to satisfy Goldwyn.

Regardless, Himes returned to his home in Venelles, but only for a short time because its owner intended to sell the house. This meant that Himes and Lesley had to journey once more to Paris to stay in friends' apartments. For part of a month they lived in the fifth *arrondissement* on rue de l'Estrapade, an area of the city that Himes loved (as did his youthful idol, Hemingway),[28] especially the Place de la Contrescarpe and the popular food markets on rue Mouffetard. But the weather was chilly and gray, and the city was deserted save "for simple-minded tourists fascinated by la gloire de la France."[29]

Next the couple traveled to Holland at the invitation of Himes's Dutch agent, settling in a large, luxurious house in Blaricum. Here Himes began thinking again of his autobiography—not without misgivings. Before he left Paris a friend in New York, Constance Webb Pearlstien, had sent him her manuscript biography of Richard Wright. Himes was not pleased. He felt that her account of his role in the Wright-Baldwin dispute was not accurate and had no place in her book. "I do not want my name used in the destruction of the memory of Richard Wright," he wrote her, "nor employed for the purpose of a derogatory reference to James Baldwin. I must reserve the right to make my own criticism when and where I see it.!"[30] At the appropriate time *he* would tell what had taken place.

Now Himes went back to his own autobiographical "Regina" and in August sent Bill Targ forty-three pages, beginning with a verbatim transcription of the disturbing letters Regine had sent him from a psychiatric clinic. He was making their relationship into a kind of case history, to which Targ reacted with mixed feelings. "The narrative is strong, compelling, reminiscent of a few of your books, including *The Primitive*," Targ wrote back. Once "past the first 16 pages of letters, it grabs and holds me. Perhaps the story should be written in the third person rather than in the first." Sometime later Himes mailed another hundred-page version, but Targ declared that the account of a black American novelist and a German girl was too preoccupied with sex to the exclusion of everything else:

> I'd like to see something more about the life around Ted. I'd like to know some of his thoughts on writing, writers, books, publishers, etc. so that we see him not only as a highly charged sexual figure but also a creative person. I'd also like to see more dialogue—some about other matters which they surely discussed, such as political scandals, celebrities in the news, movie stars, plays, books. Do they ever discuss Bardot? Camus? De Beauvoir? the War? that sort of thing.[31]

Targ was right. Himes was already encountering some of the difficulties that later plagued his autobiography. But if he tended to focus too much on his sentimental and sexual life, it was because his chief interests for the moment were his emotions. Yet for the reader there was not enough about *him* in the account to make his emotions interesting. The narrative passed over his writing, the genesis of his novels, his literary acquaintances, his politics, or even the material he had once promised to write about the black expatriate community. Obviously Himes and Targ were writing past each other, because Himes had come to view his professional career as secondary. What was important in his life were the white women he had loved and the Western racial and sexual taboos that had made these loves intolerable. He wanted to record his responses to black-white romantic liaisons, neurotic or otherwise, as typical of a black man's point of view. In effect, he saw his emotional life controlled by cultural symbols.

Himes's stay of nearly three months in Holland was not without literary significance. At one point the expatriate black writer Phil Lomax phoned him on "urgent business." Himes invited him to his house, and in private Lomax ruefully told him he had plagiarized a section of *Pinktoes,* selling it in Holland as his own. Himes was magnanimous; he not only forgave Lomax but also invited him for lunch. The two men swapped stories, and Lomax related an anecdote about a blind man with a pistol who had begun shooting at random in a New York subway. Perhaps the blind man wanted to believe he could see or perhaps he simply wanted to make others aware of his existence. The story of the blind man so intrigued Himes that it found its way into the mystery he had for years been sporadically working on. He had completed several episodes about seemingly unrelated crimes that his two detectives appeared unable to solve. What Himes needed was a unifying thread, and he decided now that "absurdity" as an end in itself was the point. Lomax's blind man became the metaphor of his theme, and Himes named his book "Blind Man with a Pistol," graciously crediting Lomax in a foreword. In his own notes Himes wrote: "Phil Lomax told me a story of the Blind Man with his pistol which was my story of all people: confusion, misunderstanding, confrontation with death . . . That was the story of all black people." Another note indicates that he had begun *Blind Man with a Pistol* as far back as 1962 in Mougins and made "several other starts" (actually seven) over the years. "All the time I wanted to write a book where no one would know who was guilty . . . When I wrote *If He Hollers* . . . the guilty were the whole white race, but no one saw it."[32]

Lomax was not the only American friend to visit Himes in Blaricum. Charles Holland, an expatriate black singer and composer whom Himes had known in Los Angeles, and his white wife Cathy also called. Years back Cathy, as a favor, had once typed a manuscript version of "Mamie Mason." Their visit made only a small dent in Himes's rigorous work schedule. He was determined now to finish the thriller for which Lomax had given him his clue. He also wanted to begin work on a novel he would call "Plan B." But Himes was also basking in growing publicity, which meant that he was being asked to lend his voice to a variety of social and political issues. In September Targ requested that he become one of the sponsors of the Fifth Avenue Vietnam Peace Parade, and as an "auctionable" contribution Himes offered a manuscript of an article he had written for *Candide* the previous year that made some references to the war. The only other donation he could think of was an invitation to Jean Giono's daughter's wedding. About a week later, at a press conference sponsored by his Dutch publisher, he answered questions about the war, his books, and his general understanding of the race question in America. The next day he was pleased to see his picture in the newspapers and afterward told Dutch television audiences that he believed only carefully planned black organized violence—as opposed to aimless riots—could produce racial justice in America. Privately he was still mulling over just such subject matter for his new novel.

The germ of the idea may have extended as far back as 1944, when he wrote "Negro Martyrs Are Needed." That article argued that a few Negro heroes must galvanize blacks for concerted action. He was not thinking of specific kinds of violence—certainly not the violence of a blind man shooting at random. This was precisely the kind of violence he opposed. *Blind Man with a Pistol* would carry that message, which was why he had to finish it now. When Sam Goldwyn, Jr., who remained unhappy with the screen treatments he had received for *Cotton*, again tried to lure him to Hollywood, Himes flatly refused. *Blind Man with a Pistol* was the most curious detective story he had ever written—perhaps that anyone had ever written. It ended with none of the mysteries solved. The solution to the crimes lay with its readers.

On November 11, 1967, Himes completed the novel, sent it off to Roslyn Targ, and drove off with Lesley into Spain. They passed through Madrid and Alicante to Gibraltar, then crossed to Tangiers to celebrate Christmas and New Year's Day. On the face of it, their journey appeared aimless, but in reality they were assessing the climate and different landscapes with the intention of settling finally in Spain.

# 12

# SPAIN

DID HIMES SENSE THAT HIS most creative years were past? If by quirks of fate and chance, he could survive far better as a writer in Europe, nonetheless Europe failed to give him (or he refused by choice) the substantive material to nourish his artistry. Himes never truly learned French nor cared to. He conversed in English with the few French people he knew, such as Duhamel and Malartic. His knowledge of French culture and social issues was minimal: At worst he was indifferent, at best he saw French life in terms of American life or, more specifically, American race relations. Some insights there were, but surely not enough. He grew more and more consumed with himself. But himself in relation to whom, to what? He came to think of himself more and more in terms of the white women he had known.

But Himes's main thoughts were focused on his American life, on what his mother had taught him, on what he had learned of love and tried to forget in prison, on his years with Jean and his American work experiences, on his immense attraction and revulsion at the libertine ways of the Harlem upper crust, and on his status as a writer—as a Negro writer—when it seemed to him that no one paid attention. Somehow, at bottom, the trouble was, as his novels attest, the desired white woman. As he thought about these things now in 1968, he still grew angry, and as he brooded about the injustices done him, he fantasized apocalyptic race wars whose outcome would bring down the whole rotten structure of American society.

The sad fact was that America too was disappointing Himes as a subject. When he did go back to New York on those brief visits, he could not help but notice that black young people sounded different from what he remembered. The scene had changed. Ironically, the younger American black writers—

John A. Williams, Melvin Van Peebles, and Ishmael Reed—who thrilled to Himes's imagination and anger and militancy produced their work with different expectations in a changed atmosphere. They may have admired Himes's courage and celebrated his writings, but he was painfully aware of the differences between them and himself. His growing self-absorption left him only dimly aware of the changing American scene. The war in Vietnam, the civil rights upheavals, and the student youth movement he dismissed as irrelevant.

When, sometime in 1968, Nicole Toutain wrote to say how sorry she was to learn about the assassination of Reverend Martin Luther King, Jr., Himes was jolted into realizing that he did not think much about King or America these days. Or, more accurately, he thought about America chiefly in terms of business negotiations. He knew and sensed that some people were saying that he ought to go back to the States and participate in the great black struggles. James Baldwin had done as much, but to what avail? What could he himself do? He was a writer, and a writer writes. On and off during 1968 Himes reworked his story "Tang," perhaps thinking he might incorporate it into his next contemplated Grave Digger–Coffin Ed thriller. "Plan B" would describe a successful violent black revolution, carefully planned, carefully orchestrated—the sort of thing he talked about on Dutch television. That would be his contribution to the race struggle in America.

Where would Grave Digger and Coffin Ed stand in these black wars? Were they basically law-and-order men or truer to their mystical black instincts? Here once again it was a question of the two sides of Himes's own psyche. In his thinking the pair would take opposing sides—and perhaps kill one another off. Was this artistic suicide? Himes never completed the book to his satisfaction, although it was published in a French version shortly before his death.[1] He knew that nearly all his books served him as some kind of catharsis (as he said frequently of *The Primitive*); they were ways of clarifying his inner conflicts. But by the time of *Blind Man with a Pistol*, he was saying that the conflicts were unsolvable. Existence was designless, purposeless, anarchic. "Plan B"—which he got around to again in September 1968—resolves life's contradictions in utter destruction. There was no place for him to go.

Yet one of the reasons Himes seriously considered Spain as a permanent residence was that he thought of it as a place for him to rest. Perhaps if he owned a fixed place to live, he would be able to write without the tensions he had experienced all his life. "Run Man Run" was a title that might well describe his own journey through the years. Like the hero of that novel who flees the pathological cop, Himes fled his own inner demons, which from time to time he projected as white males—despite the fact that many of his dearest friends, such as Van Vechten, Malartic, Duhamel, or Targ, were white men. Because he could not afford to buy a house in France, where prices for real estate were astronomical, Spain looked to him reasonable. He was receiving a small but steady income from his books, and prospects were not unpromising. As it turned out, Himes guessed right. The publisher William Morrow in the United States bought *Blind Man* in June 1968 (though not without questioning some of its inconsistencies), and Formosa Productions paid him $9,000 in October for the film rights to *Run Man Run* (which, however, it never produced).

On their return from Morocco earlier in the year, Himes and Lesley had investigated sites and properties in the vicinity of Málaga, stopping off for a period in Sitges, a charming sea resort on the Costa Brava. They returned to Paris in mid-April, promising themselves they would resume their quest sometime later.

In the interim Himes carried on business with publishers, European and American, publicizing himself whenever appropriate. In May, on the occasion of the republication of several of his detective thrillers, he left for England. Panther Books had arranged interviews for him, notably, one for the *Sunday Times* (by "Atticus") and another for BBC night television. But the chief purpose of his English visit was to drive his car to the Jaguar factory in Coventry. Its performance needed correction, he said.

On his return to Paris, he could well have witnessed some of the more strident clashes between police and students that were then devastating the Latin Quarter. Lesley and one of her friends took food and supplies to students who were occupying the Sorbonne, but Himes did not really care much about what was going on. What did concern him was the well-being of his Jaguar. He had little to fear. He was living in the sixteenth *arrondissement,* far from the worst of the riots. At one point he drove the visiting Targs to Brussels when a transportation strike prevented them from leaving the country, but this proved the full extent of his involvement with the upheavals. Long after the riots subsided, he moved to Montparnasse. "We spent our summer on the outskirts of Paris," he wrote Williams afterward, "spending most of our time keeping away from the rioting students and workers."[2]

The couple's return to Spain in the fall gave them the opportunity to search further for a place they could call home. With some misgivings they finally decided on the province of Alicante. Himes had always regarded Spain as a somewhat backward country, believing, among other things, that it manufactured inferior cat food for Lesley's cat, Griot. But once the papers were signed, he tried to assume an upbeat outlook. "We have bought a couple of lots in a development called Pla del Mar," he wrote Roslyn Targ, "on the tip of the coast jutting off Cabo de la Nao . . . Our place is called the Cabo de Moraira. We hope to build our little Spanish house."[3]

Himes and Lesley outlined the design of their house. They hired contractors and workmen, and took up temporary residence in an old palace on Duque de Zaragoza in Alicante. Here Himes planned to follow up on "Plan B." He was well under way in September on "the wildest and most defiant of my Harlem series," he wrote to Williams,[4] though some months later he would say that it had come "unstuck."

Another thing Himes wanted to do in Spain was try again to get a divorce from Jean, in order to marry Lesley. The Spanish were not so tolerant of unmarried couples living together, he believed, and he hoped to avoid legal difficulties. Above all, he wanted to make sure Lesley's future was secure. He had drawn up a will and asked Williams to find out if a divorce were possible without his having to return to the States. He was not rushed, he said, and didn't want the divorce to become more expensive than he could afford. On the other hand, he needed to get as much as possible of his life in order, since he was now much less in control of himself than before. "I am getting to be an old man and . . . absent-minded and I am beginning to suffer from loss of memory."[5] Although more financially settled, he felt oddly out of touch with life, engaged in "petty affairs" relating to building his house and "trying to do business with the Spanish."

> I have just been vegetating, staying alive, trying to keep warm. My "seeming" success hasn't meant a damn thing to me, in fact news of it never reaches me. I have been passing time on the outskirts of life; I haven't been in communication with anyone in my sphere of interest whatsoever; Lesley and I have been mostly occupied with finding some place to stay . . . As for money, the main thing in this game is to keep putting books out. Even if you have to put out a lot of fillers—who knows but what they might become classics with time. Look at Hemingway.[6]

One of Himes's chief fears was that he was losing his ability to write—not simply in terms of making money but in terms of self-realization. For his own peace of mind he needed to get down to work, but he found the constant noisy Christmas celebrations in Alicante driving him to distraction. For respite, he and Lesley drove to Barcelona at the end of December to join the Targs, who were vacationing in Spain, and then drove with them to Perpignan for New Year's. He was back in Alicante at the start of 1969, but felt exasperated. The townspeople were clamoring for another fiesta. "Maybe I'll feel tolerant when they all go back to work," he wrote Williams, so that he would "be able to get some work done." But his antagonism was no whit abated a few weeks later. "The least said about the Spanish brother, the best," he wrote. "You know, I can't stand any of the white people on this earth whom I have yet met. But I am ashamed to say I can take the Americans the best of them, despite their challenging hypocrisy and violent idiocy." As regards his writing career, he now saw it coming to an end. He would write one more thriller. "Then if I get my autobiography written, it will be it."[7]

Himes's sour mood persisted in his other correspondence through 1969. He hated Dell's cover copy for *Run Man Run*, which described the heroine's "racket" as "singing, but men were her trade . . . she never discriminated." "Who are they talking about?" he exploded. "I wrote a book about a psychopathic white detective killing two brothers and trying to kill a third. And here they go putting down this shit about some black sister out of her mind."[8] He also disliked the *New York Times* "chickenshit review" of *Blind Man with a Pistol* and wrote the reviewer that he had missed the point: It was not about black vulnerability but rather the futility of unorganized violence. Unorganized violence, he reiterated to Williams "is stupid, pointless, and makes us more vulnerable than weak."[9]

Himes was unhappy with some of the books being written about black letters in the United States. As regards his own people, he did not view himself as a celebrant or champion of the race. He liked some blacks, but on the whole he felt the race needed improvement, and he could be especially critical of expatriate blacks. Nor did he have much use for the civil rights or Black Power movements in the United States, since he believed that by themselves they could not change things. Finally, he did not know what black American critics meant when they talked about "the black aesthetic" (i.e., criteria for judging works of art relevant to African American needs). The writers he liked best and modeled himself on—Faulkner, Dostoevsky, and Hemingway—were white. He had high praise for his white contemporary Mario Puzo, whose novel *The Godfather* he enjoyed immensely.[10]

Himes did encourage young black authors. He wrote Lynn Deming, an editor at Doubleday, that he regarded Ishmael Reed's *Yellow Black Radio Broke Down* as a "work of art" and Reed as a genius.[11] The writer he praised most, however, was Williams, whose *Sons of Darkness, Sons of Light* was "a compact, definitive story of the dilemma of the Black middle class."[12] Williams's novel about a secret government plan to intern black people, *The Man Who Cried I Am*, was "a blockbuster, a hydrogen bomb, it is by far the greatest book, the most compelling book ever written about THE SCENE—the scene, scene, man . . . a milestone in American literature, the only milestone (legitimate milestone) produced since *Native Son*."[13] Himes's own apocalyptic vision of a race war in "Plan B" made Williams's book appear to him especially plausible.

The two authors enjoyed a real rapport. When Williams asked if he could visit, Himes was delighted. Williams wanted to interview him for his new magazine *Amistad,* and Himes wanted Williams to read the manuscript of the first volume of his autobiography, *The Quality of Hurt.* The two men met during the first days of May 1969, at which time Himes spoke of events in his life that he later neglected to write about in his autobiography. Williams printed much of the interview in the first volume of *Amistad* under the title, "My Man Himes." A later interview that year with Hoyt Fuller, editor of *Black World,* Himes regarded as "stupid" and hardly intelligible.

The construction of the house was so painfully slow that the Himeses left for Paris in late May. Paris had less and less appeal for Chester. It was a city, he wrote Williams, "of exorbitant prices and French exaggeration," while the weather was "as cold as a polar bear's ass."[14] To add insult to injury, a truck struck his Jaguar, grazing the rear left fender. Later he left for more interviews in England, which he alluded to afterward as a "vivisection."[15] He was particularly upset about his failure to find an American publisher for his autobiography. "I'm getting to the age where I am more and more subject to depression," he wrote Williams. "And I find these whites so motherfucking hypocritical that at times I just feel like taking a gun and shooting them all."[16] In the end, he thought that only a white female editor would be willing to publish the work, because she would understand what it was like to be exploited and subjugated by white men. Himes was again identifying himself with injured white women, yet he seems never to have regarded his own treatment of women as exploitative. To his mind, only blacks possessed the tenderness to appreciate the "mother of the human race . . . The white man has the wealth, the glory, the power, the acclaim, but the black man has the love and the capacity for love of the female of the species. And that . . . is more important."[17]

Himes's views on racial and sexual relationships were not far removed from those expressed at that time by the African American sociologist Calvin Hernton or the essayist Eldridge Cleaver. Whether these views were sufficient reasons for his editors to reject his autobiography is doubtful. In parts the prose is slipshod, and important segments of his life, such as his prison years, are scarcely dealt with. At the same time too much space is given over to minor details, such as the personalities of his cars and pets. A reader for Hodder & Stoughton in London remarked insightfully that Himes's impressions of people and places were often very funny, but that in the middle distance his perspectives were less clear. "One finds too much of certain matters—particularly gossip about publishers and agents—and the mixture of total recall in some places with the skipping of large periods in others is difficult to adjust to."[18] Himes was at a loss. He was ready to make changes but did not know which ones were advisable. He could only argue irrelevantly that the story of Willa was true except for his omission of the fact that she was descended from John Hancock.[19]

Lighter moments for Himes that summer came with news that the shooting of *Cotton Comes to Harlem* had begun in the States. Samuel Goldwyn, Jr. sent him stills of the actors—Godfrey Cambridge, Raymond St. Jacques, and Redd Foxx—which Himes liked very much. Perhaps his Harlem series might now become as popular in the United States as it had been in Europe. In a Radio-Télé Luxembourg interview, Himes gratefully acknowledged Duhamel's help in getting started but said that *Blind Man with a Pistol* belonged in better company than the Série Noire. Beyond the mystery, there lay the "absurdity." It was a serious book. As things turned out, Gallimard agreed.

In late September Himes and Lesley affixed some furnishings to a rack atop their car and drove back to Moraira. Himes really looked forward now to living in Casa Griot, so named after Lesley's cat. To their horror, they found their villa far from finished and "what had already been done looked like an imbecile child playing with mud."[20] Himes demanded that the workmen correct their mistakes, which included changing the plumbing, installing new ventilation, and reconstructing a front wall. The furnishings they had brought with them from Paris could not yet be put in the house, so they rented a ninth-floor apartment in a towerlike building nearby, where Chester hoped to get on with the second volume of his autobiography. The concierge was the only other resident in the building, and in the months that followed Himes used to complain to him about the howling winds and frequent elevator breakdowns. It was, he wrote Williams, "a Spanish nightmare." By mid-December, at his wit's end with the inadequate pace and skill of the workers, he prepared to go to court. He feared losing both the house and his money.

In January he was awarded some kind of financial rebate, and by the start of March 1970 he and Lesley at last found themselves comfortably ensconced in their new home. Himes had his own little studio, while a high fence surrounding their property kept in the marauding Griot. As for the village, he wrote, it was remote and dull and inhabited by "grubbing vegetating foreigners," but at least he had his radio and a German-made television set, which made life somewhat more tolerable.[21] Nonetheless, nostalgia for the Spain he had once known left him melancholy: "Spain can smell sweet; it used to smell that way to me too fifteen years ago in Mallorca, but lately I have only smelled the rotten odor of cauliflower."[22] If present-day Spain failed him, so did one of his friends. Van Peebles's musical play *Watermelon Man* was "a direct steal of an old short story of mine he once read, called 'The Ghost of Rufus Jones,'" he wrote Williams.[23] But other news from America was encouraging. Goldwyn had written him that the film was completed and would open soon. Himes considered going to the United States for a viewing but then changed his mind.

Himes and Lesley welcomed the opportunity to escape their isolation when they drove to Nice in May to join the Targs, who were attending a book fair. It was a lavish few days. They stayed in grand style at the Hôtel Rühl and then drove to Monte Carlo and afterward to Saint-Tropez, which by now had become the height of fashion. They went on to Aix and Arles and finally back again to Moraira. The Targs were the Himeses' first American visitors in their new home.

The couple had scarcely returned when Himes received a call from Gallimard to come to Paris in June for press and television interviews on the occasion of the publication of *L'Aveugle au pistolet* (the French title of *Blind Man with a Pistol*). As he had hoped, his book was not categorized simply as another police thriller, but instead appeared in Gallimard's more prestigious Du Monde Entier literary collection. After Paris, Himes would be expected to fly to Hamburg for more interviews. But he was tired, he said, and irritable, and expressed perhaps feigned bitterness. All "fares and expenses paid—and they think they're doing me a *favor* . . . the press is beginning to give me the 'treatment,' TV in France, TV in Germany, *Life* Mag butter-up and all that crap—they seem to think they've found themselves another 'good nigger,' but I got news for them."[24] He adopted the same tone in his *Amistad* interview with Williams: "Time to quit trying to please whitey." Perhaps, but Himes was not so fed up with the publicity that he refused to cooperate. One good reason may have been Doubleday's offer of a $10,000 advance for the first volume of his autobiography, *The Quality of Hurt*. "Beggars can't be choosers," he wrote Williams, hinting as well that Doubleday was the only publisher unafraid of a lawsuit by Willa.[25] Doubleday's offer did little, however, to lessen his hostility toward publishers, whom he once described to Williams as "lower middle-class, pretentious, indescribably ignorant whiteys."[26]

Yet when *Le Monde des livres* dedicated its center spread to Himes—a special feature normally reserved for major authors and important issues— he was undeniably proud. The event was also taken seriously in Spain and elsewhere, as he wrote to Michel Fabre, "I find I have suddenly become a celebrity in the region."[27] David Jenkins, an assistant editor of *Nova* magazine, came all the way from London to interview him. An unpublished draft of the second volume of his autobiography sums up his feelings: "I became famous in a *petit* kind of way. But that was my life. I had made it."[28]

Himes hoped that the attention lavished on him in Europe would awaken the American critical establishment. But celebrity in his native land did not come. Among blacks he had his aficionados, such as Williams and Reed, but also his detractors. Ernest Kaiser, the curator of the Schomburg Collection in New York, believed that Himes's detective series degraded Negroes and the Harlem community.[29] Himes himself was aware of how easily his works could be misinterpreted. When he went to New York the following August for the premiere of *Cotton Comes to Harlem,* he remarked to *Black News* that what he had seen was a "minstrel show." He claimed that from the start his thrillers were designed for something more than entertainment. Although he had often spoken of the haphazard circumstances under which he had begun writing detective fiction, he now discerned serious intentions. "From the beginning," he said, "my purpose was to demonstrate the absurdity of racism in black behavior as well as white behavior and more than anything else to show the result, the end product." Thus *Blind Man with a Pistol* was "the zenith of absurdity" and would one day "be considered the greatest contribution made to literature by a black American."[30]

Back in France in September 1970, Himes expressed more sympathy toward young black writers as well as a kind of cultural nationalism. On the occasion of the publication of Reed's *19 Necromancers from Now,* Himes wrote Reed, "Keep it up and we will have a literature all of our own which I believe will transcend all the others that have been put down."[31] At the same time he had to concede that the race of an author was not necessarily essential in portraying black life. He wrote Roslyn Targ: "I think the feeling of black writers toward Shane Stevens is mostly envy and the belief he is poaching in their field, 'the Black Experience,' and doing it better than they themselves. It is a common enough emotion, and one to be ignored. But I was trying to get along with the black writers when I was in New York and saw no reason to antagonize them."[32]

Chester himself produced very little during the year. He may have tinkered with "Plan B," but if so he was unhappy with the results. He sent

Roslyn Targ a short story called "Pork Chop Paradise"—in fact, a section of his unfinished "Plan B"—for possible publication. He also wrote a sketch called "Two Characters" about a couple of detectives who closely resembled Grave Digger and Coffin Ed. One is an extrovert with enormous vitality and sex appeal who treats "black and white women alike, respectfully and goodhumoredly . . . flamboyant dresser but tasteful." Like Himes's brother Joseph, he has an advanced degree in sociology. At one time he flirted with the Black Muslims but quit "when he discovered he didn't hate white people because they were white and didn't love them for that reason either." He does think that black nationalism is preferable to the passive acceptance of the white man's bounty.

Himes describes this character's opponent as his opposite. Known as King Kong in Harlem, he is sadistic, feared and hated. Gorillalike in build, mean, hypocritical, and arrogant, he is sexually "repressed and a stern Puritan with a loud condemnation of sin, but secretly envious." After twenty years in the force, he has "a roving night assignment to keep order in the streets . . . *Good criminals are dead criminals; kill first and live last,* are his tenets." He at first despises his partner, but when the partner is hurt, he pities him because he "knows the quality of hurt is part of the black experience." Roslyn responded that the sketches possessed excellent potential for a television series; the two men were opposites, but it was easy to see how they would clash and yet work together. Himes, however, did not pursue this concept, and the pieces are probably notable mainly as Himes's images of his divided self: guilt-ridden, idealized, fantasied, and down-to-earth.

Himes also sent his agent the eighty-page fictionalized version of his liaison with Regine; he hoped to include "Engaged" in a new collection of stories he would submit to Doubleday. "I confess this story moves me tremendously although obviously Lesley hates it," he wrote Roslyn. "I think it is as good a story on the 'Black Experience' as ever written and I believe in it."[33] Regine may have been confined to his fiction (for the time being, at least), but he was determined that his affair with Willa be recorded in detail in the autobiography. He could not, though, overcome the objections of his editor at Doubleday, a black woman named Helen Jackson, who told him she wanted the section on Willa's sexual relationship with her husband deleted for fear of a lawsuit. Himes reluctantly agreed but thought Jackson's other suggested revisions "high handed."

Physically, Himes was feeling miserable. His speech was further slurred by the second stroke he had suffered in Paris in 1964, and he spoke of himself as being old and tired. At the British-American Hospital in Madrid he was told that three of the vertebrae in his lower spine were grinding together, which doubtless contributed to his sour disposition. There were more fits of rage. He professed now to see racism everywhere, especially among Spaniards, whom he again claimed to despise. When he thought about his work, he had mood swings. One day he would assure himself he was a great writer; on another he feared for his reputation. He was convinced most people, white and black, did not like him, and he used to say he reciprocated their feelings. Regardless, he did have many friends; what he discounted about himself was that despite his real and imagined enemies, he could be generous and witty and quite the gentleman, especially in the presence of women.

Himes was constantly fearful of being misunderstood. When William Weatherby of Praeger publishing house proposed writing a book about him, he felt he would be unable to cooperate. "I am extremely wary of people's rationalizations, justifications, expediency, 'reality'," he wrote Roslyn.[34] He claimed that most of his serious conversations ended in his views being distorted or "considered unrealistic, demanding, intolerant, unfair, uninformed and many other derogatory appellations." The main reason was his position on race; he refused to glorify blacks or categorize them as different from other groups.

> I made a great effort to term my so-called "detective" stories by their true description, "domestic" stories. I see all manner of crime and vice an integral factor of the domestic life of any ghetto. Ghetto people, as a way of life, kill, steal, lie, cheat and use any and all means (except work, which is most often denied them) to obtain means, right suspected wrongs, nurture their emotions, afford sex fulfillment or perversions, provide self-respect or at least self-pride, to buy excitement, titillation, leisure and even peace of mind. I can go on like this forever. I believe that all people everywhere (if they are sane) know what they are doing. This is the belief with which practically no one agrees.

He felt intellectually depleted, and then there were ideological reasons:

> I would also want for some one to write [my biography] who has no personal axe to grind and will not use me to present his own opinions. I know it is very difficult to find an impartial writer . . . I do not think that southern white mentality could—or would—follow the intricacies of my thinking—go far enough for me; and I think the modern intellectual cultural black would go too far. I would like to be presented just as I am, regardless of who likes or dislikes the presentation.[35]

Himes detested biographers, and his rancor toward America was also hardening. When the Internal Revenue Service asked questions regarding his income, he wrote his attorney, "I have long been contemplating giving up my United States citizenship and several nations have assured me of their welcome." The reason he had not done so, he said, was that he would "dislike the ensuing publicity."[36] A foreword that he prepared, but later discarded, for his autobiography recalls bitter American memories:

> America hurt me terribly whether rightly or wrongly is beside the point. When I fought back through writing, it decided to kill me, whether because I was an unregenerate ex-convict who refused to wear sackcloth and ashes, a "Negro" who refused to accept the Negro Problem as my own, a "nigger" who would not conform to the existence prescribed for niggers, or a black man who pitied a white woman, I will never know. I do know that when America kills a nigger, it expects him to remain dead. But I didn't know I was dead. I still had hope. I still believed in the devil.[37]

The anger Himes felt about America was matched by his feelings about publishers, especially those in France and Holland who, he claimed, were cheating him. Perhaps American publishers stole as well, but if "I didn't get any bread from the States, I'd starve."[38] Still, he was not exactly happy with his business in the States. When finally he signed a contract with Doubleday in March 1971 for a collection of his stories, he was told there would be a further delay in the publication of his autobiography, lest Willa and possibly Regine should sue for invasion of privacy. Himes agreed to further changes in the text, masking their names: Willa would become Alva, and Regine, Marlene. Admonitions about lawsuits may also have prompted Himes to warn the critic Michel Fabre of a similar fate. Fabre had sent Himes his essay on *A Case of Rape*, suggesting the identity of the people his characters were patterned on. Himes answered: "I must object to your using the real names of living people in your article which in the U.S. constitutes an invasion of privacy and is actionable."[39] Fabre qualified his identification of characters in a revised article, softening Himes's response: "Of course it is evident that the characterizations of many real, living people are apparent in all of my fiction (as is perhaps true of all novelists) but I dare not admit it."[40]

The start of 1972 saw Himes writing frantic letters to his editor, Helen Jackson, requesting prepublication copies of *The Quality of Hurt*. He feared that further emendations would make the account of his life too palatable to readers. Although he refused to pander, he did what he could to promote the book, sending Jackson photographs for the television program *Camera Three*. Another fear was being "thrown to the wolves"—that is, being exposed to the criticism of black intellectuals. He warned Jackson: "I detest talking of writers and aspiring writers, be they black or white and I do not believe there are generations which have 'followed' me in the U.S. where the communications media completely control what the people think."[41] In all likelihood he was reacting to warnings from Williams and Reed that black feminists were especially hostile to black men who marry white women. "This attitude is worse today than it's ever been," Williams wrote him, "it's driven several people, black men and their white wives out of New York. When the sisters write for the *Times* or *Black World,* it's the same old shit, even from the most intelligent of them."[42]

Himes also felt anxious about his publisher Doubleday, which he re-called had treated him abominably when *Hollers* was first issued in 1945. Now publishers "throw the black writers to the black wolves or wolverines," he wrote Roslyn Targ. On publication he would stay in New York only a few days and return to Europe, "where at least I don't have the black racists to contend with." By "black racists" he meant a black "establishment" whose press, he said, never had any kind words for him or praise for Wright during his lifetime.[43] "I cannot see any purpose served by my participation in Doubleday's plan of exposing me to American blacks. Some black woman (or even man) is subject to stick a knife in my back . . . I have had a long and bitter relationship with my fellow blacks and if I do not participate, do not be surprised."[44]

Himes also worried about the physical image he would project. Always sensitive about his appearance, he feared his deteriorating health had made him unattractive and wrote as much to Jackson. He had a tendency to hysterical laughter, he said, and his illness had affected his speech and leg movements. Jackson reassured him, and he and Lesley flew to New York in February 1972.

Himes's anxieties were unfounded. Everywhere he went he was greeted warmly, and he even managed to spend a few happy days with his brothers in North Carolina—the first time all three had been together since their mother's funeral long ago in 1945. He acquitted himself well in his New York television appearances. Indeed, he was a charming interview subject for both television and the print media. This was especially true of one interview, conducted by the novelist Charles Wright for the *Village Voice.* In addition, Himes attended a reception with other black writers at the Carnegie Endowment for International Peace, where he gave a brief speech. Nor was he attacked by "black wolverines." A television exchange with the poet Nikki Giovanni revealed him as spirited and clearly enjoying himself. Giovanni seemed to like him, while Himes carried on about what he liked about women.

Back in Spain, Himes wrote Reed that he found the black American literary scene stimulating, but that he was anxious now to get back to the second volume of his autobiography.[45] He was sorry he was unable to stay up with "all the gang" of younger writers he had been introduced to (Clarence Major, Cecil Brown, Steve Canon, and Al Young, among others), but he no longer had the energy. He had received an issue of *Black World*, he told Reed, and hoped Reed's in-depth review of *The Quality of Hurt* would wipe out the bad impression given by Fuller's "stupid interview."[46] Himes wrote in a similar vein to Roslyn, telling how much he missed the vitality of New York, especially since he now had to face the dreary "routine" of life in Spain. For the moment at least, he yearned again for his native country.

But life in Spain was not that bad. Himes's daily routine was enlivened by visits from journalists, critics, and graduate students who wanted to interview him. One young man, the Cameroon-born Ambroise Kom, was especially welcome, but only after Himes realized that a black fellow he had seen walking down the street was not his expected African visitor. Himes had invited the stranger to his house for lunch before realizing his mistake. Another of Himes's visitors was the novelist Ronald Fair, who came with his wife in mid-April. Himes thought Fair too wrapped up in himself and too confident of "making it" in the United States. On April 23 Himes suffered another slight stroke, which took him back to the British-American Hospital in Madrid. However, he had not forgotten his encounter with Fair. A few months later he wrote, "I think he is a damn good writer, but I'm sorry to say he is also a nut."[47]

Himes's irritability reached out even to his good friend Williams, whom he believed copyrighted one of his essays for an anthology Williams was editing, in order to collect its royalties. As Williams tells it, he took out the copyright to protect Himes's material. Himes did not accuse Williams to his face but rather lavished praise on his most recent novel, *Captain Blackman*: "[This] novel makes you one of the most unbiased and bravest novelists of this or of any time."[48] Still, when Williams heard of Himes's reaction to the copyrighted essay, he was infuriated, and their correspondence ceased.

Himes's moodiness was aggravated by his declining health, which he hated to be reminded of. His arthritis was worse, and he had so much back pain that he had to use a cane to get around. When the ex-wife of his old Vermont friend Bill Smith came to Moraira, she told friends about Himes's condition, causing Himes to explode in anger. He was likewise incensed— not without reason—when he read in *Variety* that Anthony Quinn had been asked to play the role of the Haitian king Henri Christophe in a forthcoming film. Himes wrote an outraged letter to the *New York Times* Drama Section on June 14: "The idea is not only sacrilege, but arrogant stupidity . . . Why offend an indisputable large black audience . . . whose basic interest in this historic figure is that he was black?" Himes sent the letter on the same day he entered the American Hospital in Neuilly for further observations.

This time the hospital stay lasted only three days, after which Himes drove Lesley to Barcelona where he put his new car, a Fiat, on a ship headed for Genoa. (By now he felt physically incapable of driving the larger, wider Jaguar.) The couple stopped in Turin to get their new car "nationalized" and then toured bits of Italy and France, arriving in July in Paris where they lived for a month in a flat on rue des Francs-Bourgeois. There on August 9 Griot died.

Himes was devastated. He insisted on having the cat buried at the Cimetière des Animaux and grieved as he would have for a child. When a month later Madame Marabini, a Paris bookstore owner, organized an exhibition of photographs of celebrated writers' pets, Himes thanked her for the invitation and enclosed two photos of Griot. He was still thinking of his cat several months later in a letter from Spain. "It's lonely without Griot. He was such a snob. He'd treat these old retired racists like so much shit which is more than I can do no matter how much I want to."[49]

During much of the latter part of 1972, Himes was putting together a second volume of short stories—digging up ancient pieces he had written for *Coronet* and *Esquire*—and writing as much as he could of the second volume of his autobiography. Since April he had been complaining of worsening arthritis, stomach pains, and hernia, but treatment at the American Hospital in Paris in May enabled him to walk again without a cane. In September he went to London for business relating to his autobiography and while there consulted several English specialists, who concluded they could do nothing more about his other complaints. Short holidays with Lesley in Valencia and Venice toward the end of the year helped somewhat, but on the whole he felt depressed. The project closest to his heart, he wrote Reed, was the completion of his autobiography. Otherwise "life in general seems to have gone to hell."[50]

From time to time Himes's spirits picked up. The great joy of Christmas 1972 was a five-day visit from his brother Joseph and his wife Estelle. And on January 12, 1973, Himes acquired a "new baby": a six-month-old Siamese cat, "Deros Cantabile," that Lesley had ordered from England. Himes met the plane at Alicante to receive her. He was also happy to receive from Duhamel a copy of his autobiography, *Une vie de toutes les couleurs*. Duhamel thanked Himes for the kind words he had written about him, and Himes wrote back that he would be saying more good things about their relationship in his next volume. "It is unique in the history of writing and should be fascinating for Americans obsessed with the relationships between blacks and whites."[51]

There was also bad news. Himes learned that the Coffin Ed–Grave Digger series Duhamel had so successfully promoted as fiction in France was not translating profitably into American movies. *Come Back Charleston Blue,* Goldwyn's second attempt at the Harlem series, was reported to be losing nearly $2 million, which led Himes to believe that any future Harlem films would be more effective if he were to kill off one of his cops and concentrate on a single hero—an idea that Goldwyn had suggested some years before. The failure of *Charleston Blue* tempted Himes to try a script on his own, this time based on his 1959 novel *Run Man Run.* His idea was interesting. "What I want to do," he wrote Roslyn Targ,

> is to take the murders from the beginning and put them back on the denouement so the reader knows only what happened from the accounts of Jimmy and The Detective. I do not want to show The Detective actually committing a crime until the end so all the reader has to go by is Jimmy's account, the reader has a free choice to believe Jimmy or not . . . The essential point is uncertainty—mystery, no one should know positively that The Detective is the murderer until the denouement.[52]

He tried writing the script, but found it difficult to press the typewriter keys. Worse still, he would forget what he had written—which did little to moderate his tantrums.

In the spring of 1973 Himes flew to Stuttgart as guest speaker at a dinner for Black Literature Week, organized by the Stuttgart branch of the NAACP. He decided he would read a slightly enlarged version of an introduction he had written for Reed's anthology, *Yardbird Reader.* Earlier he had told Reed he did not know what to say, that he could hardly think at all and that the world was going too fast for him. The gist of his speech was that black Americans have been made into a super race, the inadvertent result of their oppression.

> We were made by torture, death, rape, punishment—you name it, we've suffered it—by all the harsh and subtle impacts of a crushing injustice. Fear taught us how to read the white man's mind, how to think faster, how to anticipate all his dangerous intentions and threatening actions. Why wouldn't we be more intelligent, inventive, creative, intuitive? We had to keep alive without friends or protectors, without wealth, arms or armor. We had to do it with our wit, our skin, our determination. In some instances we had to be holier than the white man's God, in others more depraved than the white man's lust.[53]

Implicit in much of Himes's thinking was that by transcending his suffering, he too had attained a clearer perception of life—an ironic consequence of persecution. As before, he saw *The Primitive* as his watershed book: "I consider *The Primitive* the book that opened my mind to the utter absurdity of racism and made it possible for me to write nine detective type stories," he told the French professor Claude Julien.[54] When he later signed a contract with Chatham Bookseller for the reprinting of eight of his novels, he insisted that *The Primitive* be included. Moreover, he wanted an unexpurgated edition and tried to get the original typescript from the Beinecke Library at Yale as a substitute for the New American Library edition. As it happened, the Yale version was not complete, and only Malartic could provide him with the original, which he had used for the French translation. Himes agreed to write an introduction for Chatham, but what he said about the book's genesis is erroneous. He asserted that he wrote it almost as an act of revenge, because a book he had written with a white woman was rejected by American publishers who resented its biracial authorship while he was enjoying the woman sexually. In fact, Himes had begun his book long before he worked with Willa on her novel, and none of the prospective publishers had known he was living with her. Nor is it likely that they would have cared. He was correct, however, in relating the catharsis that *The Primitive* provided him.[55] In effect, he elaborated on what he told Claude Julien: "Writing this book not only purged me but made me strong. Forever afterwards I have been shocked by the absurdity of racism. How more absurd could two people be than me and my white woman? My mind became free and highly creative and in the following eight years I wrote twelve books on the absurdity of racism and its effects on both black and white people."[56]

Himes went on to say that his manuscript caused "furious controversies" at New American Library offices, resulting in fist fights among the white editors. Finally, "five editors employing different colored ink went through it with a fine-tooth comb, deleting what was thought to be objectionable."[57] How accurate this is cannot be ascertained. Unfortunately, Chatham Bookseller closed its doors in the fall of 1973, and Himes's novel was not printed in its unexpurgated form.

Why would Himes want to distort the account of the writing of this book—not to mention so many of his others? In the main his detective books, as we have seen, were written under economic stress and contractual obligations rather than for ideological or social purposes. He did not even think of them initially as great literary works but rather as potboilers or "fillers" until he could get around to writing more serious fiction. Paradoxically, their real literary strength may lie in the fact that Himes did not feel constrained by the notion that he was writing "literature." The fact that racism served as an unconscious given in the stuff of his entertainments made the "absurdity" all the more egregious. Himes continued to say contradictory things about his other works as well. One late instance occurred in September 1973, when he told Professor Julien that his autobiographical *Third Generation* was the "unvarnished truth of my life" (with the exception of the last chapter), although some years before, as we have seen, he had told Williams that it was a "dishonest" novel. Even earlier, he had spoken of it to Richard Wright as a chiefly true account of his life.[58]

The kindest interpretation of these contradictions is that Himes's memory did him a disservice. Perhaps the unkindest view is that he remained deeply insecure about his place in letters and about what role he should play, as an African American author, in America's race struggles—and so reworked the past to portray his books as fighters in the conflict. Both views may have some validity. Himes did genuinely believe that America was incorrigibly racist—and didn't he have the scars to prove it? Further evidence beyond newspaper accounts, he assured himself, was how American editors and publishers continued to resist the terrible truths he persisted in telling.

Curiously, the further removed Himes was from overt racism, the more obsessed he became, professing to see prejudice in the most innocuous behavior. Why should he have been more aware of racism at this late point than before? He was himself imbued with the outlook and attitudes of his southern-born parents. His identity had been shaped by his own searing American experiences. He simply could not imagine a changed America in form or substance, although he was wise enough to recognize from time to time that he too often unconsciously shared the very racism he deplored. Then too he was a writer who had emerged from the socially committed 1930s and 1940s, a time when it was believed that great literature should convey a moral and social message—and Himes's message was the cruelty, the destructiveness, the absurdity of black oppression. These messages may be found in all his books, but his best writings transcend message to express a comic exuberance, a vitality, a richness of black life that all the injustices and dreadful miseries he records cannot overcome. As Malartic wrote him on reading *The Primitive*, the novel was not about race, but about what he and every frustrated artist feels in the course of his lifetime. To try to disentangle the various aspects of Himes—the writer of letters, the autobiographer, the novelist, the son, the friend, the lover, the brother, the husband—from his writings would be fruitless. They are all Himes in their bewildering welter of contradictions.

It was now becoming more and more clear to Himes that his fiction-writing career was ending. Understandably, he wanted to make sure that his work would be read correctly. He told correspondents that he would go anywhere (Lagos, for example, or Rio de Janeiro) to write and read and tell about his works. He used to rage when he thought booksellers were marketing his books as if they were mere trashy entertainments. At the moment he was particularly incensed with Spanish publishers, who he believed were as racist as the French. His anger embraced the entire Spanish nation. "I think the basic thing wrong with me is Spain," he wrote Roslyn Targ. "It's such a miserable, grabbing ignorant country and it is becoming very expensive." He did not like the jacket art of his books. "The Spanish make blacks look like they have never looked on land or sea . . . they got the moors on their mind."[59] And again he wrote: "The Spanish have treated me abominably: they have tried to make me invisible and they have cheated me in every way . . . Most Europeans do the same but the Spanish do it in a way that fills me with contempt."[60] His antagonism toward the Spanish was, in part at least, self-inflicted. He had never learned, or even tried to learn, to speak Spanish, any more than he had tried to learn French during his Paris years. Lesley, who had taken lessons years before, quite enjoyed their circumstances, which further annoyed Himes. "Everyone speaks to Lesley and ignores me as though I don't exist," he complained.[61]

Despite his complaints, Himes was not so utterly out of sorts that he did not wish to travel. In mid-December 1973 he and Lesley flew to New York to visit his brother Edward, who had become the executive secretary of the Service Workers Union. Edward still lived in Harlem and told Chester that his sense of Harlem life rang true. He especially liked *Run Man Run*. Himes's spirits picked up considerably. Then he and Lesley flew to Greensboro, North Carolina, to stay with Joseph and Estelle until the end of the year. Their visit to the United States, they promised each other, was strictly for family, and they would transact no business whatsoever while they were there.

# 13

# WHAT DID I DO?

*What Did I Do?—White American men have never liked me and I
must confess I've always felt ill at ease with white American men. I
can communicate with some white American women, but the men
never . . . I feel uncomfortable in the presence of all the white men
I ever meet unless we are combatants and then for me the situation
is normal and I am comfortable even though I might be frightened.
I suppose this is the reason white American males have never liked
me; I have never liked them. Many people (white) interpret this as a
desire to be white. Nonsense. I'm beautiful, intelligent, imaginative,
heterosexual, and brave. I have no desire to be either white or black.
My tastes in women are the same; I like white white women and
black black women.*

Chester Himes, unpublished manuscript, Amistad

AFTER HIS RETURN TO SPAIN Himes at last, in February 1974, began working
steadily on the second volume of his autobiography. The sections about
Regine he had written out in detail years before, but now his memory
sometimes failed, and he would ask Lesley to collaborate with him on writing
about events they had experienced together. He also obtained copies of his
correspondence with Van Vechten from the Yale University Library, which he
quoted verbatim, rarely suppressing negative comments about living persons
or erasing details that showed him behaving badly. In addition he contacted
friends and acquaintances for other kinds of information. To Michel Fabre he
wrote, "I am sure I will need your help from time to time," and asked about

the identity of a French writer he had once met who had written a book on Devil's Island.[1] He thanked Yves Malartic for his reminiscences and asked Marcel Duhamel to send him the exact texts of complimentary quotes about him from Jean Cocteau, Jean Giono, Jean Cau, and others.[2] He decided to incorporate the unpublished "Regina" into his memoirs, claiming that the second book about his life would be as true as he could remember it. As regards America, he had only hostile thoughts and told Roslyn Targ that the best times of his life were lived in France.[3]

Among several of his opening drafts, one began with the title "How Much Desire" and a quotation from Dante: "Alas! how many pleasant thoughts, how much desire / Conducted these unto the dolorous pass."

Another version began with Himes taking stock of his literary achievements:

> I suppose I owe my accomplishment as much to French condescension as to American racism for I despised them both with equal intensity. And I want to say right now that I consider my Harlem detective story (or domestic story) series—my nine consecutive books with a Harlem background (eight of which feature Grave Digger Jones and Coffin Ed Johnson) as a major contribution to the literature of the world, perhaps the only major contribution made by an American black writer and equalled by only a few Americans.[4]

Irony or a sense of humor seems to have eluded him. He was so utterly convinced of the value of his detective stories that he surely would have denied any imputation of delusions of grandeur.

> So I do not tell the story of the late years of my life with any degree of apology or shame but with pride and absolute belief. No doubt the above statement is going to make a good many American whites critical if not outright furious. But I base my conclusions on the judgments of world literature and I do not give a damn what any particular faction thinks. I am too old and too near death to be concerned with any level of American opinion and now the only thing I really and truly hate is old age.[5]

More than old age, Himes hated his infirmities, but "old age" provided a nice transition from volume one:

> When I was young and beautiful my greatest drawback was my pity for women. I hated to say goodbye to a woman I had loved. Even more than my lack of money and my hatred of American racism and fury at French condescension . . . was my loss of Alva. I missed her in body and soul.[6]

For Himes, his career as a writer really hinged on his remaining in Europe. Alva, however, chose to live in America. The title of another of his aborted attempts was called "I Was Scared But I Couldn't Go Home."

There is the feeling among Americans that only the overcoming of adversity
makes a black man worthy. I find that so absurd that it boggles my mind;
it clutches me in a vise of satire from which is squeezed buffoonery and
pornography . . . Therefore I ask my reader to forgive these offences in
the recounting of my later years . . . I'm goddam certain if I had had no
adversity in my life I'd be a damn sight more worthy than I am. Nobody but
me will ever know how great a writer I could have been had it not been for
the adversity.[7]

Gradually, "absurdity" tends to rival, if not displace, the theme of "hurt"
that was so prevalent in volume one. Another draft is called "I Couldn't Go
Home Because Home Wasn't There No More." It begins: "Shortly after the
first of 1955 . . . I was so lonely and depressed I decided to go to London where
I would not feel like a misfit. I had begun a new novel titled 'Drop Dead'
which I was dedicating to the entire publishing fraternity about a writer who
went around killing editors."[8] Of course, he was writing no such book. The
fiction he had been working on at the time, "The Pink Dress," dealt with
Willa, but he was now injecting surrealistic touches, retrospective fantasies
of revenge.

At a later stage, he jotted down a few lines with which he ended his
book: "That's my life for all its inconsistencies, its comedies, its humiliations,
its hurts, its ecstasies, its triumphs, its drama and its absurdities. It's funny,
really, all you got to do is to get the handle to the joke."[9]

Himes had used the phrase about "getting the handle to the joke"
once before, in a letter to Carl Van Vechten to make a case for the literary
presentation of the Negro as funny, rather than as victimized. But this
propitious start, heralding a change in mood from hurt to absurdity, from
self-pity and anger to laughter, petered out. He stopped for awhile and began
dabbling with his collections of short stories. He also wanted Doubleday to
print a collection of his mystery fiction, and in May he suggested to Stewart
Richardson, his new fiction editor, that the entire series—a total of 1,350
pages—be published in one or two volumes. They were no longer "fillers"
but classics. "My Harlem detective stories featuring Grave Digger Jones and
Coffin Ed Johnson [are] my biggest contribution to literature. I have been
brainwashed into thinking otherwise by American book reviewers, which I
know now and have always known was a mistake." These books, he added,
"contain the best of my writing and the best of my thinking and I am willing
to stake my reputation on them."[10]

Finally, Himes returned slowly and painstakingly to the second volume
of his autobiography, now titled "My Life of Absurdity." Not only was his life,

and the lives of all black Americans, absurd, but "absurdity" was central to his detective stories. "I think my Harlem stories will have a place in literature because they *are* absurd," he wrote one correspondent.[11]

All the while Himes's health was in rapid decline. The arthritis in his hip crippled him again, and even the physical effort of typing often seemed insurmountable. He drove Lesley to driving school in hopes that she would soon be able to replace him at the wheel, but this too was becoming burdensome. In late May 1974 Himes made his will and then entered the University College Hospital in London for operations on his prostate and a hernia. When oxygen failed to reach the left side of his brain, he fell into a coma. The consequence was gradually deteriorating mobility of his arms and legs. A month later he was being treated in a Spanish clinic for hemorrhages. Despite the "success" of the London procedures, he could no longer stand straight, and further prostate inflammations caused him more suffering. In September he returned to the Spanish clinic and then to the American Hospital in Paris, where other problems with his prostate were discovered.

Whatever the physical damage, Himes's illnesses that year seemed to have mellowed him. He begged the Malartics to visit him in the fall and wrote Roslyn Targ to ask her pardon for his many blunders with publishers: "I have never told anyone but for two nights I was in an intensive care ward and the one thing that kept me alive was the thought of the new will . . . I beg forgiveness for all my bad behavior and lack of thought."[12]

Back in Moraira in late October, Himes told himself he was well on the way to recovery. All he needed were injections for a couple of years, and he'd be cured. He simply wanted to live long enough to get his autobiography written.[13]

Although Doubleday offered Himes a mere $3,000 advance on his second volume, he accepted because he already owed the company more than $1,000 and in any event was not sure he would live long enough to finish the book. He wanted to finish it, he told Roslyn, not simply for the money but because he wanted his point of view known before other people began writing about his life "with great ignorance." He added that he was greatly surprised that no American critic had noted Faulkner's influence on his writing.[14]

Although Roslyn was now his principal correspondent, Himes kept up a busy letter-writing routine to retain contacts he felt essential. As for the autobiography, he tried to write at least about "a page a day,"[15] but by the end of the year progress all but stopped. On December 4, 1974, he wrote an anxious letter to Roslyn: "I am trying desperately to get down the first draft of my autobiography while my health still holds up and my memory is still sound. I hope of course to do it all." Momentarily, he was tempted to forsake the absurdity theme to search his soul for guilt. "As I write my autobiography I recall what an unmitigated pig I was towards most women, most of whom I left out of here or it would turn into a cat house. But the good thing is that I wrote. I didn't care who it hurt, who it inconvenienced, who it crippled; I was such a detestable person it makes me sick to write about myself, so I tone everything down."[16]

Toward the start of spring 1975, Himes managed to complete a version of *My Life of Absurdity*. Health permitting, he would type away with two fingers in his studio while in another room Lesley retyped his very messy drafts. Lesley wrote Roslyn that it was "the most important thing in life to him now and I think it gives him incentive to get through this difficult time . . . Perhaps he will be able to relax when summer comes."[17]

Indeed, Himes's health was so poor that he completed the manuscript only by dint of will and discipline: "I can scarcely walk and my legs are going paralyzed; some days I can't spell and other days I can't remember," he wrote Roslyn. He felt "like an exile in this isolated miserable part of Spain," adding that he realized that the draft outline of his autobiography was badly written, but hoped the second draft would be an improvement.

With death ever present in his mind, Himes feared that Jean in America might inherit his money. Since she had not granted him a divorce, he could not be sure what claim she might have on his estate. For this reason he asked that all his royalties be sent to Spain instead of to Paris, where Jean might possibly be able to draw from his French Morgan Guaranty account.[18] Meanwhile, he tried to keep up as much of a normal life as he could. In late April he returned the text of "The End of a Primitive" to Chatham, quite happy with its editing. He also sent to the editor of Wildwood House in London a blurb praising *Black Zion*, by the young British historian David Jenkins, as "the best book ever written about the effects of North American and West African slaves and their descendants."[19] He even managed to travel. In late July he and Lesley visited his cousin Robert Thomas, who was employed at the U.S. Embassy in Lisbon, but a few weeks later they returned to Paris, where Himes had a checkup at the American Hospital and learned that his blood pressure was down. Later in the fall he welcomed a succession of visitors, among them the painters Jean Miotte and Herb Gentry. Himes's near surreal fictional images made him an especially intriguing companion for visual artists.

In the meantime, Larry Jordan, Himes's new editor at Doubleday, was busy editing the draft of *Absurdity* for publication. Himes wrote him: "I am getting nervous . . . particularly concerned that my health will give out before I am finished with the book . . . Please write some information, my nerves are near screaming."[20] He was still worried about the fate of his money and now wanted to transfer $40,000 back to his bank account in Paris. "Don't be your worst enemy," wrote Roslyn Targ, in an effort to assure him his anxieties were baseless.[21]

Another checkup in Madrid, in late January 1976, was not reassuring. Himes thought the acute pain of arthritis, compounded by the deterioration of his spinal column, would drive him mad. He was becoming more irritable and impatient with Lesley, who believed (justifiably) that the second volume of his autobiography needed considerably more work. Himes was adamant. It was *his* book, he said. His health was gone, he wrote Jordan, and he felt he was going insane. "I think your editing of my book was a very good job, but I don't think I can continue."[22] When the edited typescript was returned to him, he commented that his "trouble was (still is) that too many women have tried to meddle with my life. And all women meddled with Marlene (Regine) because she was younger—they hated her [and] . . . it became tricky business. I wrote my version of the book and Lesley had to rewrite it and the typist (a woman too) had to meddle with my story."[23]

Although Himes was acutely aware that he was not up to the job of revising the volume, he blamed its inconsistencies and redundancies on others. It was impossible to work on the manuscript with editors in New York. He lived abroad because white Americans had always hated him, he wrote Jordan, yet he had to acknowledge a deep passion for America, the "bad mother," and his own responsibilities:

> I am guilty too. I spent 7-½ years in the Ohio State Penitentiary. Then I published *If He Hollers* . . . America never forgave me for that. But I am guilty too. I tried to force America to forgive me. That's what I meant when I wrote 'James Baldwin was an American freak.' Baldwin grew up criticizing me—he admit[ted] it . . . I'm America's whipping boy. And France was the first nation in the world to recognize the value of my detective stories; America didn't even read them until they were more than 5 years old.[24]

His self-absorption had made it hard for him to imagine that most Americans had not heard of him.

By early February 1976, the final version of the autobiography reached Jordan. Himes did not like it and shared his gloomy outlook with Reed: "My health is a disaster, but it will soon be over, and that will be a blessing, anyway."

He was nonetheless putting together a book of short stories, he told Reed, whose title (formerly "Black on White") had become "Stories New and Old." Himes said he was adding *A Case of Rape* and "Friends," a brutally sexual story taken from an early version of his prison novel.[25] He had even written a "Foreword" to the volume:

> All of these stories concern the relations of men and women. Most concern the relationship of Black American men and white women. All of them were written after I had first gone to Europe in the spring of 1953. The reader may readily perceive the change in my attitude toward race.[26]

It was becoming increasingly difficult for Himes to engage in any sustained concentration. When in April Miotte suggested they write a book together relating their views on art and literature, Himes made an attempt for a few weeks and then gave up.[27] During the summer he read Stephen Milliken's laudatory book about his work, which delighted him, but more often than not he lost himself in nostalgia for his sapped strength.[28] After watching the Pamplona *feria* on television, he wrote Jordan: "The summer weather is hot and the bulls are running. I wish I was running with them on these hot days, or else watching them run. This weather brings to mind Hemingway, whom I wish I was reading. But Lesley stopped by the studio on this hot afternoon to talk to me about flowers and my mind has blown. Sorry. I'll let her finish this letter to you."[29]

In early November 1976 Jordan sent Himes an edited copy of his autobiography, which the author now claimed he loved: "I have finished reading my book word by word and it reads great. There are a few passages I would have changed but they are of no consequence. It is a great book and it impresses me."[30] Later in the month, after *My Life of Absurdity* came out, the Himeses flew to New York for further consultations at the Presbyterian Hospital. Joseph visited Chester there, and Doubleday spared him publicity appearances.

Himes's health improved somewhat during the spring of 1977, allowing him to accompany Lesley on a visit to her sister in England. The occasion proved a disaster. Himes's edgy temper created a tense atmosphere, and when at one point Lesley's brother-in-law playfully tousled her hair, Himes flew into a jealous rage. On their third day—at Himes's insistence—they returned to Spain. Lesley was becoming more worried and shared her distress with Himes's brother Joseph and his wife: Chester was losing his memory, he was getting all sorts of things mixed up and screaming, screaming he was right. Everything was her fault. "The other morning he came into the kitchen and found his usual fruit on a plate, peeled and cut up. He threw all the plates off with his stick, broke everything and then said: 'I told you I don't want this.' He has two fruits *every* morning. But why break up everything? We are on the sixth walking stick at the moment." When she wanted to help him with his correspondence, he became furious. "He says that it is *his* business and not mine. I am only accused of taking over."[31] In desperation, Lesley took Himes to a German faith healer, but Himes had little faith.

Himes was becoming so restricted in his movements that it was becoming dangerous to leave him alone on their hilltop house—although Lesley did what she could to keep him moving. Sometimes she put the wheelchair in the trunk of the car and took him for drives into the countryside. But his chief pleasure was watching Deros in the garden. A sweet cat, he said, with a great personality. He liked her habit of catching small rabbits. Deros shared with Lesley the dedication in Himes's autobiography.

Himes did not like traveling any more. His cousin Robert had invited them once more to his spacious Estoril villa near Lisbon. Himes accepted but on his return wrote Roslyn that he hadn't enjoyed the visit. Among his cousin's cultured friends he liked the Africans best, but there were too many people about, too much bustle.[32]

Now Himes lived more and more vicariously on news the postman brought each morning: "I have not received any good news from either you, Mary Kling [his French agent] or any of the American publishers, and I am beginning to feel that I am not alive anymore," he complained to Roslyn.[33] Each bit of news, good or bad, affected him deeply. He was depressed because he could no longer write fiction, and Lesley, try as she might, was unable to console him.[34] His main energies were now devoted to the publication and dissemination of his works. When the director of a small theater in New York requested permission to adapt "Marijuana and a Pistol" for the stage, Himes granted permission gladly, proud that his story would join the company of works by African American writers Kristin Hunter and Alice Childress.[35] Oddly, what seemed to sustain him most was his hatred of publishers. He believed his contract with Putnam for *Pinktoes* illegal and wanted to sue, saying he would divide world profits equally with any lawyer who would win his case. To an attorney who asked him the origin of the title, Himes explained that *pinktoes* was a word coined by Los Angeles Negroes to describe adorable white women, "delectable, delicious, highly pleasing."[36]

One of the great disappointments of Himes's last years was the failure of Chatham Bookseller to publish the original version of "The End of a Primitive." When Frank Deodene, the publisher, wrote him in February 1978 that the firm was bankrupt, Himes tried to console himself by focusing his hopes on Europe. That summer he told Malartic, who was then condensing his two autobiographies into one volume for Gallimard, that he could edit them in any way he wished.[37] Malartic had been puzzled by the inconsistencies, but by now Himes did not much care. He would simply like to see a French edition of his life story.

The French had not forgotten him. At long last a translation of *Cast the First Stone* would be forthcoming in October, and at about the same time a Paris publishing house, Editions des Autres, promised to reprint *A Case of Rape* in a different translation. That autumn a French television crew came to Moraira to make a short documentary about him. Himes was hardly able to answer questions; his speech was slurred and unintelligible, although he looked gorgeous in his wheelchair with his carefully trimmed white beard and elegant sports cap. Suddenly he burst into tears, explaining to his interviewer that he could no longer write.[38]

Spain, Himes sometimes grumbled, had degenerated since Franco's death. But now he had another good reason to leave Spain—if only for a short while. In November 1978 his divorce in absentia from Jean came through, and later that month he traveled to England to marry Lesley. The small private ceremony took place in a registry office near Eastbourne with some members of Lesley's family present.

On February 12, 1979, Lesley wrote Joseph Himes from Moraira that Chester now could walk only as far as a few rooms, his memory was terrible, and he no longer wanted to go to his studio to write letters. They had few friends nearby, and it seemed pointless to go out just to drive around. In the main Himes was cheered only by hearing about his successes and the new publications of his books. He greatly liked the job Malartic had done on the two volumes of his autobiography, and when Gallimard published *Regrets sans repentir* in April, he reacted happily to the attention it received.[39]

After a series of checkups and tests at the Paris and Marseilles hospitals, doctors concluded that nothing more could be done to improve Himes's health. The Himeses thought that they would try again, and at the end of May 1980 they flew to the United States for yet another diagnosis. The Mason Clinic in Seattle unhappily confirmed previous reports from the American Hospital in Paris and could only suggest further neurological tests to check for Parkinson's disease. By now Himes seemed greatly disoriented. Later they visited both Ishmael Reed and Maya Angelou in Oakland. Angelou urged a consultation with her internist who recommended a brain scan. The scan revealed that the left side of Himes's brain was destroyed, decline was unstoppable, medication useless. On their return to Spain, Himes appeared more stable. He looked forward to reading his own interviews and delighted in a beautifully bound, limited edition of *A Case of Rape* that Bill Targ had produced for him. It took Himes several days to painstakingly sign his name to each of the 400 volumes.

Outside stimulation came from scholars, critics, students, and journalists who continued to arrive wanting to interview him. Lesley would read fan letters, critical assessments, and essays (especially from Europe), sometimes bringing tears to Himes's eyes. From time to time he was invited to speak to one group or another, but was unable to accept. In a letter to Reed in early 1981, Lesley mentioned Himes's growing popularity, but also remarked on his difficult temper: "He's a true tiger in my opinion and I wouldn't want him to change into a mouse. When he shouts from time to time, so do I. Such is life. But I don't like to see him unable to write any more."[40] Himes could indeed be easily annoyed as when, for instance, a French publisher printed a comic-strip adaptation of *Run Man Run* without consulting him.

To make daily movements easier for Himes, Lesley decided to sell Casa Griot and build a smaller house with no stairs and with doorways wide enough for a wheelchair to pass through. Casa Deros was located on their front plot looking out on the sea. It was put together quickly, with Himes and Lesley ever present to supervise construction. By August 1981 they were even able to improvise a small paella party for a few black marines from the USS *Forrestal,* and the following November they moved into their new home.

Sometime at the start of 1982, Lieu Commun, a new Paris publishing house, asked Himes for unpublished material. Because *Black on White,* Himes's proposed second volume of short stories, was still unpublished, much of his early short fiction of the 1930s and 1940s remained uncollected. These and other stories were gathered and printed in September under the title *Un Manteau de rêve.* Its cover pictured a beautifully drawn white-bearded Himes seated on his chair reading the title story, "On Dreams and Reality." When he saw the book, Himes chuckled: He had become the subject of his own fiction. During a visit around this time Michel Fabre discovered a nearly complete version of "Plan B" scattered among his papers. Since the last part of the typescript was written as an expanded synopsis with dialogue, the novel was deemed publishable.

Himes now could no longer decipher his reviews or read his fan mail, and only Lesley could communicate with him. Doctors told her that she must have no illusions; an artery near his heart was expanding, and she could only wait for it to explode. His health would not permit further operations. By July 1983 he was utterly paralyzed, and it seemed now only a question of time. Lesley used to seat him in the car or put him on the chaise longue where he would look out at Deros playing in the garden or contemplate the passing boats.

Himes's condition was not so painful as it was dangerous. He did not know about the artery. But as the days passed, his blood vessels clogged, and despite a strict diet, he had trouble swallowing. At length he refused food and became rail-thin. Doctors said his esophagus had become hopelessly twisted and placed him on a liquid diet. Lesley tried to comfort him. She told him that in America he had been awarded (thanks to Reed) the Before Columbus Foundation Prize for Excellence in Writing. Doubtless he was gladdened but spoke each day of feeling weaker.

In September 1983 Himes painstakingly signed his last piece. He had lately received a circular letter from the *International Herald Tribune* asking that he renew his long expired subscription. With Lesley's help, he concocted a letter expressing a long held bitterness. In part it read:

> I do not disagree that the *Herald Tribune* is "the only American international daily." What I am annoyed about is the fact that they never, never mentioned my books [during] my years of writing in Europe, even when my last book, *Un Manteau de rêve,* received very enthusiastic reviews from most important French newspapers and literary magazines . . . I am an American, black and very proud to be both. You have ignored me completely and this is why I borrow my neighbors' papers, FREE . . . Will you "welcome me into your daily life?" I'm not dead yet and I will have another book out in France in a week or so. It is called *Plan B* . . . It is an unfinished detective story.
>
> Please don't bother me and I won't bother you. Tell the editor that at least I have the courage to write my grievances, okay?

Himes's last months were an ordeal that Lesley called her "lonely crusade." He would allow only her to touch him or feed him. She told of his last thoughts: Himes did speak about death, at times, but was mostly concerned with his posthumous reputation as a writer. He hoped she would go on having his books printed and translated. "For him, writing was a way of living, of fighting and negating death. Of outliving oneself. Naturally, he did not enjoy life at the end, but he wanted to stay alive."[41] One day while lying in bed, instead of following her with his eyes, Himes turned his head in her direction, and she realized that he could no longer see.

Bedridden for more than a year, Himes did not speak for months. Once, before he died, Lesley thought she heard him moan softly: "Oh Lord, oh Lord." Perhaps, she said, he would say something to her, but the rest was silence. On the morning of November 13, 1984, he looked so utterly faded that Lesley called a doctor. Himes would be dead in two hours, he said. The priest she called did not arrive in time.

A funeral was arranged. Scholars and critics from Valencia, Alicante, and Madrid attended. Neither of Himes's brothers in the States was able to come, nor were there French journalists present, although Spanish reporters interviewed Lesley at some length. Among the mourners were several of Lesley's friends and neighbors. Himes had always said he wanted a small funeral. That evening Spanish television provided extensive coverage.[42]

It is customary in Spain to open the coffin to take photographs of the deceased before burial. Lesley did not want people to see Himes's emaciated face and so decided to hide the coffin until the last minute. She and a nurse covered him with a sheet and threw in chrysanthemums from the garden. The mortician was an admirer of Himes's detective stories. Perhaps he remembered Himes's fondness in fiction for runaway hearses and coffins crashing wildly in breathless manhunts. He went along with Lesley's wishes and placed Himes's coffin in an old graveyard in Benissa that was now rarely used. He knew that the journalists would rush to the old cemetery when they discovered that Himes's coffin was not in the new one. In the meantime he would return the coffin to his car and drive a devious route to Benissa's new cemetery. The coffin arrived on time for the priest to begin his benedictions. The journalists arrived too late. "I think Chester would have liked it that way," Lesley said.[43] In the antic style of his thrillers, Himes had run his last run.

# Notes

## 1. Genealogy

1. *My Life of Absurdity* (New York: Doubleday, 1976), p. 1.

2. Mary M. Jones to Estelle B. Himes, n.d., Beinecke Library, Yale University, James Weldon Johnson Collection (archive hereafter cited as Yale). Information was derived in part from Estelle Himes's manuscript, "Old Lick Log," an attempt to reconstruct her family's genealogy (Yale).

3. Edward was born on May 26, 1902, and Joseph Sandy, Jr., was born on August 4, 1908. Only Chester was given his mother's maiden name as a middle name.

## 2. The South

1. The description of childhood experiences is based partly on Joseph Himes, Jr., "As the Twig Is Bent" (unpublished memoir, n.d.). According to Joseph, Estelle occasionally taught music. "Mrs. J. S. Himes" also wrote the "Alcorn Ode," an inspirational piece that became the school's anthem:

> Beneath the shade of giant trees,
> Fanned by a balmy Southern breeze
> Thy classic walls have dared to stand
> A giant thou art in learning's hand;
> O, Alcorn, dear, our mother, hear,
> Thy name we praise, thy name we sing.
> Thy name thy sons have honored far;
> A crown of gems thy daughters are;
> When country called the flag to bear,
> The Gold and purple answered "Here."
> O Alcorn, dear, our mother, hear,
> Thy name we praise, thy name we sing.

Far as our race the claim shall need.
So far to progress thou shalt lead
Thy sons, with clashing arms of trade;
In useful arts full garbed thy maids;
O, Alcorn, dear, we proudly bear
Thy standard on to victory.

She later published a few inspirational poems in religious newspapers.

2. Joseph Himes and Edward Himes, interviews with Michel Fabre, spring 1988. Joseph stated that their mother was a snob because she was fair-skinned and also because of her consciousness of their background in the black community. But he added, "Chester made some of that up."

3. In "Present Tense" (Yale), an early version of *Cast the First Stone,* the protagonist evokes his childhood in terms strongly reminiscent of Himes's own, and remarks that he mistook Paris for Hector as the man running to escape his pursuers.

## 3. Adolescence

1. *Quality of Hurt* (New York: Doubleday, 1972), pp. 13–14.

2. *Third Generation* (Cleveland: World Publishing, 1954), p. 162.

3. *Quality of Hurt,* p. 26.

## 4. Ohio State

1. *Quality of Hurt,* p. 27.

2. Himes is listed in *Makio,* the 1926–27 student directory, as a pledge in the Alpha Phi Alpha fraternity.

3. *Quality of Hurt,* p. 26.

4. *Quality of Hurt,* p. 39.

5. "Present Tense," p. 251.

6. *Quality of Hurt,* p. 39.

7. In a 1937 story, "A Nigger," the female landlady throws out the protagonist after he savagely beats up a girlfriend. Himes's graphic blow-by-blow description is not unlike his account of bashing his girlfriend years later in Paris. See *My Life of Absurdity,* p. 118.

8. *Quality of Hurt,* p. 45. The implication that there was some kind of racial conspiracy afoot to catch him does not seem plausible. Would "fifteen or twenty" merchants allow him to walk away with their goods on the assumption that he would be caught later? The police report charges him with forging only one check. Himes's statement suggests that several of the other events he relates in his autobiography are slanted to suit his later political and ideological ethos.

9. *Quality of Hurt,* p. 46.

10. This was why they divorced, according to Joseph Himes. He believed Chester made up color antagonisms for fictional purposes. Joseph Himes, interview with Michel Fabre, spring 1986.

11. *Quality of Hurt,* p. 47.

12. *Quality of Hurt,* p. 48.

13. They lived at 2685 Fairmount Blvd., Cleveland Heights.

14. *Quality of Hurt,* p. 53. In "His Last Day" and *Cast the First Stone,* Himes provides slightly different fictional accounts of his armed robbery at the Millers'.

15. *Quality of Hurt,* p. 56.

16. Himes to John A. Williams, October 31, 1963, University of Rochester Library, John A. Williams archive (hereafter cited as Rochester).

17. Card no. 35051, "Criminal Courts Department," reads:

> Name: Himes, Chester. Offense: Robbery; Sec. G.C. 12342; Arrested by Frabel, Gill; Residence: 2254 E. 100th Street, Chicago, Ill.; File No.: Cleveland Heights; Occupation: chauffeur; Nativity: U.S.; Married: No; Sex: M; Race: C; Age: 22; B.O.: Cleveland Heights; G/J: 111/27; Argmt: 12/4 NG; Trial: 12/6; Prob. 12/7. Disposition: Change plea to guilty. O. Pen. 20 years 22; Paroled 4/1/36; Judge: McMahon; Date: 12/1/28; Photo: 32729; Inst.: 59623.

Himes's address is listed as Chicago rather than Cleveland because he had taken a room at a black hotel on the South Side at the time he was attempting to pawn the jewelry.

The back reads:

> On Nov. 25th, 1928, at about 1:30 A. M., Mr. and Mrs. Sam Miller had just returned to their home at Fairmount Blvd. Mr. Miller went to the garage to see that the doors were locked and when he stepped in the garage a colored man rose up between two cars and pointed a gun at him. He ordered victim into the house where he robbed him and Mrs. Miller $350.00 and four rings valued at about $5,000.00. He then forced victim to open the vault, at the point of a gun, and took a watch and several more rings. He then went into the garage and drove away a Cadillac Coupe. The car was located at 8:00 A. M. the following morning on Winslow Road where it was stuck in the mud.
>
> Defendant is now under arrest in Chicago.
>
> Defendant was arrested in Warren, Ohio, October 9th, 1928, in connection with robbing the Armory in Cleveland. He had several fur coats in his possession at that time. He was returned to Cleveland, where he was fined at Muni. Court and sentence suspended.
>
> Defendant is now on probation from Franklin County, on a charge of forgery and issuing checks to defraud.

The register entry of Cuyahoga County Record of Convictions, 1926–31, reads: "Judge: McMahon, No.: 35051. Name: Chester Himes. Crime: P.G. Rob. Sentence: Pen. 20 yrs. Costs: 156.65. Clerk's costs: 13.70. Sentence: 12/19/28." (Courtesy of the state records specialist, Ohio Historical Society, Columbus.)

18. Himes's parole number was 4517. He received his final release on February 3, 1939, and was restored to citizenship by Governor John Bricker on March 6. The State Archives hold no warden's reports for either the Ohio Penitentiary or the Prison Farm. The summary minutes kept by the Parole Committee for the years 1936–39 contain no record of appeals made by Himes.

## 5. The Prison Years

1. *Quality of Hurt*, p. 63. The most complete account of the fire is to be found in an article by an unnamed author, "Ohio Penitentiary 1930 Fire," *Columbus and Central Ohio Historian* 2 (November 1984): 13–16.

2. In one of the early manuscript versions of Himes's prison novel (Yale), Jimmy (or Jimmie) Monroe's father arranges for reinstatement of his disability pension and five hundred fifteen dollars retroactive compensation from the Ohio State Labor Commission. Jimmy must, however, send some of the money back to his father to pay a lawyer who negotiated with the commission. He also sends money periodically to both parents—a larger sum to his mother who is employed as a servant to an invalid. (Was the fictional invalid Himes's brother?) Jimmy's most important use of the windfall is the purchase of a typewriter on which he will begin to write his stories.

3. Estelle moved south with Joseph in 1932, when he obtained a teaching position in Arkansas. Thus Himes saw her less frequently in 1933. When Joseph moved back to Columbus in the summer of 1934 to work toward a doctorate, she followed him.

4. "Present Tense," p. 161.

5. See, for example, "Prison Mass" (1933), in which the protagonist, Brightlights (who wears a back brace), wants to believe in God but is unable to make up his mind. See also "To What Red Hell" (1934), where the convict is almost seduced by Christian doctrine but angrily turns away from it. In "I Don't Want to Die" (1933) a dying convict clings both to the hand of a priest who offers him God's salvation and to the hand of a thief who offers him friendship—without ever knowing "which offer was the greatest." Even as late as 1969, in "Prediction," the black janitor of a Catholic church wants to cross himself before blowing up a police parade. In a 1957 interview in Mallorca, Himes declared he was a "bad" Catholic; when he died in Spain, he was given a Catholic burial.

6. In "Present Tense" Himes included long letters and passages of romantic regret between the lovers, such as these: "the pitiful, brilliant, lovely, morbid, unhealthful degenerate; too bad he wasn't a real woman" and "I too was a dreamer and I became a realist" (p. 169).

7. See "Prisoners' Songs Go into Opera: Negro Convict in Ohio Pen Memorizes Words, Music of Working Chanteys," unidentified newspaper clipping, January 20, 1935, sent by Himes to Carl Van Vechten, Yale:

> Columbus, O. Jan. 19 (AP)—Prince Rico, a Georgia Negro doing a robbery 'stretch' at Ohio Penitentiary would like to weave into an opera the threads of Negro working chanties he has collected.
>
> He has spent a goodly portion of his 23 years in the custody of penal authorities in the north and south while his collection grew . . . "The songs originated in the South and were never written, due to occasional obscenity, are well known by most of the prisoners, railroad workers and hoboes of the Negro race," he explained in polished phrases. One mournful chantey, in which you can almost hear the thud of the chain gang pickaxes, goes:
>
> Every mail day
> Mail day I get a letter

Cryin': son come home,
Lord, Lord, my son come home.

One finds almost the same sort of indomitable whimsicality in these chanteys as in Rico's statement about putting them into an opera. He's serving a ten to 25 year sentence for robbery from Franklin County. It started in 1933.

The article also includes the "Ballad of Lightning Jim" and other extracts.

8. Himes was transferred to the London Prison Farm on September 21, 1934, and given prisoner number 5326.

9. See "Present Tense," p. 381.

10. See untitled version of prison novel, pp. 462–67, Yale.

11. See untitled version of prison novel, p. 380, Yale.

12. Untitled version of prison novel, p. 381, Yale.

13. See "Present Tense," pp. 218–21.

14. Himes to Van Vechten, February 18, 1947, Yale.

15. Himes's first periodical appearances were "His Last Day" (*Abbott's Monthly* 5 [November 1932]: 32–33, 60–63); "Prison Mass" (*Abbott's Monthly* 6 [March 1933]: 36, 61–64; [April 1933]: 20–21, 48–56; [May 1933]: 37, 61–62); "Her Whole Existence: A Story of True Love" (*Abbott's Monthly* 6 [July 1933]: 24–25, 53–56); "A Modern Marriage" (*Atlanta Daily World,* August 2, 1933, p. 2); "I Don't Want to Die" (*Abbott's Monthly and Illustrated News* 6 [October 1933]: 20–21); "He Knew" (*Abbott's Monthly and Illustrated News* 1 [December 2, 1933]: 15).

16. Himes to Williams, October 31, 1962, Rochester.

17. "I Don't Want to Die," p. 21.

18. "His Last Day," in *Collected Stories of Chester Himes* (London: Allison and Busby, 1990), p. 293.

19. Himes to Miss Amrine, n.d. (1934), Yale.

## 6. Free at Last

1. Himes to Langston Hughes, n.d. (1937?), Yale; Himes to Williams, October 21, 1962, Rochester. Himes was then living at 1711 East 68th St., Cleveland.

2. Himes to Henry Lee Moon, several letters written between September 15, 1937, and May 29, 1942, Schomburg Center Library, New York. These letters were made available through the help of Christine McKay. During that period, Chester and Jean Himes moved several times in Cleveland: from 2434 East 63rd St. to 10722 Olivet Ave. (in August 1938), then to 10622 Massie Ave. (by September 1939), and to Suite 4, 2260 East 93rd St. (by February 1940). In the summer of 1941 they went to Louis Bromfield's Malabar Farm in Lucas, Ohio (see p. 46).

3. Himes repeatedly claimed that this gradually became the reason for their separation in 1952, implying that he could not bear being provided for by his wife. His brother Joseph gives no credence to this excuse. In his 1985 interview with Michel Fabre, Joseph said that Chester simply used people unscrupulously.

4. Himes to Williams, October 31, 1962, Rochester.

5. Ruth Seid (pseudonym Jo Sinclair) to Michel Fabre, 1988, private collection.

6. Seid to Fabre, 1988, private collection.

7. Dan Levin to Edward Margolies, 1989, private collection.

8. Himes to Williams, October 31, 1962, Rochester. Himes claimed he wrote some fifty vignettes called "This Cleveland," for which he got a dollar each. However, none could be found in the newspaper's files, and only one such draft, called "Christmas," remains among Himes's papers at Yale. He told Van Vechten, "I wrote by-line articles for the CIO weekly organ, the *Union Leader* and then the daily vignettes for the editorial page of the *Cleveland News* which were very popular (one or two were reprinted in the *New Yorker*). I wrote for two or three Cleveland magazines." Himes to Van Vechten, September 13, 1946, Yale.

9. *Quality of Hurt*, p. 72.

10. The stories are respectively "With Malice toward None" *Crossroad* 1 (April 1939); "A Modern Fable—of Mr. Slaughter, Mr. McDull, and the American Scene" *Crossroad* (Summer 1940) (a political commentary in satirical style); and "Looking down the Street: A Story of Import and Bitterness" *Crossroad* (Spring 1940).

11. Jean Himes, telephone interview with Edward Margolies, December 1990. She added that she helped Himes write the book.

12. Himes to Van Vechten, September 13, 1946, Yale.

13. *Quality of Hurt*, p. 73.

14. "Most of the brothers used to clothe themselves from the salvage from the Hollywood big shots. I had more expensive clothes then than I've ever had since. But the Communists had a use for me . . . I was to apply for work in various firms which did not employ Negroes. This is when and where I got all my material for *Lonely Crusade*." Himes to Williams, October 31, 1962, Rochester.

15. In October 1941 the Himeses lived in Apt. 2 at 1464 Central Ave., Los Angeles. Information about Himes's California years is also derived from a newspaper article, "Chester Himes Paints Local Scene in Novel," following a review of *If He Hollers Let Him Go* in the Los Angeles *Tribune*, March 12, 1945. By December 1941 the Himeses lived at 4433 Crocker St., and by May 1942 at 1056 N. De Carmo Dr., Los Angeles.

16. This essay, "Negro Martyrs Are Needed," was published in *Crisis* in May 1944. It drew the attention of the Federal Bureau of Investigation, which opened a file on Himes (No. 105–2502).

17. See Michael Carter, "This Story Had to Be Told," clipping, Washington *Afro-American* (?), n.d.

18. *Quality of Hurt*, p. 75.

19. The Himeses made their home atop City Terrace in the Boyle Heights district, occupying a little house evacuated by a Nisei family. "It was an isolated house next to a reservoir, with only a Mexican couple for neighbors and I used to keep my Winchester rifle within reach at all times." Himes to Williams, October 31, 1962, Rochester.

## 7. Arrivals and Departures

1. *If He Hollers Let Him Go* (New York: Doubleday, 1945), p. 1.

2. CBS speech, 1972, Amistad Research Center, Tulane University (archive hereafter cited as Amistad).

3. *Quality of Hurt*, p. 76.

4. CBS speech, 1972, Amistad.

5. CBS speech, 1972, Amistad.

6. *If He Hollers Let Him Go*, p. 146.

7. From November 1945 to May 1946 the Himeses lived at 121 Bainbridge Street, Brooklyn, N.Y.

8. Joseph's wife, Estelle, bore the same name as his mother.

9. "Second Guesses for First Novelists," *Saturday Review of Literature* 29 (February 16, 1946): 13.

10. *Quality of Hurt*, p. 93.

11. Himes to Van Vechten, August 12, 1946, Yale.

12. Van Vechten to Himes, n.d., Yale.

13. Himes to Van Vechten, September 13, 1946, Yale.

14. Himes to Van Vechten, February 28, 1947, Yale.

15. Himes to Van Vechten, February 18, 1947, Yale.

16. Himes to Van Vechten, May 23, 1947, Yale.

17. *Lonely Crusade* (New York: Knopf, 1947), pp. 6–7.

18. *Lonely Crusade*, p. 91.

19. Himes to Van Vechten, August 8, 1947, Yale.

20. Himes to Willard Motley, n.d., Library of Marquette University, Milwaukee, Willard Motley archive.

21. "History as Nightmare," *New Leader* (October 25, 1947): 11, 15.

22. The reviews of *Lonely Crusade* were, on the whole, less unfavorable than Himes pretended. The advance notice in *Kirkus Reviews* (July 15, 1947, p. 372) was unfavorable largely for reasons of style. In the *New York Times Book Review* (September 4, 1947, p. 20) the book was reviewed briefly; the reviewer, Nash K. Burger, noted the "somewhat familiar pattern of such fiction" in Lee's struggle, but said that the author "was wise enough to present Lee's story in human, not stereotyped ideological terms." Arna Bontemps wrote the review for the *New York Herald Tribune Weekly Book Review* (September 7, 1947, p. 8, VII). He found that Himes examined a difficult problem with passion and pride. The *New Yorker* (September 13, 1947, p. 126) devoted only fifteen lines to this "bitter story": "Mr. Himes considers this problem intelligently and convincingly; regrettably, though, he seems to think that an ugly narrative is necessarily a powerful one." In the *Atlantic Monthly* (October 1947, p. 138) Stoyan Christowe began by calling the novel a "top best-seller," "a brave and courageous probing in the Negro psyche," but noted that "the book reads not like a novel but like excerpts from extended social studies." In *Commonweal* (October 3, 1947, p. 604) George Streator found the theme of the novel "highly probable" and remarked on the similarity between its plot and incidents and people in real life. He made some fun of the ending in the style of a "camera finish" but did not comment on the writing itself. Eric L. McKitrick in the *Saturday Review of Literature* (October 25, 1947, p. 25) saw the book as a "turbulent story seething with violence" and the hero as "tortured constantly with his fancied deficiencies as a man." John Farrelly, the reviewer for the *New Republic* (October 6, 1947, p. 30), thought "the story is much too extended and repetitious." He saw Lee Gordon as "an exaggerated figure not so much as an individual as a catalogue of the Negro's emotional distortions." In February 1948 a

two-page review by Milton Klonsky appeared in *Commentary* (pp. 189–90), devoted in large part to anti-Jewish graffiti, before the reviewer lashed out at the novel. It was "in the direct line of descent from its predecessors, more sensational, more insipid for all that, and even more clumsily written." *Reader's Digest* (March 1948, pp. 43–44) reprinted, in condensed form, an editorial published in *Ebony* in November 1947 under the title "Time to Count Our Blessings"; it lambasted a virulent malicious story of a Negro whose "high shouldered air of bravado, disdain, even arrogance is typical of too many Negroes today" (p. 43).

But the worst attacks came from the Communists. Theodore Ward led the assault in "Five Negro Novelists, Revolt and Retreat" (*Mainstream*, Winter 1947): 100–110. Lloyd W. Brown followed suit in *New Masses* (September 9, 1947, pp. 18–20): "I cannot recall ever having read a worse book on the Negro theme." Not only was Himes a renegade, he also "illustrated the flowering of the Myrdal-Wright thesis on the Negro question, emphasizing the fear-hate complex." Brown concluded, "Let Chester Himes go his miserable way, but let him go alone on his lonely crusade, accompanied only by the ghosts of Uncle Tom and the nameless wretched slave who betrayed Nat Turner and his people" (p. 20).

23. "Dick [Richard Wright] had no offer to review it, although he wrote a fair preface for the French edition" (Himes to Williams, October 31, 1962, Rochester). To Van Vechten, Himes wrote on September 11, 1947 (Yale), about Constance Curtis's review in the *Amsterdam News:* "I thought it was good. And the review in *Newsweek*. Vivian Wolfert wrote that one . . . There was a review in the *Cleveland News* which Bill Cole says is good. Oh yes, *New Masses* gave me a thorough going over."

24. The only completed work by Himes bearing this title is a corrected copy of *Lonely Crusade,* which he later gave to his translator Yves Malartic. "Immortal Mammy" may have been an earlier projected title for this work.

25. On May 18, 1948, Himes sent Van Vechten his outline of "Stool Pigeon." Van Vechten's response is unknown.

26. "The Dilemma of the Negro Novelist in the United States," in *Beyond the Angry Black,* ed. John A. Williams (New York: Cooper Square Publishers, 1966), p. 54.

27. *Quality of Hurt,* p. 111.

28. *Quality of Hurt,* p. 132.

29. Himes to Van Vechten, November 23, 1952, Yale.

30. On April 14, 1952, the prison novel was sold under the title "Debt of Time"; in early May, it was called "Solitary"; it then became *Cast the First Stone.* On November 23, 1952, Himes sent the several typescript versions to Van Vechten. He explained that the version called "Day after Day" was written about 1936–37; the one called "The Way It Was," in 1939–40; and the version called "Black Sheep," in the winter of 1949.

31. *Quality of Hurt,* p. 135.

32. *Quality of Hurt,* p. 137.

33. Himes to Malartic, n.d. (1952), private collection.

34. "I am quite interested in a woman, Vandi Haygood, who was formerly married to Billy Haygood . . . If all goes well and I get my divorce we will probably marry some time next year . . . Jean and I are separated and we will be divorced as soon as I have sufficient money on hand so that it can be done decently. We have

agreed to do it mutually." Himes to Van Vechten, November 11, 1952, Yale. Jean was, in fact, very unwilling to grant Himes a divorce.

35. Supposedly because *Invisible Man* was published in 1952 to much critical acclaim. The scene is portrayed in *The Primitive*.

36. Himes to Van Vechten, February 1, 1953, Yale.

## 8. Interim

1. Himes to Van Vechten, May 12, 1953, Yale.

2. *Quality of Hurt*, p. 200. Himes was also invited to a few literary parties, one of which his publisher Corréa gave in honor of Henry Miller, but Himes professed to find such parties pretentious and dull.

3. Himes to Van Vechten, April 12, 1953, Yale.

4. Himes to Yves and Yvonne Malartic, May 1953, private collection.

5. Himes to Van Vechten, June 1, 1953, Yale.

6. Himes to William Targ, June 6, 1953, Amistad.

7. Himes to Ellen Wright, June 27, 1953, Amistad.

8. Himes to William Targ, July 6, 1953, Amistad.

9. Himes to Malartic, October 21, 1953, private collection.

10. *Kirkus Reviews*, November 1, 1953, p. 716.

11. Edmund Fuller, in the *Chicago Tribune Review of Books* (January 10, 1954, p. 5), wrote that the novel was "a strong addition to [Himes's] growing list of books" and that it was endowed with "much tragic power," although the structure and conception did not equal the writing. Martin Levin, writing in the *Saturday Review of Literature* (March 13, 1954, p. 51), thought that in spite of its excesses, the novel was of great interest. Milton S. Byam, in *Library Journal* (79 [January 15, 1954]: 145), remarked that the subject degenerated into crises, but that the "very objective writing" vitalized the picture. Frederic Morton, in the *New York Herald Tribune Review of Books* (January 10, 1954, p. 6), was impressed by the "controlled force" but found the novel "a far less modulated work which yet seizes the reader with a strong if incoherent impact of its own." On the same day *New York Times* reviewer John Brooks wrote about this "searing book with its terrible pathos of the oppressed set against each other" (p. 29). Riley Hughes, in *Catholic World* (April 1954, p. 72), declared: "By tying his story to a Freudian mother complex formula, ruthlessly applied, Mr Himes removes his characters as far from the readers' sympathy as they are from convincing reality." On February 7, 1954, the *San Francisco Chronicle* was more appreciative of this "sincere piece with a dismal theme," which left "much food for thought" (p. 12).

12. *Third Generation* (Cleveland: World Publishing, 1954), p. 45.

13. Himes to Richard Wright, n.d. (spring 1955), Beinecke Library, Yale University, Richard Wright archive.

14. Himes to Williams, October 3, 1962, Rochester.

15. According to Joseph Himes, Chester was wrong in saying, or implying, that their mother hated his father because he was black. She ended up despising him for his failure to "achieve." Interview with Michel Fabre, spring 1985.

16. Himes to Trierweiler, June 28, 1955, Amistad.

17. Trierweiler to Himes, December 7, 1955, Amistad.

18. Fragment, Himes papers, Amistad.
19. Fragment, Himes papers, Amistad.
20. Trierweiler to Himes, December 7, 1955, Amistad.
21. Yvonne Malartic, interview with Michel Fabre, August 1985.
22. Unpublished fragment, "It's Funny Really," Himes papers, Amistad.
23. Himes quoted in Trierweiler to Himes, n.d. (late April 1955), Amistad.
24. Fragment, Himes papers, Amistad.

## 9. Celebrity

1. Himes to Charles Orengo, January 6, 1956, private collection.
2. Unpublished notes, Himes papers, Amistad; Trierweiler to Himes, June 19, 1956, Amistad.
3. Fragment, Himes papers, Amistad.
4. Himes to Van Vechten, March 15, 1956, Yale.
5. Himes to Walter Freeman, January 4, 1956, Yale.
6. Himes to Van Vechten, April 26, 1956, Yale.
7. Fragments, Himes papers, Amistad; see *My Life of Absurdity*, p.36.
8. The character Becky is based on Jean Himes; Ronny is Vandi's husband; Harold is Horace Cayton; and Walter and Lucille are Ralph and Rose Ellison.
9. Himes to Walter Freeman, March 3, 1956, Yale.
10. Unpublished fragment, Himes papers, Amistad. See *My Life of Absurdity*, p. 31: "Sex and violence held me in a vise . . . I needed women desperately, not just for sex but for safety, to help me control my temper. And I needed women too, to help restore my ego, which had taken such a beating in New York."
11. Unpublished fragment, Himes papers, Amistad.
12. Himes to Freeman, April 10, 1956, Amistad.
13. Himes to James Silberman, May 9, 1956, Yale.
14. Fragment on *Pinktoes*, n.d., Himes papers, Amistad.
15. Himes to Van Vechten, June 16, 1956, Yale.
16. Himes to Van Vechten, June 16, 1956, Yale.
17. Ralph Ellison to Horace Cayton, n.d. (June 1956), private collection.
18. Himes to Jean Himes, July 29, 1956, Amistad; Himes to Van Vechten, October 8, 1956, Yale.
19. Himes to Jean Himes, October 11, 1956, Amistad.
20. Located at 9, rue Gît-le-Coeur, the Hôtel Rachou soon became known as the "beat hotel" where Gregory Corso, Allen Ginsberg, and many others stopped on their way from San Francisco to Katmandu. William Burroughs and Brion Gysin also lived there.
21. Himes to Van Vechten, August 28, 1956, Yale.
22. Fragment, Himes papers, Amistad.
23. Unpublished notes, Himes papers, Amistad.
24. Fragment, Himes papers, Amistad. Himes's views are not unlike those of his friend, ex-GI William Gardner Smith, whose novel *Last of the Conquerors* (1948) tells of less racism among the defeated Germans than among Americans. Himes was wrong in his use of "sexually" here, for Regine had been deeply in love with Harrington,

with whom she found peace and protection, as a late February 1956 letter to him indicates.

25. Himes to Van Vechten, October 8, 1956, Yale.

26. In November and December 1956 Himes wrote scores of such letters in an effort to round up some money. His letters to Freeman and Van Vechten are at Yale.

27. Himes to Thomas Bledsoe, December 6, 1956, Amistad.

28. On December 12, 1956, Himes wrote Freeman that he had been trying desperately to write a detective story called "Trouble Wears a Skirt" but had managed only sixty-four pages. In the Himes papers (Amistad) two fragments, in part scribbled on the back of an envelope, read:

> "*For Love of Imabelle*, Notes for a story"
> 1. Jackson crossed himself; he was not a Catholic but he was a religious man
> 2. Troubled in mind. The woman spelled trouble. Trouble was on his mind.
> 3. Got racket. Sisters of Mercy
> Begin with pitch. Bang + blow—got back to her room. Trunk was gone
> Jackson always crossing himself
> Jackson short fat man turned grey
> Went to church the Lord told him to, etc.
> Counting money—stacking it neatly in rolls—putting rolls in oven—150 of
>     Jackson's $ 10's.
> Jackson's eyes red with suspicion. He had seen it done before. But this time
>     it was for keeps with all his money—worked and hustled for.
> Put money in stove
> Jackson crossed himself
> Bang—smell of gunpowder.
> Officer breaks in the door.
> Jackson said he ain't done nothing. Swears to God. Slim took him for more
>     money.

This is probably the story Himes got from the painter Walter Coleman (see p. 102).

29. Himes to Otto Fischer, December 16, 1956, draft, Amistad.

30. Regine Fischer to Himes, December 1956, Amistad.

31. Marcel Duhamel to Himes, December 26, 1956, private collection.

32. *Blind Man with a Pistol* (New York: Vintage Books, 1989), p. 119.

33. *For Love of Imabelle* (Chatham, N.Y.: Chatham Bookseller, 1973), p. 111.

34. Untitled notes for autobiography, Himes papers, Amistad.

35. Duhamel's advice was not given in writing, and Himes and Duhamel said different things at different times about the latter's inspirational role.

36. *A Rage in Harlem* (New York: Panther Books, 1969), p. 51.

37. Himes to Van Vechten, April 23, 1957, Yale.

38. *My Life of Absurdity*, p. 126.

39. Himes to Van Vechten, July 22, 1957, Yale.

40. Himes to Malartic, July 7, 1957, private collection.

41. Himes to Van Vechten, August 28, 1957, Yale.

42. *My Life of Absurdity*, pp. 160–61.

43. Autobiographical fragment, Himes papers, Amistad.
44. Himes to Van Vechten, December 17, 1957, Yale.
45. Himes to Van Vechten, December 19, 1957, Yale.
46. Unpublished autobiographical fragment, Himes papers, Amistad.
47. *Big Gold Dream* (Chatham , N.Y.: Chatham Bookseller, 1973), pp. 7–8.
48. Igor Maslowski, "*La Reine des pommes* de Chester Himes," *Mystère-Magazine,* June 1958, p. 7. The critic also called the book "one of the most extraordinary detective stories I have read since I have been writing this column."
49. *My Life of Absurdity,* p. 181.
50. Himes to Malartic, December 1958, private collection.

## *10. Three Women*

1. Lesley Himes wrote that if Himes was troubled, he had no reason to be: she knew about Regine, and she herself was quite independent and "in fact had another lover at the time." Lesley Himes to Edward Margolies, July 21, 1994, private collection.
2. Himes to Lesley Packard, July 28, 1959, Amistad.
3. According to Lesley, they never actually arrived at the club. Himes realized he was incapable of driving, turned around halfway, and went home. Himes, she believes, may well have been remembering another occasion.
4. Himes, conversation with Edward Margolies, March 1963.
5. Otto Fischer to Himes, January 13, 1960, Amistad.
6. *My Life of Absurdity,* p. 200.
7. Lesley Himes, interview with Michel Fabre, April 1986.
8. Himes to Van Vechten, September 8, 1960, Yale.
9. Himes to Van Vechten, September 8, 1960, and n.d. (August 1960), Yale. Himes vaguely contemplated visiting Africa, like Wright who had gone to the Gold Coast and published his reflections about it in *Black Power* (1953). In fact, Himes knew only a few Africans, mostly students he had met in Paris cafés.
10. *My Life of Absurdity,* p. 217.
11. Himes to Herbert Hill, June 26, 1961, Amistad.
12. Himes to Van Vechten, July 29, 1961, Yale.
13. Himes to Van Vechten, July 29, 1961, Yale.
14. Van Vechten to Himes, August 8, 1961, Yale.
15. Himes to Lesley Packard, September 15, 1961, Amistad.
16. Himes to Lesley Packard, n.d. (1961), private collection.
17. Himes to Lesley Packard, n.d. (1961), private collection.
18. Himes to Lesley Packard, n.d. (1961), private collection.
19. *My Life of Absurdity,* p. 238.
20. Himes to Van Vechten, December 16, 1961, Yale.
21. Herbert Hill, memorandum to Arthur Cohn, April 16, 1962, Amistad.
22. *My Life of Absurdity,* p. 247.
23. The essay was eventually published as "Harlem, ou le cancer de l'Amérique," in *Présence africaine* 45 (spring 1963): 46–81.
24. Van Vechten to Williams, October 15, 1962, Rochester.
25. Himes to Williams, November 6, 1962, Rochester.

26. Himes to Carl Brandt, November 29, 1962, Amistad.

27. Himes to Van Vechten, November 29, 1962, Yale.

28. The advances Himes had drawn on books he had never completed were sums of 5,000 new francs on "Murder Wears a Skirt" and 3,213 francs on "It Ain't Funny." Gallimard had also agreed to further advance 2,000 francs on his next book, at the same time acquiring preference rights on another five books; the advances due would compensate for those already paid. Yet Himes was furious about the royalty statement he was given in December 1962: It stated that he had received a total of 3,393,360 francs between December 27, 1956, and June 12, 1959, which he felt was nonsense. Obviously, in his eyes, all the advances on this statement charged against *La Reine des pommes* had been taken from the advances given on "A Jealous Man Can't Win," "If Trouble Was Money," *Run Man Run,* and *The Big Gold Dream.*

Himes complained to Marcel Duhamel: "I was charged 400,000 frs for 'The Lunatic Fringe' . . . This book (which I still have) is one-half of a manuscript about some white people in Mallorca. You did not want this book at all. The killer was suffering from amnesia, which is taboo for Série Noire and you did not like the idea. You did not pay me a single franc on 'The Lunatic Fringe.'" Himes to Duhamel, December 17, 1962, carbon copy, Amistad.

In addition to small advances, Himes was charged with such large sums as 500,000 and 400,000 francs, which he questioned. He was given credit for having earned 331,597 francs for the reprinting of *La Reine des pommes* over five years, but there was no record of that sum ever having been paid, he claimed.

29. Duhamel to Himes, December 28, 1962, carbon copy, Amistad.

30. Lesley wrote that she knew he was staying with Marianne although Chester may not have known that she knew. She added that she knew their relationship "would never work." Lesley Himes to Margolies, n.d. [July 1994], private collection.

31. Himes to Williams, January 21, 1963, Rochester.

32. Himes to Williams, February 12, 1963, Rochester.

33. Himes to Williams, February 25, 1963, Rochester.

34. Van Vechten to Williams, March 7, 1963, Rochester.

## 11. Lesley

1. Himes to Michel Fabre, September 16, 1971, private collection.

2. Guy de Bosschère, "Chester Himes: *Une Affaire de Viol,*" *Présence africaine* 48 (1963): 239–40.

3. Himes wanted to revise "Cotton" extensively at Plon's request and make copies of the revised version, then titled "The Cops and the Cotton," to send to America, England, and Germany. The novel was first translated into French as "De Bourres et de Coton" (*bourre* meaning both "cops" and "padding") but came out as *Retour en Afrique.*

4. Himes to Van Vechten, January 8, 1964, Amistad.

5. Years later, when Himes was bedridden, he received a letter from a young Belgian lawyer who told him that reading *A Case of Rape* had helped her enormously in a case she had with a black client. She was now able to see problems in a very different light. Himes was unable to respond, but Lesley corresponded with her afterward.

6. Himes to Van Vechten, April 15, 1964, Amistad. The items have not been located, but there exists a clipping with that photograph in Himes's papers (Amistad).

7. Himes to Van Vechten, May 12, 1964, Amistad.

8. Michel Salomon, "Juifs et noirs dans l'Amérique d'aujourd'hui," *L'Arche* 89 (June 1964): 22–26, 61.

9. "Les souris et le fromage," a political fable, appeared in the July 13, 1964, issue of *Le Nouvel Observateur.*

10. Unpublished notes, Himes papers, Amistad.

11. Himes to Van Vechten, October 23, 1964, Yale.

12. *My Life of Absurdity,* p. 290.

13. Himes to Maître Suzanne Blum, December 18, 1964, Amistad.

14. *My Life of Absurdity,* p. 297.

15. Himes, conversation with Edward Margolies, March 1963, at the Albert Hotel.

16. *My Life of Absurdity,* p. 295.

17. Himes to Lesley Packard, n.d. (1965), Amistad.

18. Himes to William Targ, November 25, 1965, Amistad.

19. Unpublished fragment, pp. 1–2, Himes papers, Amistad.

20. Himes to Malartic, February 10, 1966, Amistad.

21. *My Life of Absurdity,* p. 310.

22. Himes to Williams, March 25, 1966, Rochester.

23. Himes to Williams, March 25, 1966, Rochester.

24. Himes to Malartic, March 25, 1966, private collection.

25. Lesley Himes to Margolies, July 21, 1994, private collection.

26. Himes to William Targ, September 11, 1966, Amistad.

27. Himes to Williams, April 24, 1967, Rochester.

28. In later years Himes vehemently denied Hemingway as an influence. He liked one or two of Hemingway's novels, he said, but not the short stories. Lesley Himes to Margolies, July 21, 1994, private collection.

29. Himes to Roslyn Targ, August 16, 1967, Amistad.

30. Himes to Constance Webb Pearlstien, July 26, 1967, Amistad.

31. William Targ to Himes, September 8, 1967, Amistad.

32. Notes, Himes papers, Amistad.

## 12. Spain

1. "Plan B" has since been published in the United States under the title *Plan B* (Jackson: University Press of Mississippi, 1993).

2. Himes to Williams, December 18, 1968, Rochester. To be fair, Lesley says that Himes paid for some of the supplies she was carrying to the students.

3. Himes to William and Roslyn Targ, December 12, 1968, Amistad.

4. Himes to Williams, September 1968, Rochester.

5. Himes to Williams, December 3, 1968, Rochester.

6. Himes to Williams, December 3, 1968, Rochester.

7. Himes to Williams, January 2, 1969, Rochester.

8. Himes to Williams, February 6, 1969, Rochester.

9. Himes to Williams, March 8, 1969, Rochester.

10. Himes to Putnam's (Puzo's publisher), March 10, 1969, Amistad.

11. Himes to Lynn Deming, May 8, 1969, carbon copy, Amistad.

12. Letter to the editor, *New York Herald Tribune Book Review,* May 5, 1969.

13. Himes to Williams, June 13, 1969, Rochester.

14. Himes to Williams, June 5 1969, Rochester.

15. Himes to Williams, July 8, 1969, Rochester.

16. Himes to Williams, July 19, 1969, Rochester.

17. "Reading Your Own: My Favorite Novel," *New York Times Book Review,* June 4, 1967, p. 4.

18. Robin Denniston, reader's report on *Quality of Hurt* for Hodder & Stoughton, Himes papers, Amistad.

19. Himes to Williams, August 9, 1969, Rochester.

20. Himes to Williams, November 2, 1969, Rochester.

21. Himes to Williams, April 4, 1970, Rochester.

22. Himes to Williams, April 17, 1970, Rochester.

23. Himes to Williams, April 7, 1970, Rochester.

24. Himes to Williams, June 23, 1970, Rochester.

25. Himes to Williams, July 7, 1970, Rochester.

26. Himes to Williams, July 16, 1969, Rochester.

27. Himes to Fabre, November 7, 1970, private collection.

28. Unpublished autobiographical draft, Himes papers, Amistad.

29. Ernest Kaiser, conversation with Edward Margolies, March 1972.

30. Himes to Mrs. Geiger, editor at New American Library, n.d., Amistad.

31. Himes to Ishmael Reed, October 16, 1970, private collection.

32. Himes to Roslyn Targ, October 10, 1970, Amistad.

33. Himes to Roslyn Targ, October 10, 1970, Amistad.

34. Himes to Roslyn Targ, February 10, 1971, Amistad.

35. Himes to Roslyn Targ, February 17, 1971, Amistad.

36. Himes to Robert Manley, April 10, 1971, Amistad.

37. Himes papers, June 6, 1971, Amistad.

38. Himes to Williams, June 18, 1971, Rochester.

39. Himes to Fabre, September 16, 1971, private collection.

40. Himes to Fabre, September 28, 1971, private collection.

41. Himes to Helen Jackson, January 20, 1972, Amistad.

42. Reed to Himes, January 12, 1972, Amistad.

43. Himes to Roslyn Targ, January 17, 1972, Amistad.

44. Himes to Roslyn Targ, February 1972, Amistad.

45. Himes believed he could make the second volume even more "personal" than the first. Himes, conversation with Michel Fabre, spring 1972. Many reviewers had expressed disappointment that Himes did not treat his childhood and youth in greater depth in his first volume. He had written about the women in his life in his novels, and in his mind *Third Generation* and *Cast the First Stone* (although fiction) were sufficient treatment of his youth and prison years. His growing to manhood and becoming a writer are documented in a longer version of his prison novel, "Yesterday Will Make You Cry."

46. Himes to Reed, March 1972, private collection.

47. Himes to Jackson, June 10, 1972, Amistad.

48. Himes to Williams, May 30, 1972, Rochester.

49. Himes to Reed, November 14, 1972, private collection.

50. Himes to Reed, November 14, 1972, private collection.

51. Himes to Duhamel, January 10, 1973, Amistad.

52. Himes to Roslyn Targ, April 26, 1973, Amistad.

53. Unpublished fragment, Himes papers, Amistad.

54. Himes to Claude Julien, September 6, 1973, private collection.

55. Himes told Lesley he had begun the novel as "a primitive" but that the process of writing it had purged him of his naivete—hence the French title, "The End of a Primitive." Actually, as has been noted, he had thought of that same title for quite another novel he was contemplating while living in the United States.

56. Unpublished introduction for Chatham Bookseller's edition of *The Primitive,* Himes papers, Amistad.

57. Unpublished introduction for Chatham Bookseller's edition of *The Primitive,* Himes papers, Amistad.

58. Himes to Julien, September 6, 1973, private collection.

59. Himes to Roslyn Targ, September 27, 1973, Amistad.

60. Himes to Roslyn Targ, November 26, 1973, Amistad.

61. Himes to Roslyn Targ, November 26, 1973, Amistad.

*13. What Did I Do?*

1. Himes to Fabre, February 18, 1974, private collection.

2. Himes to Duhamel, February 25, 1974, Amistad.

3. Himes to Roslyn Targ, February 27, 1974, Amistad.

4. Unpublished fragment, Himes papers, Amistad.

5. Unpublished fragment, Himes papers, Amistad.

6. Unpublished fragment, Himes papers, Amistad.

7. Unpublished fragment, Himes papers, Amistad.

8. Unpublished fragment, Himes papers, Amistad.

9. Unpublished fragment, Himes papers, Amistad.

10. Himes to Stewart Richardson, May 5, 1974, Amistad.

11. Himes to Raymond Witkins, April 30, 1974, Amistad.

12. Himes to Roslyn Targ, September 27, 1974, Amistad.

13. Himes to Roslyn Targ, November 3, 1974, Amistad.

14. Himes to Roslyn Targ, August 28, 1974, Amistad.

15. Himes to Malartic, August 28, 1974, private collection.

16. Himes to Roslyn Targ, December 24, 1974, Amistad.

17. Lesley Himes to Roslyn Targ, n.d. (1975), Amistad.

18. Himes to Roslyn Targ, April 26, 1975, Amistad.

19. Himes to an editor of Wildwood House, March 23, 1975, Amistad.

20. Himes to Larry Jordan, May 11, 1975, Amistad.

21. Roslyn Targ to Himes, November 16, 1975, Amistad.

22. Himes to Jordan, January 21, 1976, Amistad.

23. Himes to Jordan, December 27, 1975, Amistad. Lesley stated that she did no writing, nor did the woman who was typing the final drafts. The latter only corrected spelling mistakes. "Chester was so paranoid at this time . . . I even thought the book should not go to print at this point." Lesley Himes to Margolies, July 21, 1994, private collection.

24. Himes to Jordan, February 7 (?), 1976, Amistad.

25. Himes to Reed, February 28, 1976, private collection. Neither of these works appears in *Black on White,* which was published posthumously.

26. Unpublished draft, Himes papers, Amistad.

27. Miotte's interview, however, was incorporated in his book *Chester Himes / Miotte* (Paris: SMI, 1977).

28. Stephen F. Milliken, *Chester Himes: A Critical Appraisal* (Columbia: University of Missouri Press, 1976).

29. Himes to Jordan, July 12, 1976, Amistad.

30. Himes to Jordan, November 4, 1988, Amistad.

31. Lesley Himes to Joseph and Estelle Himes, July 4, 1977, Amistad.

32. Himes to Roslyn Targ, July 16, 1977, Amistad.

33. Himes to Roslyn Targ, November 5, 1977, Amistad.

34. Lesley Himes to Yves and Yvonne Malartic, November 23, 1977, private collection.

35. Himes to Billy Byron, November 14, 1977, Amistad.

36. Himes to Richard Dannay, n.d. (1977), Amistad.

37. Himes to Malartic, August 7, 1978, private collection.

38. Michel Fabre was instrumental in this production and went to Moraira with the film crew.

39. Himes to Malartic, March 27, 1979, private collection.

40. Lesley Himes to Reed, February 2, 1981, private collection.

41. Lesley Himes, interview with Michel Fabre, March 1990. We are indebted to Lesley Himes for much private information about her husband's last years.

42. The Spanish journalists included Santiago Corcoles for *Cultura* and C. R. Minguela for *Las Provincias.*

43. Lesley Himes, interview with Michel Fabre, March 1990. Later Lesley had a plaque affixed on the niche in the cemetery. It reads "Chester Himes / Escritor / Missouri, USA, 1909 / Moraira, 1984 / Su esposa Lesley."

# CHRONOLOGICAL LIST
# OF THE WORKS
# OF CHESTER HIMES

Himes's works are listed in order of publication. Because of the importance of his French career, titles that appeared first in French translation are listed ahead of American printings.

*Fiction*

"His Last Day." *Abbott's Monthly* 5 (November 1932): 32–33, 60–63.
"Prison Mass." *Abbott's Monthly* 6 (March 1933): 36, 61–64; (April 1933): 20–21, 48–56; (May 1933): 37, 61–62.
"Her Whole Existence: A Story of True Love." *Abbott's Monthly* 6 (July 1933): 24–25, 53–56.
"A Modern Marriage." *Atlanta Daily World*, August 2, 1933, p. 2.
"I Don't Want to Die." *Abbott's Monthly and Illustrated News* 6 (October 1933): 20–21.
"He Knew." *Abbott's Monthly and Illustrated News* 1 (December 2, 1933): 15.
"The Meanest Cop in the World." *Atlanta Daily World*, December 7, 1933, p. 2.
"Hero: A Football Story." *Abbott's Monthly and Illustrated News* 1 (December 30, 1933): 5, 7.
"Crazy in the Stir." *Esquire* 2 (August 1934): 28, 114–17.
"To What Red Hell." *Esquire* 2 (October 1934): 100–101, 122, 127.
"Every Opportunity." *Esquire* 6 (May 1936): 99, 129–30.
"The Visiting Hour." *Esquire* 6 (September 1936): 76, 143–44, 146.
"The Night's for Cryin'." *Esquire* 7 (January 1937): 64, 146–48.
"Scram!" *Bachelor* 1 (February 1938): 26–27, 64.
"Salute to the Passing." *Opportunity* 17 (March 1939): 74–79.
"With Malice toward None." *Crossroad* 1 (April 1939): n.p. [5 pp.]

"A Modern Fable—of Mr. Slaughter, Mr. McDull, and the American Scene." *Crossroad* 2 (Summer, 1939): n.p. [5 pp.]

"Marijuana and a Pistol." *Esquire* 13 (March 1940): 58.

"Looking down the Street: A Story of Import and Bitterness." *Crossroad* (Spring 1940): n.p. [5 pp.]

"Face in the Moonlight." *Coronet* 9 (February 1941): 51–63.

"The Things You Do." *Opportunity* 19 (May 1941): 141–43.

"Strictly Business." *Esquire* 17 (February 1942): 55, 128.

"Lunching at the Ritzmore." *Crisis* 49 (October 1942): 314–15, 333.

"In the Night." *Opportunity* 20 (November 1942): 334–35, 348–49.

"Two Soldiers." *Crisis* 50 (January 1943): 13, 29.

"Heaven Has Changed." *Crisis* 50 (March 1943): 78, 83.

"So Softly Smiling." *Crisis* 50 (October 1943): 314–16, 318.

"All He Needs Is Feet." *Crisis* 50 (November 1943): 332.

"Money Don't Spend in the Stir." *Esquire* 21 (April 1944): 75, 174–75.

"All God's Chillun Got Pride." *Crisis* 51 (June 1944): 188–89, 204.

"He Seen It in the Stars." *Negro Story* 1 (July/August 1944): 5–9.

*If He Hollers Let Him Go.* Garden City, N.Y.: Doubleday, 1945. 249 pp.

"Let Me at the Enemy—an' George Brown." *Negro Story* 1 (December 1944–January 1945): 9–18.

"A Penny for Your Thoughts." *Negro Story* 1 (March–April 1945): 14–17.

"The Song Says 'Keep on Smilin'.' " *Crisis* 52 (April 1945): 103–4.

"There Ain't No Justice." *Esquire* 23 (April 1945): 53. [Subtitled "Article."]

"My But the Rats Are Terrible." *Negro Story* 1 (May–June 1945): 24–32.

"Make with the Shape." *Negro Story* 2 (August–September 1945): 3–6.

"A Night of New Roses [i.e., "Neuroses"]." *Negro Story* 2 (December 1945–January 1946): 10–14.

"The Something in a Colored Man." *Esquire* 25 (January 1946): 120, 158.

"One More Way to Die." *Negro Story* 2 (April–May 1946): 10–14.

*Lonely Crusade.* New York: Alfred A. Knopf, 1947. 398 pp. Reprint, Chatham, N.J.: Chatham Bookseller, 1973. 398 pp.

"Journey Out of Fear." *Tomorrow* 7 (June 1948): 38–42.

"To End All Stories." *Crisis* 55 (July 1948): 205–20.

"Mama's Missionary Money." *Crisis* 56 (November 1949): 303–7.

*Cast the First Stone.* New York: Coward McCann, 1952. 346 pp.

*The Third Generation.* Cleveland: World Publishing, 1954. 350 pp.

*The Primitive.* [Originally entitled "The End of a Primitive."] New York: New American Library, 1956 [copyrighted in 1955]. 152 pp.

"Friends." *Unusual* 1:3 (1955): 1–11. [Unbound supplement to this issue.]

*For Love of Imabelle.* [Originally entitled "The Five Cornered Square."] Greenwich, Conn.: Fawcett World Library, 1957. 157 pp. Reprinted as *A Rage in Harlem.* New York: Avon, 1965. 192 pp. *La Reine des pommes.* Translated by Minnie Danzas. Série Noire. Paris: Gallimard, 1958. 248 pp.

*Il pleut des coups durs.* [Originally entitled "If Trouble Was Money."] Translated by C. Wourgraf. Série Noire. Paris: Gallimard, 1958. 249 pp. *The Real Cool Killers.* New York: Avon, 1959. 160 pp.

*Couché dans le pain.* [Originally entitled "A Jealous Man Can't Win."] Translated by
Janine Hérisson and Henri Robillot. Série Noire. Paris: Gallimard, 1959. 186 pp.
*The Crazy Kill.* New York: Avon Books, 1959. 160 pp.

*Dare-dare.* [Originally entitled "Run, Man, Run."] Translated by Pierre Verrier. Série
Noire. Paris: Gallimard, 1959. 256 pp. *Run Man Run.* New York: Putnam, 1966.
192 pp.

*Tout pour plaire.* [Originally entitled "The Big Gold Dream."] Translated by Yves
Malartic. Série Noire. Paris: Gallimard, 1959. 250 pp. *The Big Gold Dream.* New
York: Avon Books, 1960. 160 pp.

"The Snake." *Esquire* 52 (October 1959): 147–49.

*Imbroglio négro.* [Originally entitled "Don't Play with Death."] Translated by Jeanne
Fillion. Série Noire. Paris: Gallimard, 1960. 249 pp. *All Shot Up.* New York: Avon
Books, 1960. 160 pp.

*Ne nous énervons pas!* [Originally entitled "Be Calm."] Translated by Jeanne Fillion.
Série Noire. Paris: Gallimard, 1961. 255 pp. *The Heat's On.* New York: Putnam, 1966.
220 pp. Reprinted as *Come Back, Charleston Blue* (after the title of a film adapted
from the novel). New York: Berkley, 1972. 192 pp.

*Pinktoes.* [Published in English.] Paris: Olympia Press, 1961. 207 pp. New York:
Putnam/Stein & Day, 1965. 256 pp.

*Une Affaire de viol.* Translated by André Mathieu. "Postface" by Christiane Rochefort.
Paris: Editions Les Yeux Ouverts, 1963. 174 pp. Reprinted as *Affaire de viol.* Translated
by Françoise Clary and Michel Fabre. Introduction by Michel Fabre. Paris: Editions
des Autres, 1979. 163 pp. *A Case of Rape.* New York: Targ Editions, 1980. 105 pp.

*Retour en Afrique.* [Originally entitled "Back to Africa."] Translated by Pierre Sergent.
Collection Actualités 6. Paris: Plon, 1964. 249 pp. Reprinted as *Le Casse de l'Oncle
Tom.* Paris: Plon, 1971. 246 pp. *Cotton Comes to Harlem.* New York: Putnam, 1965.
223 pp.

*Blind Man with a Pistol.* New York: Morrow, 1969. 240 pp. Reprinted as *Hot Day, Hot
Night.* New York: Dell, 1970. 238 pp.

*Black on Black: "Baby Sister" and Selected Writings.* New York: Doubleday, 1973. 287 pp.
[Includes the following unpublished stories: "Baby Sister, a Black Greek Tragedy";
"Black Laughter," 1946; "Christmas Gift," 1944; "Da-Da-Dee," 1948; "A Nigger";
"Pork Chop Paradise"; "Prediction"; "Tang," 1967; and a previously unpublished
political essay, "If You're Scared, Go Home."]

"Life Everlasting." *First World* 2 (Spring 1978): 60–61.

"Trac noir." *Lui* 188 (September 1979): 50–52, 56, 120, 122.

*Le Manteau de rêve.* Translated by Hélène Devaux-Minié. Paris: Editions Lieu Commun, 1982. 217 pp. [Includes five stories previously unpublished in English: "On
Dreams and Reality"; "The Ghost of Rufus Jones"; "Spanish Gin," 1957; "One Night
in New Jersey"; "In the Rain."]

*Plan B.* [Originally entitled "Plan B."] Translated by Hélène Devaux-Minié. Paris:
Lieu Commun, 1983. 210 pp. *Plan B.* Jackson: University Press of Mississippi, 1993.

"La Révélation." *Le Monde,* January 6–7, 1985, p. xi.

*Faut être nègre pour faire ça.* Paris: Lieu Commun, 1986. 224 pp. [Includes three stories
previously unpublished in English: "Daydream"; "The Way of All Flesh"; "I'm Not
Trying to Hurt You."]

"One Night in New Jersey." *Mediterranean Magazine* 1 (March 1987): 44–48.
*"Baby Sister"; "Joue, Gabriel, joue!"; "Naturellement le nègre . . ."* Translated by Maurice Cullaz and Hélène Devaux-Minié. Preface by Michel Fabre. Paris: Editions de l'Instant, 1987. 200 pp. [Includes "Blow, Gabriel, Blow," and "Naturally, the Negro," both previously unpublished.]
*Un joli coup de lune.* [Originally entitled "The Lunatic Fringe."] Translated by Hélène Devaux-Minié. Paris: Lieu Commun, 1988. 122 pp.
*The Collected Stories of Chester Himes.* London: Allison & Busby, 1990. 429 pp. Reprint. New York: Thunder's Mouth Press, 1991. 429 pp. [Although this collection was intended to be comprehensive, several stories were omitted.]

## Nonfiction

Letter in *"Native Son:* Pros and Cons." *New Masses,* May 21, 1940, pp. 23–26. [Reply to "The Meaning of Bigger Thomas," *New Masses* 35 (April 30, 1940): 26–28.]
"Now Is the Time! Here Is the Place!" *Opportunity* 20 (September 1942): 271–73, 284.
"Zoot Suit Riots Are Race Riots!" *Crisis* 50 (July 1943): 200–201, 222.
"The People We Know." *The War Worker,* first half November 1943, pp. 6–7; second half November 1943, p. 19.
"Negro Martyrs Are Needed." *Crisis* 51 (May 1944): 159, 174.
"Democracy Is for the Unafraid." *Common Ground* 4 (1944): 53–56.
"Second Guesses for First Novelists." *Saturday Review of Literature* 29 (February 16, 1946): 13.
"A Letter to the Editor." *Commentary* 5 (May 1948): 473–74. [Protests Milton Klonsky's review of *Lonely Crusade* in *Commentary* 5 (February 1948): 189–90.]
"A Short History of a Story." *Crisis* 56 (November 1949): 307–8.
"Harlem ou le cancer de l'Amérique." *Présence Africaine* 45 (spring 1963): 46–81.
"Le Billet de Chester Himes: La nouvelle école." *Jazz Hip* 33 (1963): 8–9.
"Les Souris et le fromage." *Le Nouvel Observateur,* July 23, 1964, p. 9.
"La Colère noire." *Adam,* November 1964, pp. 68, 70–73, 132.
"The Dilemma of the Negro Novelist in the United States." In *Beyond the Angry Black,* edited by John A. Williams, pp. 52–58. New York: Cooper Square, 1966.
"Reading Your Own: My Favorite Novel." *New York Times Book Review,* June 4, 1967, p. 4. [On *The Primitive.*]
"A Letter of Protest to His Publishers from Chester Himes in Spain." *Negro Digest* 18 (May 1969): 98. [On the Dell paperback edition of *Run Man Run.*]
Letter to *Jazz Hot* (Paris), dated April 18, 1972. *Jazz Hot* 38 (July–August 1972): 14.
"Preface." In *Yardbird Reader I,* edited by Ishmael Reed, pp. xvii–xviii. Berkeley, Calif.: Yardbird Publishing Cooperative, 1972.
*The Quality of Hurt.* New York: Doubleday, 1972. 351 pp. [First volume of autobiography.]
*My Life of Absurdity.* New York: Doubleday, 1976. 398 pp. [Second volume of autobiography.] *Regrets sans repentir.* Translated by Yves Malartic. Paris: Gallimard, 1979. 398 pp. [Condensation in one volume of both volumes of the autobiography; condensed by Yves Malartic.]

# INDEX

Hancock, John, 78, 151
Harlem Renaissance, 29
Harper's, 77
Harrington, Ollie, 79, 92, 93, 97, 102, 105,
  117, 123, 132
Harvard University, 8
Haygoods: Vandi, 52, 56, 62, 70, 75–76,
  77, 80, 81, 84, 86–88, 92–93, 97, 106;
  William, 52, 62
Haynes, Leroy, 79, 105
Heath, Gordon, 133
Helsinki, University of, 133
Hemingway, Ernest, 9–10, 34, 36, 52, 121,
  137, 142, 149, 170
Henri Christophe, 158
*Herald Tribune* (Paris), 111, 114, 116, 124
Hernton, Calvin, 150
Highsmith, Patricia, 68
Hill, Herbert, 118, 124
Himes, Chester, birth, 7; in black
  underworld, 26–30; convictions, 28,
  29–30; childhood, 9–16; death, 174–75;
  departure for Europe, 77–79; divorce
  from Jean, 172; education, 14, 15, 21,
  23–25; first published stories, 36–38;
  homosexual relationships, 33–35, 77;
  injury from fall, 21–22, 24, 25, 26,
  40, 42, 139; marriage to Jean, 41, 60;
  marriage to Lesley, 172; in prison,
  30–38, 39; separation from Jean,
  74–75; strokes, 129, 135, 154, 158
  **Works:** "All God's Chillun Got Pride,"
  52; *All Shot Up* (*Imbroglio négro*), 110,
  112, 113; "An American Negro in Black
  Africa," 124; "Baby Sister," 123–24,
  125–26, 131; "Bars and Stripes Forever,"
  34; *The Big Gold Dream* (*Tout pour
  plaire*), 105, 108–09; "Black Boogie
  Woogie," 85, 86; *Black on Black*, 37;
  *Black on White* (*Un Manteau de
  rêve*), 173, 174; *Blind Man with a Pistol*
  (*L'Aveugle au pistolet*), 16, 126, 143,
  144, 146, 147, 149, 151, 152, 153; "Blow
  Gabriel Blow," 113, 123; *A Case of Rape*
  (*Une Affaire de viol*), 94, 97, 98, 107,

  118, 130, 131–32, 134, 156, 170, 172, 173;
  *Cast the First Stone*, 32, 33, 34, 35,
  36, 45, 47, 61, 62, 68, 70, 71, 72, 74,
  76–77, 107, 127, 128, 172; *Come Back
  Charleston Blue*, 160; *Cotton Comes to
  Harlem*, 130, 133, 134, 138, 139, 141–42,
  144, 151; *Cotton Comes to Harlem*
  (film), 151, 152, 153; "Crazy in the
  Stir," 36, 37; *The Crazy Kill*, 101, 102;
  "Da-Da-Dee," 69; "Day after Day,"
  41; "The Ghost of Rufus Jones," 152;
  "He Knew," 37; "Headwaiter," 40; *The
  Heat's On*, 114, 116; "Hero: A Football
  Story," 36; "His Last Day," 37; "Idle
  Hours," 42; *If He Hollers Let Him Go*,
  36, 47, 50, 51–52, 55–56, 57, 58, 62–63,
  70, 87, 89, 98, 133, 136, 143, 157, 169; *My
  Life of Absurdity*, 157–58, 159, 164–68,
  169, 170, 172; *Lonely Crusade* (*La
  Croisade de Lee Gordon*), 44, 47, 58, 59,
  60, 61, 62, 63, 64–68, 70, 74, 75, 77, 80,
  94, 117, 119; *For Love of Imabelle* (*La
  Reine des pommes*; *A Rage in Harlem*),
  100, 102, 105, 106, 109, 110, 115, 120, 121,
  134, 136; "The Lunatic Fringe," 84, 91,
  95, 96, 106, 110, 128; "Marijuana and a
  Pistol," 171; "A Modern Marriage," 36,
  37; "The Night's for Cryin'," 40; "On
  Dreams and Reality," 173; "The Pink
  Dress," 106, 166; *Pinktoes* (*Mamie
  Mason*), 20, 91–92, 93, 94–95, 108,
  118, 119, 124, 125, 136, 137, 143, 144, 171;
  *Plan B*, 144, 146, 150, 153–54, 173, 174;
  "Pork Chop Paradise," 154; "Present
  Tense," 33; *The Primitive* (*La Fin d'un
  Primitif*), 73, 75, 76, 80, 81, 84, 85–86,
  88–89, 91, 92–93, 95, 119, 128, 142,
  146, 160–61, 162, 168, 171–72; "Prison
  Mass," 36, 37; *The Quality of Hurt*, 14,
  25, 150, 151, 152, 156, 158, 159, 172; *The
  Real Cool Killers* (*Il pleut des coups
  durs*), 104, 105, 108; "Regina," 107,
  141, 142–43, 165; *Regrets sans repentir*,
  172; *Run Man Run* (*Dare Dare*), 28,
  73, 89, 108, 112, 146–47, 149, 160, 163,

Platt, Dr., 141

Plon, 90, 94, 103, 105, 108, 118, 125, 128, 129, 130

*PM*, 58

Pocket Books, 130

Poe, Edgar Allan, 15

Portugal: Lisbon, 168, 171

Poston, Ted, 46

Potter, Larry, 139, 140

Powell, Adam Clayton, 53, 125

Powell, Bud, 124

Praeger, 155

Prostitutes, 21, 25, 26, 40, 90

Pueblo del Rio Housing Project, 49

Putnam, 134, 136, 137, 171

Puzo, Mario, 149

Pythian Theater, 25

Quinn, Anthony, 158

Racism, 42, 44–46, 57, 59, 64, 91, 92, 132, 136, 144, 153, 155, 157, 160–61, 162, 165; in American South, 8, 12, 126; in the armed forces, 49; in California, 47–48; in Cuba, 131; in England, 136; in France, 93, 94, 126, 134, 136; in Ohio, 23–24; in Spain, 155, 163

Radio-Télè Luxembourg, 151

Raft, George, 35

*Raisin in the Sun, A* (Hansberry), 123

Ramseger, Dr., 113, 119, 120

Rasmussen, Birgit, 138

Reach, James, 128

*Reader's Digest*, 74

Reed, Ishmael, 146, 149, 153, 157–58, 159, 160, 169–70, 172, 173, 174

Residencia Tanger, 84

Reynolds, Grant, 40, 49, 96

Richardson, Stewart, 166

Rico (Prince), 33–34, 35, 41, 48

Rimbaud, Arthur, 69

Riots, 136, 144, 147

Rochefort, Christiane, 131

Rockefeller, Winthrop, 53

Roditi, Edouard, 112

Rogers, Buddy, 35

Roosevelt, Franklin D., 42, 52, 68

*Roots* (Haley), 124

Rosenkrantz, Baron Timme, 104

Rosenwald Foundation, 50, 52, 62

*Running Wild*, 35

Safford, Frank, 61

St. Jacques, Raymond, 151

Samuel French Literary Agency, 127, 128

*Sanctuary* (Faulkner), 101

*Saturday Evening Post, The*, 35

*Saturday Review of Literature*, 57

Schneider, Agnes, 103

Schomburg Collection, 153

Schulberg, Bud, 71

Scotia Seminary, 5, 8

Seaver, Edwin, 78–79

Seid, Ruth, 43, 58

Seltzer, Louis B., 44

Série Noire, 98, 119, 133, 138, 139, 151

Shaking Quakers, 42

Silberman, James, 91, 94

Simmons, Art, 93, 133

Sinatra, Frank, 70

Sinclair, Jo. *See* Seid, Ruth

*Sissie* (Williams), 127

Sissle & Blacke, 54

*Skippy*, 35

*Sky Above, the Mud Below, The*, 123

Smith, Bessie, 104

Smith, Bill, 63, 72, 158

Smith, Dick, 40

Smith, William Gardner, 79, 92, 103, 111, 132

Société de Culture Africaine, 97

*Soir*, 109, 113, 125, 126

*Sons of Darkness, Sons of Light*, 149

Sorbonne University, 97, 147

South Carolina, 4, 5, 40; Charleston, 6; Cheraw, 12–13; Orangeburg, 6; Spartanburg, 4

Soviet Union, 46

Spain, 146–48, 152, 157–58; Alicante, 144, 147–50, 159, 175; Barcelona, 84, 107, 148, 159; Benissa, 175; Costa Brava, 147; Deya, 84; Gibraltar, 141, 144;